BEYOND INTERPRETATION

BEYOND INTERPRETATION

Toward a Revised
Theory for Psychoanalysis

John E. Gedo, M.D.

INTERNATIONAL UNIVERSITIES PRESS, INC.

New York

Library of Congress Cataloging in Publication Data

Gedo, John E
   Beyond interpretation.

   Bibliography: p.
   Includes index.
   1. Psychoanalysis. 2. Psychoanalysis—Cases,
clinical reports, statistics. I. Title. [DNLM:
1. Psychoanalytic theory. 2. Psychoanalysis.
WM460.3 G296b]
RC504.G38   616.8'917   78-13894
ISBN 0-8236-0499-3

Second Printing—1980

Manufactured in the United States of America

This book is dedicated to my wife, Mary Mathews Gedo, who has become the historian of culture I have always wished to be.

Contents

Preface

This book is a response to the widely felt sense of crisis in contemporary psychoanalysis. The analytic community is in disfavor with a public beguiled by a smorgasbord of alternatives advertised as quick, cheap, and palatable; governmental support has eroded in an intellectual climate of pragmatism and populist resistance to complexity; even the sources of future recruits to our ranks are threatening to dry up in an era that glorifies a life of activity in contrast to one of contemplation. Perhaps more serious than these external pressures is a crisis of confidence on our own part concerning the effectiveness of psychoanalysis as therapy and the adequacy of our theories as a valid psychology.

These signs of the imminent collapse of an old régime should not lead us into pessimism; to the contrary, these are exciting times for the heirs of Sigmund Freud—a time of challenge and of revolutionary opportunities. The clinical method of psychoanalysis has continued to serve admirably as the primary observational tool for the study of man's inner life, and the progressively expanding data base it has produced has continued to lead to refinement of the psychoanalytic theories of psychopathology and of normal development. The theoreticians of the past generation succeeded in systematizing a confusing and sprawling array of psychoanalytic psychology; in the more recent past, the major difficulties of this theoretical system have been convincingly shown to be attributable to certain epistemological weaknesses—in other words, to be in need of the same kind of revision that the whole scientific corpus developed around the turn of the century must undergo.

In this work, my aim is *not* to develop an epistemologically sound metapsychology. I believe that such a task is being adequately carried out by others, whose most relevant works will be cited in appropriate contexts throughout this book. I am addressing myself principally to the other area of major psychoanalytic concern: the revision of our theories about our clinical procedures. My aim is to demonstrate that our current psychological insights properly applied in the therapeutic arena, give us unprecedented opportunities to assist our analysands to alter their subsequent functioning. As a result, we can in good conscience recommend psychoanalytic treatment to any nonpsychotic person seriously interested in self-inquiry.

In order to substantiate this claim, as well as to illustrate the therapeutic principles I am advocating, I present three lengthy accounts of completed analyses in this book. My discussions of these narratives focus on the genesis of each patient's personality organization and on the psychoanalytic transactions that were required to effect changes in it. The discussions not only serve as material to support the theory of psychoanalytic technique presented here; in addition, they highlight a number of issues of real significance in the lives of my patients—issues that have hitherto received scant attention from psychoanalysts.

The observations in question are in no sense novel—it is the significance I attribute to them that is a departure from accepted thinking. Existing psychoanalytic generalizations do not take certain matters into account, and our clinical theories (even those of the boldest dissidents in the psychoanalytic community) are ill-suited to handle these data. Consequently, I am suggesting a set of new clinical constructs as a framework for organizing both these observations and the more familiar data also found in the course of these analyses.

In other words, the second major aim of this book is to articulate a new clinical theory for psychoanalysis, one that is based on the broadest possible range of psychoanalytic data. At the same time, I try to make this theory congruent with recent metapsychological proposals that meet the requirements of the philosophy of science. Moreover, I pay particular attention to the necessity to give internal coherence to these proposed conceptualizations. We should thereby repair the effects of the continual patching that has disarrayed the formal integrity of Freud's theories since his death.

The central concept around which my tentative revision of psychoanalytic psychology is built is that of human personality as a hierarchy of personal aims. The infant's biological needs constitute the earliest of these goals; by the end of the second year of life, these have been supplemented by a variety of subjective wishes; the entire hierarchy, in both conscious and unconscious aspects, will form the person's primary identity, or, as I would prefer to call it, the "self-organization." The formation of the self-organization and its later transformations, especially through the acquisition of systems of values, should be viewed in epigenetic terms as the core of personality development. A brief outline of this developmental sequence is provided in the theoretical section of this book. And finally, I close the circle by returning to the topic of our theory of technique, by reassessing the mode of action of psychoanalytic therapy in the light of a psychology centered on a hierarchy of personal aims.

I must resist the temptation to burden the reader with the history of the intellectual path I have followed to arrive at these views. One segment of that journey, however, cannot go unmentioned: my collaboration with Arnold Goldberg, which produced *Models of the Mind* (1973). That monograph was an effort to find a consistent and inclusive framework that could accommodate all of the essential clinical findings of psychoanalysis. There, we brought together into one hierarchical schema the disparate modes of psychic functioning encountered in psychoanalytic work. The outlines of the theory of technique elaborated in this book were initially presented in *Models of the Mind* as a logical corollary of that hierarchical schema.

In the intervening years, our paths have diverged, and I do not know whether Goldberg would endorse my current version of the ideas we developed together before 1973. As this book will show, my own psychoanalytic views have changed in certain respects, and this circumstance compels a reconsideration of some features of the hierarchical model that was our joint creation. Perhaps the most significant aspect of *Models of the Mind* I no longer stand behind is its use of Heinz Kohut's proposals concerning narcissism as a developmental line. Kohut is one of several contributors whose clinical innovations are taken up in some detail in this book; I trust that I have been able to clarify the extent of my disagreement with his concepts without depriving him of credit for the important influence he has had on my psychoanalytic evolution.

As to the future, let us adopt the motto of Danton: *Toujours de l'audace!*

Chicago
May 1978

Acknowledgments

The experience of discussing portions of this work in preliminary versions with various professional audiences has been invaluable for the integration of the ideas I am presenting. I should like to thank the participating members and program chairmen of the following groups for these opportunities: The Panels on New Horizons in Metapsychology and New Theories of Object Relations of the American Psychoanalytic Association, the Chicago, Michigan, and St. Louis Psychoanalytic Societies, the Philadelphia Association for Psychoanalysis, the Michigan Psychoanalytic Institute, and Study Groups of the Boston, New York, Los Angeles, and Seattle Psychoanalytic Societies.

Drs. M. Robert Gardner, Meyer S. Gunther, George H. Klumpner, Leo Sadow, Nathan Schlessinger, and David M. Terman kindly read all or parts of this manuscript and offered many helpful critiques. Their encouragement for my effort was truly a *sine qua non* for persisting in this solitary task. Insofar as this book has achieved coherence, I am indebted to the invaluable suggestions of an anonymous reader and to those of Natalie Altman. Jacqueline Miller has been unfailingly helpful and efficient in the preparation of successive versions of the manuscript.

CHAPTER ONE

A Psychology of Personal Aims

The Conceptual Baseline

Aside from the basic points of view of its metapsychology (cf. Rapaport and Gill, 1959), the highest conceptual level in psychoanalytic theory is embodied in the various models of the mind. Each of these stands as a graphic analogue for one of the clinical theories of psychoanalysis. An attempt to find one consistent and inclusive epigenetic framework that would accommodate all of the essential clinical theories of our psychology resulted in a schema presented in *Models of the Mind* (Gedo and Goldberg, 1973) as a supraordinate, hierarchical model of psychic functioning at every phase of the life cycle.

This hierarchical schema brought together all of the disparate modes of psychic functioning encountered in the course of applying the psychoanalytic method with adults in the full gamut of nosological conditions. To this end, we found it necessary to base the hierarchy on a series of parallel developmental lines. On a tentative basis, we chose the specific lines of the typical situations of danger, the typical mechanisms of defense used to ward these off, the lines of reality testing, of narcissism, and of object relations.

We described five modes of psychic organization, each one characteristic for one of the successive developmental phases of childhood. In adults, the five modes are available simultaneously, i.e., in a synchronic manner, except for those

1

individuals whose development has been prematurely arrested. In such cases, some of the more differentiated modes have had no opportunity to be established. The actual model we drew shows the acquisition of successive modes of functioning along the horizontal axis, i.e., along the diachronic or time scale. The vertical dimension of the diagram is used to indicate the potential availability of the existing repertory of modes within each developmental phase, i.e., at one point in time. The various modes are interrelated in the behavior we can observe in specific ways that yield a psychoanalytic diagnosis of the personality organization.

The successive developmental phases were marked off from each other by a series of nodal events. These consisted of the acquisition of certain essential capacities, e.g., new structures such as the superego; a new phase was conceptualized in terms of these functions' attaining a degree of stability that precludes regressive loss of autonomous functioning in that regard. The question of the irreversibility (or its lack) of these functions was entered on the graphic model by means of arrows.

Construction of the hierarchical model revealed that previous models of the mind in psychoanalytic use had referred to differing phases of development. In other words, the various phases of development and their characteristic modes of functioning turned out to be optimally illuminated by one or another of the traditional clinical theories of psychoanalysis. Indeed, these poorly correlated, disparate aspects of psychoanalytic thinking turned out to be referable to distinct developmental conditions; they are not competing explanatory schemata, as they were generally thought to be in the past.

To recapitulate briefly, by means of certain continuities that characterize human development, the so-called developmental lines, we succeeded in demonstrating that a number of familiar psychoanalytic models of the mind (the reflex-arc model, object-relations models, and the classical tripartite and topographic models) do in fact usefully portray psychic life at every phase of childhood development as well as in those circumstances in later life which reflect regressions to the functional state of earlier phases. Used complementarily, the various clinical theories of psychoanalysis do not seem to leave any gap in portraying mental life throughout the life cycle. To put the matter the other way around, each of the models of the mind Freud proposed as guides to his clinical theories is still serviceable if applied to the appropriate mode of structuralization within the overall hierarchy (see Figure 1).

The hierarchical model we developed is congruent in its basic organization with the manner in which Piaget has built his empirical findings about cognitive development into his ideal schemata. Although Piaget's data can be correlated with our hierarchical model without undue difficulty (as will in part be shown below), the model we constructed differs radically from Piaget's theoretical system in having no pretensions about representing the actualities of mental organization—it is explicitly a schema for the ordering of the *observer's* conceptualizations.

The particular lines of development we chose for inclusion in the hierarchical model were those representing issues that permit the observer to make nosological distinctions among the psychopathological conditions encountered in psychoanalytic practice. The developmental line of object love was omitted on empirical grounds, i.e., because we did not find it to be especially helpful in making such diagnostic assessments. However, the epigenetic schema we did outline remained completely different from the first such effort within psychoanalysis, that of Erikson (1959). We followed him only in using the epigenetic *principle* for constructing the hierarchical model.

The hierarchical model portrays the course of expectable development and does not indicate the presence of psychopathology as such. However, in view of the fact that psychoanalytic diagnosis must be made by observing the un-

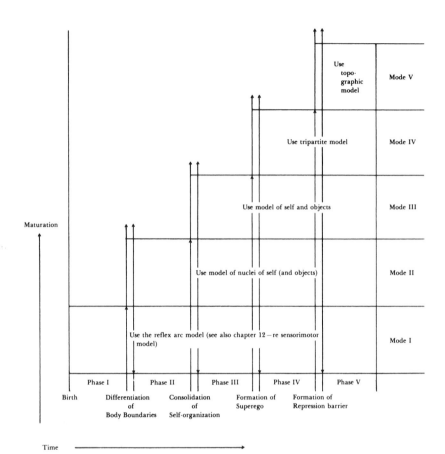

FIGURE 1
THE HIERARCHICAL MODEL: MODES, PHASES, AND
APPROPRIATE SUBORDINATE MODELS OF THE MIND
(AFTER GEDO AND GOLDBERG, 1973)

folding and resolution of the transferences within the psychoanalytic situation, the hierarchical schema lends itself to use as a diagnostic instrument by permitting the charting of short- and long-term shifts in the mode of psychic organization in the course of treatment. This procedure pays heed to the familiar principle that diagnosis cannot be based on the observation of behavior on a short-term, cross-sectional sample. In other words, a psychoanalytic nosology will have to take into account various patterns of expectable changes in modal organization as a consequence of setting the analytic process in motion. To repeat the essence of this viewpoint: in the course of every psychoanalysis, each of the modes of functioning included within the hierarchical model will come into focus repeatedly, of necessity in the guise of the typical manner in which the patient has dealt with the developmental crisis represented by that mode within the adult personality. From this perspective, an adequate psychoanalytic nosology will have to be a great deal more complex than anything psychoanalysts have thus far contemplated. Such a nosology will have to focus on the manner of resolution of each of the normative crises of childhood and the interrelationship of their derivatives in adult life.

At the time *Models of the Mind* was written, our clinical experience had barely begun to suggest the outlines of a future psychoanalytic nosology based on such criteria. We contented ourselves there with correlating regressions to specific modes of psychic organization in adult life with typical problems encountered clinically in persons diagnosed in accord with traditional categories as modified by the clinical work of Kohut (1971), differentiating the classical transference neuroses from more archaic character types he had labeled "narcissistic disturbances" and from borderline and psychotic syndromes. Given such a skeletal diagnostic schema, the typical problem encountered when functioning has attained expectable adult levels (Mode V) is the experience of frustration. In Mode IV, characteristic for conditions in the transference neuroses, the typical problem is that of intrapsychic conflicts. With deeper regression, we encounter the persistence of various illusions, lending the personality that specific flavor we tend to label "narcissistic" (Mode III). If the regression threatens the cohesion of the sense of self (Mode II), the problem has entered the realm of the psychoses or borderline conditions. Finally, functioning has reverted to Mode I in those states of overstimulation that Freud (1893) labeled "traumatic."

Our conceptual work in *Models of the Mind* culminated in proposals to classify the therapeutic measures necessary to deal appropriately with each of these five contingencies as specific "modalities" of psychoanalytic treatment. These issues are taken up in detail in later chapters. Here, I should note that we believed each of these modalities to be absolutely necessary to every psychoanalytic effort, even if in varying proportions, depending on how often the analysand functions in which mode. In other words, the use of the various modalities should be a routine feature of psychoanalytic treatment technique; it is *not* a departure from classical procedures, as Eissler (1953) seemed to suggest when he called any intervention on the part of the analyst other than verbal interpretation a "parameter." (See Gedo and Goldberg, 1973, pp. 159-60.)

I should add that the systematic use of multiple therapeutic modalities in every analysis has resulted in treatments that no longer conform to the criteria usually employed for describing the course of a psychoanalysis. At the same time, I have not as yet had sufficient experience with these methods to suggest new criteria for the typical course of analyses conducted in this manner, and so I shall leave such considerations out of account in this work, with the reminder that such criteria are never supposed to be prescriptive in any case. Analyses, after all, are not made to conform to any given program; they may be described, retrospectively, in terms of certain familiar patterns.

Toward a New Paradigm for Psychoanalytic Psychology

Progress in psychoanalysis has always, of necessity, followed a cyclical course (cf. Gedo and Pollock, 1976, pp. 229-

232): the acceptance of any innovation in the general theory of mental functioning necessitates a revision of the special theory of therapy. This revision, in turn, leads to changes in the technical procedures of treatment. Although these new techniques have not altered our basic methods of observation in the past 80 years, they have generally created major accretions to our data base by bringing into focus phenomena that have always formed part of the psychoanalytic situation but have hitherto been overlooked or dismissed as epiphenomenal. The accumulation of new observations will then require setting in motion another revolution of the cycle because their explanation will necessitate revision of the psychoanalytic theory of the mind.

The hierarchical view of mental functioning elaborated in *Models of the Mind* introduced the developmental viewpoint into psychoanalytic theory as a *systematic* feature of its approach to behavior. This proposal included a series of corollaries about the theory of psychoanalytic treatment, but the thorough reconsideration of that theory required by this new approach was barely hinted at in that book. Through the clinical work I have performed in the intervening years I have attempted to exploit these insights in the service of obtaining better therapeutic results as well as more significant observational data.

Psychoanalyses performed with the foregoing principles in mind yield clinical observations that have not received much emphasis in the past. Perhaps the most cogent among these is the finding that, in a substantial proportion of analyzable individuals, the genesis of the psychopathology turns out to involve crucial transactions between the young child and his caretakers during the first two years of life. Some of the experiences of the second year, including some preverbal material, are capable of analytic rediscovery through reconstructions based on transference developments. In many instances, the legacy of these early experiences determines the specific configuration of the Oedipus complex

(see Chapter 4 for one striking illustration); in many others
(see, for example, Chapter 6), the principal problems of subsequent adaptation turn out to be direct derivatives of the
vicissitudes of the preoedipal phases, i.e., issues of tension
regulation, of the integration of mutually exclusive personal
aims, or of the persistence of illusions. Even personalities
whose early development was favorable may carry into later
phases certain structuralized potentials for action which
create insoluble "intrapsychic conflicts" that cut across the
usual tripartite division of the mind into ego, id, and superego
(Chapter 8 will provide an illustration)—behaviors traditionally classified in psychoanalytic discourse as consequences of
the repetition compulsion. At any rate, although Freud's dictum about the Oedipus complex forming the nucleus of the
neuroses is still valid, the focus of analytic attention has
decisively shifted to an earlier era, which seems to stamp
the personality with its "primary identity" (Lichtenstein,
1964).

The illustrative material I have selected is reasonably rep-
resentative of my clinical experience over the last two decades. In one sense, it reflects the widely shared impression
that persons with circumscribed neuroses no longer seem to
form any significant proportion of the analytic patient popu-
lation. Although, of course, there is no practicable way of
substantiating this opinion, I do not think that this state of
affairs actually represents any change in the personality organization of our analysands. To the contrary, I believe that
it represents an evolving shift in the conceptualization of the
data of observation—at least it does in my personal instance.
When I now review my extensive notes about the people I
worked with at the very start of my analytic training, I see
the simple formulations of an Oedipus complex (at most,
complicated by some regressive evasions of its unresolved
conflicts) as rather inadequate, if not downright inaccurate,
summaries of the complex clinical data. Nor have I seen clinical reports by other analysts that would lead one to believe

that the model of neurosis illustrated by Freud through his observation of Little Hans (1909a) is an adequate one for the data they now obtain by means of the analytic method. These remarks are not to be taken as a depreciation of psychoanalytic knowledge twenty or, for that matter, 80 years ago; quite the reverse, I feel that psychoanalysis has every reason to be proud of the collective progress it has made in our time.

The role of early development in the genesis of various disturbances of character has, of course, been a commonplace of the psychoanalytic literature of the past decade, and it has given rise to increasing demands on the part of theoreticians for a new set of constructs more relevant for these conditions than are the traditional terms of psychoanalytic psychology. Most of these voices have called for concepts specifically applicable to these archaic modes of functioning; by contrast, in *Models of the Mind* we predicted that an emerging psychology of "the self" would eventually become the core of a new synthesis within psychoanalytic theory.[1]

The clinical results I shall report here, based on the consistent application of the theory of therapy suggested by the hierarchical view of psychic life, demonstrate that our traditional constructs may leave much to be desired in illuminating our data even in cases where archaic issues are relatively negligible in pathogenesis. The more important the early issues prove to be in the psychic life of an analysand, the less satisfactory those traditional theoretical tools are for comprehending it. Under the circumstances, the time has finally come to stop the 40-year effort to make do with the theoretical legacy of Freud through piecemeal patching: we should develop a comprehensive, coherent, and epistemologically sound new framework for the clinical generalizations of psychoanalysis.

The conceptual innovations introduced in the present

---

[1] More recently, G. Klein (1976) has articulated such a proposal, but his effort was unfortunately left incomplete by his untimely death.

work grew out of the increased precision of my observational skills as a result of systematic use of the hierarchical schema for ordering my clinical data. The clinical generalizations I then obtained have impelled me to develop theories more relevant for the new data than the traditional hypotheses of psychoanalysis seemed to be. The process culminated in the elevation of the epigenesis of the self-organization, understood as a hierarchy of personal aims, into the central organizing principle of this hierarchy. This theoretical option simultaneously eliminates the incoherence of using conflicting subsystems within psychoanalytic theory (see Chapter 15); at the same time, it permits us to dispense with the entire set of physicalistic metaphors Freud was constrained to borrow from nineteenth-century science—that of mental apparatus, energies, and forces—which no longer meet the requirements of contemporary epistemology.[2]

It must be kept in mind that the clinical theories of psychoanalysis should remain essentially inductive, i.e., they must not be derived from metapsychological assumptions alone, although they should conform to an explicit set of the latter. Theories must be founded on observations made in the psychoanalytic situation proper; at best, these may be supplemented by data from the direct observation of children.

A definition of "self" that might have served as the axis of a new psychoanalytic psychology was actually first proposed by Lichtenstein (1964, 1965). It was something of a paradox that Lichtenstein discerned the outlines of such a definition in certain propositions of Hartmann which had inadvertently burst the boundaries of ego psychology in postulating a supraordinate organizing or synthetic principle within mental life. More recently, Schafer (1970a) has also singled out these

---

[2]The change I am advocating now imposes an obligation and provides an opportunity to reconsider the various components of the hierarchical model proposed in 1973 in order to bring them into conformity with the new premises of the theory I offer here.

features of Hartmann's theoretical work as the Achilles heel of an otherwise consistent system adhering to a mechanistic, natural-science model of the mind: they amount to what Gilbert Ryle called "a ghost in the machine" and what Schafer (1976) aptly mocks as "the mover of the mental apparatus."

Lichtenstein's scrupulousness in crediting the leader of ego psychology with planting the seed of its eventual destruction is probably justified. His version of developmental psychology postulates the acquisition of a "primary identity" that stamps all of the individual's actions with their uniqueness, endures through all subsequent developmental vicissitudes, and crucially limits his freedom of action. Lichtenstein was correct in pointing out that this developmental psychology transcended existing psychoanalytic theory. Although he therefore hailed Freud's work on narcissism, in which Lichtenstein saw the earliest tentative statement of this conceptualization, as equal in significance to that of the tripartite model and of the structural theory, this did not lead him to claim that the new psychology of the self he was espousing would take priority of place within psychoanalytic psychology; Lichtenstein merely labeled it a metapsychological "fourth dimension." I am in agreement with the implication conveyed by Lichtenstein's metaphor: a psychology of the self has as profound a significance for psychoanalysis as relativity theory had for physics. I am now advocating a reassessment of the role of the self, understood in the terms proposed by Lichtenstein, as an organizer of subsequent psychic life (cf. Spitz, 1959).

In *Models of the Mind* we stressed that the "self" amounts to "more than the passively recorded percepts of the activities of one's own person in the past. By virtue of their continuing dynamic effects [these memories] must be understood, in addition, as an actuality in the real world—the organized personality as a whole" (pp. 63-64). To that concept I would now add that the personality as a whole is most fruitfully understood as a hierarchy of potentials for actions, i.e., of both or-

ganismic and subjective goals, as modified by a system of
values.

In my view, goals are to be understood as mental dispositions to action *ipso facto* laden with affect (Basch, 1976a).
This viewpoint agrees with Toulmin's conclusion (1975) that psychology in general must abandon Aristotle's artificial cate-
gorization of human aims into cognitive, affective, and volitional varieties. The principal merit of the recent theoretical work
of Schafer (1976) may well be his success in consistently
avoiding the fruitless division of mental life into these outworn
and arbitrary categories. A psychology based on the hierarchy
of personal aims thus promises to obviate the former
difficulties of psychoanalytic theory with the problem of "affects."

In my proposed theory, I distinguish two sets of human
aims, which I have named "goals" and "values." I have chosen these terms as extensions of the familiar concepts of ambitions and ideals, which have long been used to refer to personal aims within the realm of subjective intentionality.[3] The
range of psychoanalytic clinical material requires that we also
take into account the effects of prepsychological infantile experience on the patterning of later motivations. In other
words, the hierarchy of personal aims must integrate the
realm of subjectivity with a nonexperiential one involving organismic needs (see Chapter 2). When this hierarchy is established, probably in the latter half of the second year of life,
every piece of behavior comes to subserve both meaningful

[3]Perhaps the most significant theoretical contribution of Kohut's recent
work was his coupling of infantile ambitions and ideals in what he referred
to as the "nuclear self." This concept went considerably beyond Kohut's
only published definition of "self" (1970) or his usage of that term in his
1971 book, and in the direction of the ideas I am articulating here. Kohut
has not pursued this line of inquiry in any systematic manner. In his second book (1977) he specifically denies that a precise definition of the "self"
is desirable for the time being. With some inconsistency, however, he does
suggest a "broader" use for the term than the one in his 1971 book. This
broadening involves the adoption of the view Goldberg and I developed in
1973.

wishes and objective biological needs. The onset of these conditions is marked by the child's acquisition of reflexive self-awareness.

George Klein (1976) has supplied a list of personal aims which he calls the "vital pleasures"; his examples can serve as a tentative indication of what I have in mind by the concept of a goal. My use of Klein's specific categories does not mean that I regard the list he has developed as definitive or final. Klein divides human aims as follows: tension reduction, sensual pleasure, pleasure in functioning, effectance (i.e., power goals), pleasure in pleasing, and pleasure in synthesis. Some of these aims presuppose subjectivity and can therefore be regarded as ambitions; others, such as tension reduction, do not necessarily involve self-awareness, so that in principle they might operate on a nonexperiential level.

If we also divide values into subjective and nonexperiential varieties, we may construct a diagram of goals and values divided into those of the psychological realm and those that originate prior to its onset (see Figure 2). Subjective values are usually called ideals; among these, the moral standards have perhaps been mentioned most frequently. Prepsycholog-

	GOALS	VALUES
Subjective	Ambitions	Ideals
Prepsychological	Biological aims	Biological patterns

FIGURE 2
CLASSIFICATION OF PERSONAL AIMS

ical values involve biological patterning in terms of scales such as more/less, simpler/more complex, familiar/novel, endogenous/exogenous. These issues have not as yet been explicitly faced in psychoanalytic discourse. The epigenetic view of development implies that the nature of ambitions and ideals will depend on the prior configuration of biological aims and patterns. Conversely, it would dictate the view that these biological attributes will be assimilated into the realm of subjective motivations.

CHAPTER TWO

A Revised
Theory of Psychoanalytic Therapy

The Evolution of the Psychoanalytic Theory of Therapy

From its inception in the matrix of the therapeutic experiments of Breuer and Freud, the effectiveness of psychoanalysis as a clinical procedure has posed a continuing challenge for successive psychoanalytic theories of mental life. A series of differing rationales about the mode of action of Freud's treatment efforts was necessitated in part by gradual changes in his therapeutic procedures during the first two decades of his clinical work. The standard "psychoanalytic situation" finally crystallized in the course of the analysis of the Rat Man (Freud, 1909b; see also Nunberg and Federn, 1967). It consists of the "basic rule" of free association in the setting of a maximum feasible number of treatment sessions of agreed duration. Regularly using the couch, preserving the analyst's relative anonymity, making financial arrangements in advance, etc. are other aspects of the procedure which are usually considered routine. Adherence to these technical precepts has probably served as the actual criterion by which most observers have determined whether a therapist's work is truly psychoanalytic. This attitude has promoted an unfortunate tendency toward ritualizing our treatment

15

techniques at the expense of paying adequate attention to the principles of psychoanalytic practice, principles based on rational deduction from our most current conception of psychic functioning. Nonetheless, it would be grossly inaccurate to imply that the analytic theory of technique has been completely neglected since the procedure itself has become standardized. Dissatisfaction with the oversimplified precept of early psychoanalysis—derived from the topographic theory of mental function—that the task of the treatment is to make the unconscious conscious actually preceded Freud's revision of psychoanalytic psychology in the 1920's. The most articulate statement of the shortcomings of therapy based on this principle was made by Ferenczi and Rank (1924), who stressed the sterility of an interpretive strategy focused on verbalizable mental content. A combination of historical factors, more personal and political than scientific, discredited these proponents of the primacy of affective reliving—perforce in a largely nonverbal fashion—of crucial childhood feeling states within the transference setting (cf. Gedo, 1968). Progress in the psychoanalytic theory of technique took place along a different track, one that exploited Freud's (1923) refinement of the concept of resistances in his redefinition of the ego as one of the major structural divisions of the mind.

General acceptance of the structural theory enshrined Freud's new dictum: "Where id was, there ego shall be" as the sovereign technical principle of psychoanalysis. The actual interpretive strategies needed to implement such a program were spelled out over the course of two decades following Freud's metapsychological revolution, perhaps most notably by Anna Freud in *The Ego and the Mechanisms of Defense* (1936). At the same time, seeds of the realization that the tripartite model of the mind Freud proposed in 1923 could not properly organize the full range of observations of psychoanalysis as a general psychology began to appear in Hartmann's work on adaptation (1939). The progressive broadening of the field of application of psychoanalytic treatment during the last thirty years has gradually highlighted the inadequacy and over-all shallowness of explanations of the therapeutic process predominantly based on the structural viewpoint. Two major and mutually exclusive schools of thought attempted to fill this theoretical gap. "Ego psychology," dominant in the United States, placed its reliance on an economic point of view wedded to the presumed vicissitudes of psychic energies. The crucial concept, developed by Hartmann (1952), was that of neutralization. To illustrate the persisting influence of this theory, in spite of long-standing demonstrations that it is epistemologically untenable, let me cite Kohut's recent discussion (1971, pp. 48, 186-187, 208) of the treatment of "narcissistic personality disturbances," in which therapeutic results are attributed to the "progressive neutralization" of infantile narcissistic drives. The alternative viewpoint, which has triumphed in much of the rest of the psychoanalytic community, has been associated with the name of Melanie Klein. In its rejection of the structural point of view, Kleinian theory has, in essence, returned to a topographic one, so that its therapeutic technique employs the interpretation of unconscious fantasies, including fantasy systems assumed to be universally present as biological attributes of being human (cf. Segal 1974). The illegitimacy from a scientific standpoint of such an a priori interpretive approach should be apparent.

Models of the Mind (Gedo and Goldberg, 1973) was, I believe, the first attempt to arrive at a theory of technique based on a contemporary understanding of the epigenesis of mental life and the pathologies potentially produced by its developmental vicissitudes. Most relevant to my thesis here is our conclusion that the appropriate interventions of the analyst do not consist of interpretations alone. This view was derived from the clinical finding that functional regressions through the entire range of potential modes of the organization of psychic life take place in the course of every analytic process, no matter what the presumed diagnosis may be.

There is a specific therapeutic modality appropriate for the problem typical of each of the separate modes of function. On the one hand, most analytic patients for long periods achieve expectable levels of adult functioning in the analytic setting itself; at these times they may be capable of reaching their own conclusions about the significance of their self-observations. In such circumstances, the analyst can generally best assist this introspective work by lending his presence as an impartial witness, without further intruding on the analysand. On the other hand, whenever patients regress to the more archaic modes of mental organization, verbal interpretation—either of the resistances or of the wishes against which they have been erected as defenses—will prove to be insufficient or altogether inappropriate. Depending on the degree of regression, various interventions may be needed; in *Models of the Mind,* we devised the terms pacification, unification, and optimal disillusionment to characterize the interventions appropriate to the three archaic modes within the hierarchy (see Figure 3). Modell (1976) has recently indicated his agreement with this overall point of view about psychoanalytic technique; he has chosen to refer to the operations necessitated by any and all of the primitive modes of mental organization through a term of Winnicott's as providing a "holding environment." Modell has correctly emphasized that the classical technique of psychoanalysis, when properly utilized, automatically does this. In other words, what is under discussion here involves no actual departures from the usual analytic *procedures:* the issue is one of explicitly recognizing certain aspects of the psychoanalytic situation as legitimate and even essential factors in the process of treatment. Loewald (1960) made the same point in his discussion of the therapeutic action of psychoanalysis: ". . . a mature object-relationship is maintained with a given patient if the analyst relates to the patient in tune with the shifting

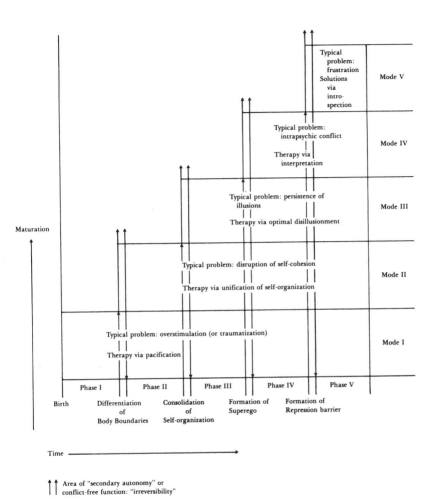

FIGURE 3
HIERARCHICAL SCHEMA OF PROBLEMS TYPICAL FOR
SPECIFIC MODES OF FUNCTIONING AND THEIR THERAPIES

levels of development manifested by the patient at different times..." (p. 20). It follows from this statement that the therapeutic aim of psychoanalysis must be conceptualized as the completion of interrupted developmental processes. Majority opinion has been more conservative on the score of the "model technique" of psychoanalysis. To be sure, it has been widely recognized that certain essentially nonverbal transactions must have taken place in order to make the analyst's central interpretive task possible. These transactions have been variously conceptualized as the creation of a "therapeutic alliance" (Zetzel, 1956) or as the performance by the analyst during the initial phase of treatment of certain "diatrophic," i.e., maternal, functions (Gitelson, 1962). According to these schemata of the analytic process, the nature of the analytic situation provides a holding environment (more or less automatically, depending on the perceptions of each analysand) as a prerequisite of the actual work; conversely, analyzability for Zetzel and Gitelson can be gauged in rough measure by the fact that the patient is able to form a therapeutic alliance without any specific effort on the part of the analyst.

This same principle was codified by Eissler (1953), when he defined as technical "parameters" the noninterpretive interventions necessitated by the individual needs of the analysand—legitimate departures from the basic technique only insofar as it is later possible to interpret their meaning and to explain to the patient the reason for the analyst's reluctant compliance with his special need. More recently, however, there has been some implicit shift away from the definition of psychoanalysis exclusively in terms of interpretation in Greenson's (1965) reformulation of the analytic process, which he regards as contingent on a "working alliance." As I understand this concept, it looks upon the manifold transactions that make interpretive work possible at each stage of an analysis, not as preliminaries to the principal task of the treatment, but as expectable and continuing aspects of the job itself. Needless to say, such a view also implies broader criteria of analyzability than those advocated by more conservative authors.

The Hierarchical View of Mental Life and the Theory of Therapy

My own outlook on the theory of therapy is a logical corollary of the epigenetic approach to psychological development. I believe that the unfavorable outcome of any phase-specific developmental crisis can be reversed only by dealing with those results of all antecedent developmental vicissitudes that later gave rise to maladaptation. These results constitute the functional handicaps that subsequently determined the disadvantageous dispositions requiring alteration in treatment. In other words, in psychoanalytic work we cannot afford to neglect any of the modes of psychic functioning present in the material; moreover, everyone who comes for assistance with any psychological problem whatsoever will inevitably respond to the analytic situation with the full gamut of functional possibilities. Hence, the provision of a holding environment, interpretive assistance, and witnessing the analysand's introspective efforts are unavoidable concurrent tasks in every analysis.

It follows, then, that the aims of psychoanalytic treatment transcend the realm of psychic life consisting of subjective wishes and ambitions. In other words, the patient's need for any aspect of an effective holding environment must not be equated with a wish. It is true that in the course of life he may have learned about some of the circumstances that favor his optimal adaptation so that he may secondarily develop subjective wishes for such "gratifications." For example, a wish for the availability of the mother, as betrayed by a child's anxiety about separating from her, does not indicate that his need for external assistance to maintain the integration of his behavior constitutes an *intention* on his part about which subjective awareness could ever be achieved.[1] To re-

---

[1] For an illustration, see Case 1 (Chapter 4). Specifically, note that the patient's wish for the continuous availability of a caretaker did become conscious after appropriate interpretation of his defenses against this humiliating knowledge. He was never able, however, to arrive at any understanding of the reasons for such a wish. The key to therapeutic change was the

state this point a little differently, it is the repetitive phenomena that Freud (1920) characterized as arising "beyond the pleasure principle" that require the provision of the holding environment in the analytic situation. These compulsive repetitions have never been understood through introspection; Frank (1969) has therefore aptly called them simultaneously unrememberable and unforgettable.[2]

It is perfectly true, of course, as Eissler stated in his work on technical parameters, that establishing better adaptation through a symbiotic relationship, which is what the provision of a holding environment amounts to, does not constitute an analytic end-result, or any kind of therapeutic success, for that matter. The "reduction" of the parameter, or (to put the same thing into more neutral language) the gradual elimination of the symbiotic bond through systematic verbalization, as demanded by Eissler, is indeed the actual curative step. By assisting the analysand to perceive the specific nature of his need and the manner in which the analyst has been able to meet it within the therapeutic relationship, we can help him to learn to perform the same functions for himself, presumably much as young children optimally learn to do so in the matrix of a "good enough" family environment (as Winnicott would have said). This process clearly does not involve the uncovering of unconscious wishes; it consists instead in apprehending hitherto unknown needs and developing rational programs for their fulfillment. Once the rationale of such in-

---

analyst's realization that the patient truly needed to have his activities monitored in order to avoid confusion.

[2] There has been no significant disagreement with Freud's conclusion that the explanation for these phenomena must be sought beyond the boundaries of psychology. His *specific* hypothesis to account for them, that of the death instinct, has found little support, except for the followers of Melanie Klein. One might see the transposition of the concept of the death instinct into the realm of psychology (as a source of unconscious fantasies) as one of the cardinal fallacies of Kleinian theory. This arbitrary metamorphosis of a biological concept into a psychological one illegitimately confuses distinct levels within a complex system.

terventions is understood in these terms, it serves conceptual clarity to define an "interpretation" proper as any therapeutic effort to bring unconscious wishes into awareness.

Another way to state this is that analysis should, in secondary-process language, raise the unrecognized biological goals of the human organism to the level of the person's conscious awareness in order to weave these aims into the self-organization in an optimally adaptive manner. It is the potential necessity for noninterpretive therapeutic interventions of this kind in every analysis that requires psychoanalytic psychology to go beyond purely "clinical" theories, such as those proposed by Schafer (1976) or G. Klein (1976). To repeat, such clinical contingencies show that our theories must include more within their purview than is contained in the patients' subjective material. In stating this, I am seconding the views of Rubinstein (1976), who was the first to emphasize that, in postulating a realm of unconscious mental life, psychoanalysis is centrally focused, even in its *clinical* concerns, on matters beyond the reach of the analysand's subjectivity and introspection.

If I have begun my discussion of the mode of action of psychoanalytic therapy with a lengthy exposition of those aspects of treatment which should accurately address themselves to certain objective needs of the analysand, I have chosen to do so because the consequences for the theory of therapy of my theoretical proposals in this work also point in a different direction. In general agreement with the critics of Freud's mechanistic constructs, I am impelled by my clinical experience to highlight the realm of subjectivity. It is for that very reason that, at this point in my argument, I wish to emphasize that man is also constrained to pursue organismic goals which always remain subjectively alien to him. Nonetheless, psychoanalysis as a therapy must be able to explicate for its patients the consequences of unrecognized psychobiological needs for their emotional life. I trust I have made it sufficiently clear that objective needs such as tension regulation or the capacity to make adaptive choices among conflicting alternatives can only be studied in a natural-science framework, i.e., that they do not lend themselves to introspective observational methods. In such matters, the analyst as an empathic observer must detect the patient's functional deficits, and he must convey to him the truth about these conditions.

The foregoing statements are particularly germane for the modalities of treatment applicable to the two modes of psychic organization which, in the adult, are the most regressed or "primitive": pacification (the return to tolerable levels of stimulation in Mode I) and unification (the integration of a coherent set of goals in Mode II). The third therapeutic modality which is implicit in a holding environment, the provision of "optimal disillusionment" (in Mode III) is no different in principle; in actuality, however, the task of identifying the patient's illusions depends on the analyst's assessments of reality. As various authors (Wallerstein and Smelser, 1969; Schafer, 1970b) have noted, such judgments are inevitably influenced by the observer's past experiences; to put the matter relatively simply, everyone is both culture- and character-bound in his view of reality. However difficult the task may be as a consequence of our personal limitations, appropriate and objective responses to the analysand's misperceptions of the actualities form part and parcel of every successful analysis (see Gedo, 1977b). It is quite probable that one of the "personal" factors entering into the "art" of psychoanalytic treatment and distinguishing the most skillful clinicians is the capacity to identify accurately whatever is truly illusory in the patient's perceptions of himself and of others, without confusing the presence of unusual but realistic configurations or actual originality with such distortions.

Having placed great stress on the necessity to incorporate the provision of a holding environment into the theory of psychoanalytic technique as a universal requirement of the therapeutic endeavor, I must now redress the balance by restating the obvious fact that interpretation, the modality of treatment devised for the handling of unconscious conflicts (in Mode IV), is an indispensable element of our therapeutic repertory, fully as important as the modalities I have emphasized thus far. Construed in the narrow sense, as a specific type of verbal intervention designed to elevate all aspects of a mental conflict into conscious, secondary-process thinking, interpretation always involves the identification of a wish and of the countermotives which oppose it. Optimally, each conflict in the present should be traced back to its childhood antecedents, if necessary with the aid of hypothetical reconstructions of the past.

CHAPTER THREE

Orientation for Clinical Section

It will become apparent from a reading of the case protocols I have prepared for this book that the evolution of my psychoanalytic technique has gone so far that traditionalists may choose to regard my clinical work as basically different from psychoanalysis as they have defined it. The theoretical justification for rejecting such criticisms has been stated in detail in Chapter 2. Here, it may be appropriate to discuss this issue from a more pragmatic point of view. I am convinced that the interventions I have attempted to systematize as the most appropriate therapeutic responses to the problems typical for early modes of psychic organization when they come into the forefront in the course of psychoanalytic treatment have, in fact, always been practiced by successful analysts. These aspects of the "art" of psychoanalytic clinicians have merely received no explicit attention in the literature on the technique of treatment, or they have been described as exceptional measures, reluctantly employed in particularly difficult cases as "parameters" (Eissler, 1953).

Consistent application of the hierarchical model of psychic life to the data obtained in the psychoanalytic setting led me to a very different conclusion. As I look back, I can see that, in the course of every analysis I have attempted, I have encountered behaviors organized in accord with each of the five modes we had described in *Models of the Mind*. In other words, every psychoanalytic encounter presents us with episodes of overstimulation, with temporary disruptions of a cohesive sense of self, and with a multiplicity of behaviors based on a variety of illusions. Yet the traditional theory of treatment addresses itself only to the problems typical of the more advanced modes of psychic functioning, the conflicts typical of Mode IV and the frustration experienced in Mode V.

Perhaps a more meaningful way to restate this issue is the reminder that the psychoanalytic view of psychopathology has far outdistanced our explicit rationales for the variety of interventions needed to deal with the broad range of problems we now treat. It is widely agreed that we can no longer make do with Freud's central conception with regard to the etiology of disturbed psychic functioning, the designation of the oedipal constellation as the "nuclear complex" of the neuroses. For one thing, the term "neurosis" in that statement was defined much more narrowly than is currently customary: we no longer find a focus on discrete syndromes, such as phobic or hysterical symptoms, to be sufficiently useful. We tend to seek an understanding of the whole personality in depth, and such an effort requires consideration of the developmental vicissitudes of phases both preceding and following the oedipal period. Symptoms that represent compromise formations (between dangerous wishes and the defenses against these) are still properly explained in terms of Freud's original proposals, but such explanations will not suffice for the complexities of human behavior beyond isolated actions.

To repeat, we no longer attempt to illuminate all of human behavior in terms of derivatives of the unresolved conflicts of the Oedipus complex. For some time now, the very lack of adequate resolution of the oedipal issues in childhood has been attributed, with increasing conviction and emphasis, to vicissitudes of the developmental stages that precede the oedipal crisis. This shift in viewpoint must be credited to the direct observation of young children by Mahler and her collaborators (Mahler et al., 1975), to the clinical discoveries of the school of Melanie Klein, of Kohut

(1971, 1977), and of Kernberg (1975). It is furthermore a reflection of our having replaced other concepts of development by the epigenetic one. The logic of this approach places
relatively greater weight on experience that has occurred
earlier in the lifespan, because the effects of resolving an
earlier crisis will influence a wider array of subsequent developmental vicissitudes. This point of view is, of course,
congruent with the widely shared clinical assumption that the
less opportunity the child has had to develop psychologically,
the more vulnerable he will be to environmental failures.

The theory of psychopathology developed by Freud
(1914) was applicable to the "transference neuroses"; individuals suffering from these conditions have managed to
traverse the earliest developmental phases of psychic life in a
more or less expectable fashion. This is the reason for
Freud's finding that their typical difficulties center on the
nuclear complex of the neuroses, i.e., on the vicissitudes of
the oedipal constellation. During the first half-century of the
history of psychoanalysis, only personalities organized in this
manner were thought to be analyzable. With the growth of
the epigenetic viewpoint in recent years, most of us have
come to regard such an ideal developmental course during
the preoedipal years as a theoretical fiction. Instead, we regard the specific outcome of the oedipal crisis as a function
of the particulars of the child's preoedipal experience.

Starting with the technical experiments of Ferenczi, which
I have described elsewhere (Gedo, 1968b) and with increasing emphasis since the death of Freud, the scope of
psychoanalytic treatment has been expanded beyond the
"transference neuroses." I am excluding from consideration
therapies that apply psychoanalytic psychology to the entire
range of psychiatric disorders by means of treatment procedures that definitely depart from that of psychoanalysis proper because they are designed to provide indefinitely what
Winnicott (1960) called a "holding environment." When used
with proper indications, such nonanalytic psychotherapies, as

I have elaborated on elsewhere (Gedo, 1964), can be of great value. As is well known, however, the classical technique of psychoanalysis proper has also come to be applied with some frequency to an increasing range of individuals with severe disturbances of character.

According to the more conservative school of thought within psychoanalysis, among these character disorders only those in which oedipal conflicts play a central role in the pathogenesis are analyzable. When this is in fact the case, the prominent preoedipal components of behavior are correctly understood as regressive defenses against the nuclear oedipal anxieties. More radical analysts, notably the followers of Melanie Klein and of other British theorists stressing the importance of object relations, have asserted that disorders based primarily on vicissitudes in the preoedipal phases of development can also be analyzed.

Probably the most coherent presentation of the more radical point of view has been that of Kohut (1968, 1971, 1977). In his view, there are two distinct types of analyzable disorders: the traditional transference neuroses based on conflicts concerning love and hate for the persons of the child's familial surround, and what Kohut has called "narcissistic personality disturbances." According to Kohut, the central problems in the latter do not involve significant sexual or aggressive wishes relating to other people; instead, he sees these difficulties as consequences of a lack of stability in the cohesion of the self.

In his initial contributions on this subject, Kohut (1966, 1971) thought of cohesiveness of the self as the consequence of adequate cathexis of the body (or perhaps of its mental representation?) with narcissistic libido—clearly, an unacceptably concrete use of the libido theory for an author who does not generally deal with psychic energy as though it were an entity in the physical world. More recently, Kohut (1977) has not used the libido concept, but he has not retracted his earlier statements, and it is not clear what he now has in mind when he uses the concept of a cohesive self. At any rate, it would now make better sense to abandon the term "narcissistic personality disturbance"; it would be more logical to refer instead to "self-cohesion disturbances," if we wish to use Kohut's clinical viewpoint.

Most recently, Kohut (1977) has begun to speak of these different types of disturbance as the problems of "guilty man" and of "tragic man," respectively. By guilty man, Kohut means an individual in conflict about the sexual and hostile wishes of the classical oedipal situation; his tragic man alludes to a person whose principal problems involve the realization of his ambitions and ideals. Kohut believes that these are distinct syndromes, a contention with which I disagree on the basis of my clinical experience, such as the first two cases included in this book. Although Kohut overstates the distinctiveness of transference developments along these lines in particular patients, I believe he is correct in stressing that either object-related or narcissistic transferences may be used defensively to screen more basic pathological problems; the latter may or may not turn out to be conflicts around the same type of issue as the one involved in the presenting transference configuration.

To repeat: in my clinical experience, patients who can be successfully analyzed do not fall into two groupings of the kind postulated by Kohut. It is true that I have encountered occasional instances in which the Oedipus complex seems to play little or no part in the pathogenesis, but such conditions do not imply that the principal difficulties lie in the "narcissistic" realm. On the contrary, such findings are generally related to an arrest of psychological development at extremely primitive levels, an arrest that involves both the sense of self and relationships to others.[1] Although Kohut's effort to in-

---

[1] In the absence of early arrests in development, i.e., in persons whose childhood development included the experience of an Oedipus complex, problems in the two spheres discussed by Kohut (1977, pp. 132–33) as "guilty man" and "tragic man" cannot be differentiated as a matter of

troduce distinctions into the category of analyzable disorders is, in principle, a step in the right direction, it does not, unfortunately, do justice to the complexity of psychoanalytic clinical material. Nor has Kohut proposed any modality of treatment other than interpretation to deal with the specifics of the psychoanalysis of either guilty or tragic man.

In his most recent work, Kohut (1977) comes close to endorsing the offer of empathy (apparently viewed as an interpersonal process, not merely an instrument for the recognition of psychological configurations in others) as the therapeutic tool of psychoanalysis, at any rate, one more important than insight. However, this view seems to apply equally to the treatment of both guilty and tragic man.

If we review the foregoing controversies vis-à-vis the theory of treatment, we see at once that they are related to the question of the central importance of the transference reliving of the "infantile neurosis" for the successful outcome of the analytic process. It is probably no exaggeration to state that many analysts gauge the results of psychoanalysis mostly in terms of whether or not the infantile neurosis has reemerged as a "transference neurosis" as a result of the work. A frequent corollary of this emphasis on the "working through" of the nuclear complex of the neurosis, although one that is always of questionable legitimacy, is the assumption that material referable to preoedipal issues can be dealt with, at least in those instances which are truly "analyzable," as the results of defensive regression away from the central, neurosogenic conflicts.

The traditionalist position I have just summarized, possi-

---

legitimate principle. In my clinical experience, and contrary to Kohut's explicit statements about his own (1977, p. 225), conflicts about love and hate for other people invariably co-exist with problems in the realm of the "self" (however those are defined). It should be kept in mind, however, that this issue is quite distinct from the question of separating narcissistic libido from object libido as separate lines of development (cf. Kohut, 1966; see also Kohut, 1971, p. 220).

bly somewhat arbitrarily, is not based on the epigenetic view
of development, but on its only serious alternative, that of
preformation. In accordance with this linear model, the
course of development is seen as an automatic progression
through a series of predetermined stages. Freud's initial exposition of the Oedipus complex may have been conceived
according to this conception of development, which is no
longer considered to be tenable within biology. Although
most psychoanalytic theorists have followed Hartmann (1939)
in rejecting the theory of preformation, we have by no means
reached unanimity on this score—adherents of the Kleinian
school in particular, as well as the followers of French struc-
turalism, have failed to espouse the epigenetic viewpoint. But
the failure to adopt it has been much more widespread with
regard to the theory of therapy, ever the last to be influenced
by innovations, than it has been in our developmental
psychology. Hence, many analysts who have adopted epigenetic positions with regard to explicitly developmental issues
paradoxically continue to believe that preoedipal material in
analysis can be interpreted simply as a regressive evasion
of the Oedipus complex.

The inadequacy of such a reductionist position might best
be illustrated through examples of successful analytic treatment of patients whose development has been altogether arrested in one of the earliest phases of development. Although
such patients obviously cannot re-experience an infantile
neurosis within the transference, in view of the fact that
psychological development in childhood never reached the
stage of self-other differentiation in which such a constellation could come into being, the resolution of archaic conflicts
through transference repetition does take place. In *Models of
the Mind*, such an analysis was described in detail, through a
discussion of a case reported by G. Zavitzianos (Gedo and
Goldberg, 1973, pp. 136-149; see also Gedo, 1966, 1967).
The resumption of development in the course of a successful
analysis of such a problem may enable the analysand to ex-

perience oedipal issues for the first time—not as the transference repetition of forgotten childhood psychic constellations, but as new object relationships in the present. Indeed, the distinction between the transference repetition of forgotten childhood complexes and the experience of a new mode of relatedness within the therapeutic setting is not always easy to make; failure to make it has often led to erroneous reconstructions of the past and to false theoretical inferences based upon these.

To recapitulate my argument: material referable to early modes of psychic organization appears in every analysis, and it does so not only as a manifestation of regressive resistance to the Oedipus complex—although, to be sure, one effective method of defense used by most analytic patients is to switch from one problem to another, without coming to grips with any. To put the matter into a truly epigenetic context, the conflicts of relatively later phases of development, such as the Oedipus complex in its entire configuration, actually consist of mental attributes maintained as a consequence of other ongoing conflicts that are legacies of earlier phases of development. Hence, the issues of later developmental crises are seldom resolved as a result of simply confronting the analysand with their continuing influence as transference repetitions. This statement is amply confirmed by the growing body of follow-up studies after "successful" analysis (e.g., Schlessinger and Robbins, 1975; Oremland et al., 1975). Nor is it based on empirical findings alone; rather, it is a necessary corollary of the epigenetic view. Only by altering the outcome of each of the earlier developmental vicissitudes does a more favorable resolution of later conflicts become possible, because the specific mental dispositions that proved to be vulnerable during the developmental crisis of the later phase were the direct products of those earlier crises. The psychoanalytic theory of therapy, like our nosology, is therefore in need of drastic expansion in the direction of greater complexity.

It should be added that the goal of altering the consequences of maladaptive resolution of early developmental vicissitudes is always only a theoretical ideal, more or less impossible to reach in actual practice. This is why psychoanalytic treatment cannot be expected to eradicate the conflicts of the Oedipus complex. As the various follow-up studies have shown, it usually leads at best to greater or lesser mastery over them. Such mastery can be maximized by careful attention to the optimal resolution of the legacies of earlier developmental stages; it is vitiated by treating these archaic problems as resistances to the main task of analysis—a focus on the Oedipus complex in isolation.

The clinical material I present in later chapters will illustrate an approach to the analytic task that pays equal attention to the derivatives of developmental vicissitudes at any and all stages. The crux of my technical recommendations is that each mode of functioning and its typical problems calls upon the analyst to intervene in a distinct manner. The optimal analytic situation (Mode V) is one in which it is sufficient to assist the analysand with his introspective efforts. More frequently, self-analysis encounters defensive obstacles that call for interpretations by the therapist (Mode IV). In response to more archaic material, he may be called upon to interfere with the patient's illusions (Mode III) through confrontations about the actualities, to give assistance in integrating the behavior of a patient threatened with an inability to correlate his various goals (Mode II), or with overcoming traumatization (Mode I). The manner in which the analyst has to move back and forth between these multiple frames of reference will have to be demonstrated by detailed case reports, in this book and elsewhere. I believe that the protocols of terminated analyses presented in Chapters 4, 6, and 8 will suffice at least to suggest that psychoanalyses conducted according to the foregoing theory of technique have a greater chance of success, in terms of both process criteria and in those of external adaptation, than those guided by a literal application of traditional theory.

So as to understand how psychoanalytic treatment actually operates, we must also keep in mind that modalities of intervention may be classified for didactic purposes, but are not always easy to categorize in that manner *in vivo.* In other words, a verbal interpretation about some intrapsychic conflict may have an impressively pacifying effect—to give only the most obvious of examples about the "multiple functions" (Waelder, 1930) performed by every transaction within the treatment situation. This phenomenon accounts for the fact that psychoanalysts have accepted the illusion that they are able to treat a wide spectrum of psychopathological conditions successfully through the sole medium of interpretation. To be sure, in order to maintain this fashionable fiction, it has been customary to disavow much of the activity that takes place in a successful analysis that is not directed to the analysand's unacceptable wishes or to the unconscious defenses against becoming aware of these.[2] Psychoanalyses performed with the foregoing principles in mind yield clinical observations that have received insufficient emphasis in the past.

In order to be able to bring attention to observations of this type, I shall be obliged to use accounts of analyses from my own private practice. I am aware that this choice creates insuperable problems from the viewpoint of scientific critics; there is no way of eliminating my subjective biases, the possibility of tendentious patient selection, and even the reliability of the data may be called into question. Nonetheless, I hope that it will be apparent that, in spite of the changes in

---

[2]The ubiquity of this disavowal is nicely illustrated by an exchange that took place in a seminar chaired by Rudolph Loewenstein. Loewenstein was asked whether it is permissible to communicate with an analysand by whistling a tune. Loewenstein was vehemently opposed to such a departure from analytic abstinence (as he saw the issue), and the majority of participants echoed his view. By dint of persistent questions over many hours, dissidents from this position were able to elicit a broad range of examples of noncompliance with these standards. In his characteristically graceful manner, Loewenstein ended the discussion by concluding that it is orthodox to tell a patient Jewish jokes, but whistling is out!

technique I wish to illustrate, the case protocols I have prepared are based on the classical psychoanalytic *method:* the
use of free association on the part of the analysand in the
presence of the analyst as an empathic witness who responds
from a position of freely hovering attention.

Some readers may regard it as a more serious problem
that my clinical records were not compiled for research purposes and contain only scattered details. They consist, for the
most part, of periodic progress notes written with the aim of
clarifying the analytic process for my own guidance. Hence, I
have been restricted in the range of case material available to
me to a handful of terminated analyses in which my recollection is sufficiently vivid to supplement these skeletal notes. If
I offer this clinical material without further apology, it is with
the conviction that the best I can do in any case is to *illustrate*
the issues I have in mind. No amount of case material, in
whatever detail and however checked for reliability, would
suffice to rule out alternative interpretations, questions about
therapeutic technique, and other doubts about my conclusions. Consequently, I have chosen to compromise by presenting the case material at sufficient length, I hope, to convey the flavor of the person and of his analysis but without
going into the specifics of day-to-day material.

As a result of this condensation, the case histories that follow may give a misleading impression of certainty—an air
suggesting the confident application of a complete and
finished schema. I have no way of refuting such a conclusion,
beyond asserting that, if anything, the contrary comes closer
to the truth about my usual working methods. I can only cite
the corpus of my psychoanalytic writings to bear witness to
the fact that my intellectual style is characterized by skepti-
cism about accepted formulations (cf. Gedo and Goldberg,
1973; Gedo and Pollock, 1976) and by a preference for
novelty—a style that should be evident from a reading of this
book. The interpretations I report as a matter of course in
the retrospective accounts in this book were actually ham-

mered out in the clinical situation in the usual trial and error manner characteristic of psychoanalysis.

Another way to phrase the same assertion is to restate my conviction that psychoanalytic treatment must go beyond the refinding of the familiar content configurations generally encountered in the material of any analysand's free associations. It must discover, instead, the personal significance of the ubiquitous themes of human psychic life in their specific interrelatedness for that individual. The case protocols prepared for this book summarize the significant meanings found by my patients, with my assistance, in the process of our common endeavors.

I have made every effort to protect the anonymity of my patients by eliminating and, wherever necessary, altering certain identifying information. I have also chosen to report only about the analyses of individuals unconnected with the mental health professions and otherwise unlikely to come to the notice of my readers. The other criterion I have used to make my selections was that of trying to present patients whose principal problems were centered at different developmental levels, in order to have clinical data of the broadest possible range available for consideration.

Although each of the analyses I describe was terminated on the basis of mutual agreement about the attainment of reasonable goals, I do not wish to claim that any of these treatments was either entirely complete or wholly successful in its outcome. One of the analyses (Chapter 8) was explicitly an effort in which only a sector of the personality came under scrutiny. For the purposes of this book, however, the pragmatic criterion of therapeutic success must take second place; the case material is cited to illustrate certain technical procedures and principles and to challenge the theoretical framework hitherto employed to illuminate psychoanalytic observations. For the purpose of facilitating theoretical inquiry, I attempt to present the case material itself without making use of the construct language of psychoanalysis, reserving formulations at the level of clinical generalizations and theories for the discussions that follow each case presentation.[3] Finally, I should perhaps call attention to the manner in which I have used traditional metapsychology in the "initial formulations" of each case. In my use of the familiar theoretical constructs of psychoanalysis, I have tried to minimize those of their unacceptable features which stem from their epistemological weaknesses (see Toulmin, 1978). To put this in another way, the clinical theories derived from Freud's metapsychology that I have found to be pertinent for the formulation of my case material do not utilize the aspect of metapsychology that has been most objectionable from a philosophical point of view: the postulate of psychological energies and their transformations. I should note, perhaps, that these constructs were also left out of account in *Models of the Mind.*

---

[3]With two exceptions: I have occasionally made use of the developmental concepts of oedipal and preoedipal phases as well as of transference. Although these terms, when used in their strict sense, belong to the traditional metapsychology of psychoanalysis, they have also been used in a much looser manner to refer to certain observable behavioral phenomena. In other words, in using the "Oedipus complex," I am referring to the child's intense, ambivalent involvement with his parents, including the erotic sphere; my use of "transference" designates the repetition in a treatment situation of past transactions with significant figures.

CHAPTER FOUR

First Clinical Illustration: A Disturbance of the Self-Organization

This man of 25 was sent to me specifically for analysis by a female psychologist who had been seeing him in psychotherapy for about a year in the out-patient department of a well-known medical center, but at the time of referral was leaving that clinic. From the initial consultation, the patient impressed me as a likeable and enormously talented young man immobilized by the very multiplicity of his goals, none of which did he experience as truly his own. He said he was a graduate student, but he had in fact dropped out of school, in so complicated and gradual a manner and with such an accumulation of unfinished obligations that he could not even reregister without having first met these old commitments, a task that would require many months of effort. On the other hand, he definitely did not consider himself to be a part of the adult world; he continued to live on the campus of the university he had formerly attended, very much part of the student community, undecided about what he might wish to be "when he grew up"—all this in spite of the fact that he had been completely self-supporting for several years and was a full-time *employee* of the university, playing an important, albeit self-taught, technical role in a long-term project involving the administration of the institution. Moreover, he felt himself to be completely isolated from the *students,* who were then almost uniformly caught up in the facile political enthusiasms of opposition to the Vietnam war, an issue he tended to view with the moral detachment and sense of tragedy of a Thucydides scholar. On the other hand, he expressed his distaste for mid-America and its constraints by adhering to such manifestations of the counterculture as a consuming interest in rock music, underground films, and taking various drugs, and by adopting a manner of dress which was both theatrical and eccentric.

It was in connection with these behaviors that we succeeded in establishing our mode of working together: when he asked me what my attitude to his drug-taking would be, I replied that I doubted whether he could afford to pay for drugs as well as the analysis at the same time—a statement that made him laugh with surprise and delight and one that was literally borne out by subsequent events. As for his clothing, within a few days of starting our work, and in response to his own declarations about feeling a lack of authenticity, I told him that his dress made me feel he was impersonating someone else, like a character out of a Toulouse Lautrec poster. With a glow about being understood, he confirmed somewhat sheepishly that he had copied the costume of the star performer in the most celebrated of these works. With these, as with subsequent interventions, he was able to deal in the spirit of having received information of value rather than criticism.

In line with his general uncertainty about direction (in both senses of the word), the patient arrived seeking the analysis recommended by his therapist, but could not immediately accept it when it was offered to him. Initially he attributed his reluctance to financial problems; however, mere confrontation with the fact that his indecision about committing himself to his job had resulted in receiving scant remuneration alerted him to the need to put his dealings with his employers on a more commercial basis. This decision produced the immediate result that he was able to ask for and received a substantial increase in salary through a change in job classification, which also made him eligible for significant insurance coverage for the analysis. It seemed that he had been able spontaneously and rapidly to identify with my forthright attitude about expecting appropriate payment for my work. These developments clarified the fact that he could actually afford analysis provided he were willing to accept some financial help his mother was eagerly offering him if he would only get treatment to straighten himself out. But if *she* wanted him to be healthy, he felt it impossible to move in that direction; similarly, he had had to break his engagement when he had seen the satisfaction with which his mother and his fiancée had been daydreaming about his future. Moreover, he had become unable to complete most of his courses in his master's program when, after his initial year, he had won a prestigious award generally reserved for students who had promise of developing a brilliant university teaching career. His feeling about this was best expressed during the terminal phase of the analysis when an interviewer asked him to explain his difficulty in completing this course work: with complete spontaneity, he burst out with the hitherto unformulated answer, "I had no wish to become a culture salesman."

When we began the analysis, it was already clear that he could not permit himself to surrender to his parents' expectations. In practice, this meant those of his mother, because his father's ideas for him were so foreign to his nature that he could disregard them without much feeling. He was enabled to effect a compromise and accept money from his mother when, in an effort to clarify his strange passivity in relation to his mother, I asked him how she could possibly prevent him from dealing with this as a loan, i.e., making repayment, if necessary to her estate upon her death if she refused it earlier. His "negativism" turned out to have many determinants, of course, but the one that first came to the fore was his shame about the profound gratification he experienced from his unique rapport with his wonderful mother, e.g., her unconditional willingness to *pay* for his analysis. He was the inheritor of the mantle of mother's revered father who had died when the patient was four. Grandfather had been a Hungarian musician who had come to this country as a young man, married and settled here, and became an outstanding figure in the musical life of the large midwestern city where the patient had been raised. Among other activities, he had been responsible for a successful series of children's concerts held throughout the entire metropolitan area, so that his grandchildren were aware of his accomplishments as long as they continued to live in their native city.

The patient felt that his grandfather's death had been *the* turning point of his life; since then, in some subtle way that he could not specify, nothing had been quite right for him, in spite of the fact that his mother had soon developed her special attachment for him, in obvious preference to his two siblings. From the older of these, a brother about three years his senior, he had always remained distant. This brother had been quite jealous of him during childhood and had taken every opportunity to attack and torture the patient, and because the two boys shared one room these assaults had been rather frequent. In the face of this persecution, which he never reported to his parents, the patient had remained outwardly passive; instead of fighting back, he had turned to the manipulation of a toy microcosm he had constructed inside a small box. This behavior had the flavor of a contemptuous dismissal of his older brother, an attitude that had continued into adulthood. Although his brother was married, was soon to present his parents with their only grandchild, and had a good position with a large business as a junior executive, he had clearly followed in the nonintellectual tradition of the father's side of the family and therefore could not communicate with the patient.

In contrast, the youngest of the siblings, a girl about three years the patient's junior, interested him intensely, and he

felt poignant guilt toward her because of the mother's preference for himself. This feeling had reached an apex in the
year preceding his winning the graduate fellowship, when his
sister, then a high school senior, had suffered an emotional
crisis, characterized by mutism, which had been dealt with
through a psychiatric hospitalization. The patient had tried
frantically to make the parents understand that the girl's
negativism was a response to their rigid expectations, and his
intense concern was still in evidence at the start of the
analysis, although by that time his sister had successfully
graduated from college. As a matter of fact, it soon transpired that the patient's readiness to do something definitive
about his emotional problems was somehow the result of having become convinced that his sister, although a markedly
shy and virginal bluestocking, was set on a satisfactory life-
course as a scholar and would not need family assistance for
psychiatric care in the future.

Although maternal grandfather had been self-consciously
Hungarian, the mother had been raised in a German-
speaking household and became a thoroughly Americanized
school teacher. She married a colleague from a lower-class
Irish Catholic background who eventually became a school
administrator. Mother returned to work around the time the
patient began school, so that he had suffered no real hard-
ship as a consequence of her professional commitments. He
recalled that it was at night that he could not manage without
her presence in the house in later childhood; although
adequate sitters had been available, he could never calm
down sufficiently to go to sleep while she was out, but immediately fell asleep when he heard the parents' car coming
into the garage. This inability to manage his own tensions
was still troubling him, and the only way he could get along
was to be utterly without scheduled obligations. He would
eat, sleep, work, seek companionship, or withdraw, completely on the spur of the moment; when he was bound to
the clock, his disrupted diurnal rhythms caused him to lose

track of the schedule and fail in whatever he undertook. One of the most important early discoveries of the analysis was the insight that such failures were in most instances not *motivated*—on the contrary, they made him extremely anxious and humiliated him; they were the *consequences* of disorganization. If, occasionally, he deliberately promoted such outcomes, it was in order to hide from himself the fact that most of the time he could not prevent them, or because he was trying, unsuccessfully, to master the humiliation of previous failures.

In contrast, his mother was superbly organized and an excellent organizer. Although at the conscious level he resented the help she continually offered him in this regard, his associations soon revealed that he expected and needed the same help from the analysis. He had given his mother many cues that he required her guidance, as he was now cuing the analyst that he needed the availability of a calm person who could keep track of a program arranged in accordance with the relative importance of its various parts. The analyst's statement that getting his head examined was for the patient the most crucial of his current enterprises and that all else had to be subordinated to coming to his sessions at the correct time made sense to him, and he gradually gained the ability to make some order out of the chaos of his previous drifting, at least during the working week.

Of course mother had tended to overstep the boundaries of his need; she had tried to organize him not in harmony with his own predilections but in terms of her own preferences, and he had reacted to this with outrage and negativism. In the analysis, he often repeated this pattern—sometimes on the basis of transference distortions. The most persistent of these was his conviction that, like his mother, I wanted to see him safely married and furnished with professional qualifications. More often, he was enraged by efforts on my part to structure "reality," however realistically, in ways that made more sense to me than they did to him. The best example of this early in the treatment was his decision to spend the first summer vacation period in helping a friend who wanted to make an underground movie by serving as his cameraman. Confrontations with the fact that this was yet another illustration of his quixotic propensity to rush to the aid of others when he could ill afford the time (or money or energy) it would take merely firmed up his determination. It was only years later, after the film had actually been put together and the camera work generally judged to have been successful, that it became apparent that I had overlooked a transference issue embedded in this matter. Impressed with the profound intellectuality of this student of the history of ideas, I had been incapable of imagining that he could have a meaningful personal commitment to a technical job. Not that this prejudice of mine had been incorrect per se, but in taking him for granted in this regard, I had repeated the behavior of his mother. Unlike myself, she was a person totally incapable of valuing abstractions; in fact, she was a splendid teacher of retarded children because she was a veritable genius of everything concrete. Her son had inherited much of her endowment, and she could not imagine that he would be interested in anything but the utilization of these talents for practical ends; his passionate interest in aesthetics, theoretical physics, or social science made no sense to her. In dismissing his hobby, in which he followed his mother's way of life, I had repeated her blunder of trying to categorize him exclusively within too narrow a framework.

One respect in which the patient had always been willing to accept his mother's help was when she performed her role as a mediator between him and his father. Everyone in the family recognized that father was a difficult and irascible person, although the full extent of his pathology was never faced. Though he was a competent school administrator, at home he behaved more like one of the children than head of the house. He seemed to be actually jealous of the maternal devotion his wife lavished upon their children, and because of her clear preference for the patient, the latter became the specific target of his hostility. As he grew older, the patient came to understand that his father's limitations of character had come about as a result of a difficult childhood capped by the early death of his own father. He could not quite grasp why a woman of his mother's sensitivity and warmth had chosen to devote herself to such a damaged person, but he never doubted that the parents' marriage had been mutually satisfying.

Whenever I misunderstood the analytic material, the patient responded with an intense transference resistance characterized by total hopelessness about the possibility of communicating with me. Interpretation of the genetic roots of this sequence in terms of his father's fixed conviction about the patient's primary badness—an attitude that had indeed defeated all of the boy's efforts to explain himself when accused of ill-will or selfishness—led to memories of the childhood regime which had contributed so much to his chronic state of overstimulation. The most unbearable aspect of this had been his utter lack of privacy; not only did he have to share a bedroom with his brother; in addition, there were no doors on this room, and the lights and noises of the main areas of the household penetrated the space where the children were put to bed with the injunction to go to sleep.

To be sure, the patient had been and remained unusually susceptible to excitement; for a long time, every minor success, including an analytic session in which he felt he had communicated something of importance to me, was so stimulating to him that he became disorganized and might miss the next session altogether or arrive late for it. However, with consistent interpretation of his propensity to get overstimulated with no methods for pacifying himself as one of the major problems of his life, he gradually gained the ability to anticipate these untoward reactions and thereby to increase his tension tolerance.

The patient's view of himself was, needless to say, complex and inconsistent; however, in spite of his bewilderment about what he added up to, he could always cling to the knowledge that competent outside observers had found him to be very superior in endowments. Nevertheless, whenever he felt himself to be unusually talented, this hopeful fantasy made him fear that he must be crazy to have such thoughts. He had, in fact, when in first grade, been selected by a state-wide program that identified and followed unusually gifted children, and throughout his school years certain instructors, including many of the most accomplished ones, had not hesitated to label him a genius. His childhood model and idealized hero had been Albert Einstein; when his parish priest had announced that salvation depends on baptism within the church, he had indignantly abandoned Christianity: any dogma that made no provision for an Einstein's greatness had to be inadequate.

He proved to be similarly independent-minded on certain other crucial matters, such as the need to get away from his father's parochial prejudices. He could not share the latter's fear of the Jews or his panic about the gas lines in the basement—which father insisted on having disconnected for reasons he could not satisfactorily explain. His decision to enroll at a famous university bitterly hated by his father as a hotbed of Eastern radicalism received essential support from his mother. The only intellectual defeat he had ever sustained occurred when he entered college with the hope of becoming a nuclear physicist: he found that his mathematical abilities were not sufficient in scope to permit him to compete successfully in that field (i.e., not at the level of a world's champion). Although clearly disappointed, he shifted in good grace to the field of social science and made a brilliant undergraduate record. He had difficulty in courses only when *he* found the instructor to be inadequate, because in such circumstances he would withdraw with the feeling of hopelessness which his dealings with his father had aroused in him.

During the early phases of the analysis, two parallel

themes predominated. On the one hand, everywhere he went the patient felt drawn into attempts to rescue or to help needful people. His fervent commitment to an ethic of goodness went beyond any need to make reparation to his sister: it had the quality of an immoderate ambition. This was of one piece with his general attitude of having to be above mundane matters; this in turn made it very difficult for him for a long time to recount his associations as they occurred, without transforming them into clever abstractions. He also showed lack of moderation in his choice of women, getting involved in an affair with a rising pop singer whose frenetic lifestyle was hardly compatible with his felt need for order and calm. When her infidelities and general unreliability drove him into wishing to disengage from her, his sense of values did not permit him to drop her, no matter how bothersome she had become, so long as she expressed a need for him. He also found it difficult to settle for any woman less extraordinary than she was; his interest was aroused only when he met someone with a creative gift. If he could not be the Café Singer Lautrec had immortalized, he could at least share in a woman's success in that field, vicariously.

Another area of immoderate ambition affected his work habits. Not only did he do his own work, spending countless hours—mostly during the night—disentangling the inevitable chaos on a large project; he also did much of the work of his immediate superior, a middle-aged woman often incapacitated by depression. He did not hesitate to go to people at the top of the administrative hierarchy with incisive suggestions about how they should perform their work. Although his interventions were at first regarded as mere impertinences, he gradually gained the attention of the more competent authorities and was promoted into the planning phase of the operation. He had had no previous exposure to this technical field, but he mastered it within a few months through independent study, and the pattern of doing much more than his own assigned work soon reasserted itself, again earning a mixture of appreciation and hostility from his as-sociates. In the meantime, much of the analytic work consisted of matter-of-fact examination of these behaviors, with attempts to differentiate arrogance and unwarranted claims of uniqueness from his really superior performances. He was highly gratified at having found an impartial and expert witness who echoed neither his father's malevolent depreciation nor his mother's automatic assumptions that he possessed special merit.

The second principal theme of the first year of analysis was the manner in which the analytic experience had become essential for him if the patient wanted to maintain his sense of direction and purpose. Every interruption of the schedule of appointments, at first even that of an ordinary weekend break, disorganized him. After he had learned about this pattern, which he conceptualized as being equivalent to the necessity of utilizing a program in computer work, he became able to bridge the gap from one scheduled appointment to the next, i.e., to maintain his sense of cohesive purpose as long as nothing interfered with his four weekly sessions. It was quite remarkable how *impersonal* his use of the analyst remained: he regarded me as if I had been an unfailing information bank. Thus, he took it for granted that I would be able to fill in the gaps in his grasp of the data of his grandfather's Hungarian background, and it never occurred to him that my performance on this score could only mean that I am also Hungarian—from his point of view, *all* adequate psychoanalysts had to be able to function as Hungarians. When my work struck him as actually superior, he might respond with dreams such as one in which he was viewing a magnificent exhibit of marine life at the Art Institute. His associations led to his ecstatic and solitary childhood expeditions to the natural history museum of his native city—the director had been a friend of his grandfather!—and to the shift of his major interests from natural science to aesthetics. What particularly pleased him about his analysis was the profusion of pictures in my office.

On the other side, he was perpetually afraid that he

would learn something discreditable about me. In this connection, it was significant that he knew that his former
therapist had left her job to make a second marriage, and
some months later he thought he had seen her wheeling a
baby buggy and leading a toddler along beside it by the
hand. Needless to say, this was a misidentification and a
transference reaction which alerted me to the probability that
he had felt deserted by his mother, not immediately upon the
birth of his younger sister but several months later, during
the grandfather's terminal illness. And indeed, as the history
became filled out, it turned out that his mother had thrown
herself with tremendous energy into nursing her father; she
had taken her two younger children to his house with her
every day, and the patient's principal early memory was that
of riding his tricycle, all alone, back and forth on the
sidewalk in front of the grandparents' house. There were
some indications that, after her father's death, his mother
had been under great stress because her husband absolutely
could not tolerate any sign of her mourning; it was from this
period that the patient's feeling that nothing was right any-
more actually dated: if mother was not perfect, nothing could
be right.

As the emotional climate of this period of his childhood
was being reconstructed, early in the second year of analysis,
the patient realized that his paramour was a psychotic woman, and he grasped the impossibility of his grandiose quest to
repair her pathology through the magic of personal contact.
He also realized that such efforts were in identification with
his mother's caretaking attitude toward everyone, especially
with her success in coping with her husband's paranoia—even
at the cost of relinquishing her deep emotional need to
mourn for her father. We were thus able to reconstruct the
emotional consequences to himself of the childhood situation:
with his grandfather's death, he had also lost a greatly admired and benevolent figure who had both put his father
into the shade and had to a certain extent succeeded in coun-

tering the latter's hostile influence. As a child, the patient could not turn to anyone as a replacement for grandfather until he gained the capacity to utilize more remote idealized models, such as Einstein. It was, of course, no coincidence that he chose a great man who had been subjected to irrational persecution, such as the malevolent treatment he was experiencing at the hands of his own father, the anti-Semite.

What was of even greater importance had been the fact that the strain of caring for three children under the age of six, a paranoid husband, and a dying father had obviously been too much even for his superbly competent mother, and his absolute trust in her perfection had broken down. It was at this time that he had withdrawn into the solitary daydreams of manipulating the microcosm he had created in his toy box; and it was the repetition of this disillusionment that he was continuously anticipating with dread in the analytic transference.

About the middle of the second year of analysis, there was a period of stubborn unwillingness to associate, which brought into focus his lifelong anal retentiveness. Constipation had been a chronic problem for him. He finally recovered memories of his reaction to his sister's birth, when he had been about two-and-a-half. This response had been a combination of clinging to his mother and fecal retention. His attitude of refusal to progress and to attempt to do original work could now be ascribed to his boundless childhood admiration of his mother's miraculous creation of new life, compared to which his feces had seemed humiliatingly worthless. Insight into these feelings was followed by his creating a beautiful woodcut, which he sent out as his Christmas card. Upon receiving this, I felt confident in affirming to the patient that he possessed major artistic talent; whereupon he was able to realize that he had never attempted to utilize this before because he was color-blind, so that he felt he could never hope to excel in the principal media. He also gained insight into the hostile component of his retentive and negativistic behaviors, i.e., into the wish to defeat his mother, and now his analyst, by remaining infantile and unsuccessful, thereby tarnishing the excellence of these caretakers.

By the end of the second year of treatment, repeated interpretation of his disruption whenever the analysis was unavailable so that he could not borrow organizing functions from me had helped the patient to master the consequences of what he now referred to as "disorder and early sorrow." The fact that his need for my collaboration was made explicit helped him to realize that his mother had never taken credit for performing similar services for everyone in the family, so that he had been able to make use of her without acknowledging to himself what she had been doing for him. As he consolidated this knowledge, he learned to tolerate my absences, even if they were relatively unexpected ones, by keeping in mind his expectable reactions to them. He was able to remain functionally intact by preparing a schedule in advance, to which he could then adhere without too much difficulty—and with increasing flexibility.

In such circumstances, the negative reaction to being left to his own devices began to take place after the resumption of our work. It therefore became possible to focus on the vengeful motive behind these regressions. We were thus able to reconstruct the childhood situation in which he attacked his mother by analogous regressive reactions, e.g., the fecal withholding. She had been unable to reverse these developments because she had responded to them as evidence of her humiliating imperfection as a mother. Consequently, instead of confronting the boy with his anger and investigating its causes, she increased his rage through the irrelevance of her subsequent preoccupation with her own lack of worth (i.e., the defeat of her own inordinate ambitions).

Following this period of reconstructive work, the patient was able to remain well organized through a six-week summer vacation break. Henceforth, he underwent disorganization only in extraordinary circumstances in which he felt helpless, such as being held up at gunpoint on one occasion, or, in the context of termination, after the extraction of a wisdom tooth. His job performance had been so superior that he received an increase in salary which made him completely self-supporting, including payment of his analytic fees. In the fall, he fell in love—for the first time—with a young woman decidedly more solid than anyone he had ever dated before. In the hope of impressing this scholarly person, the patient resumed work on his long-abandoned master's thesis, the major stumbling block to his re-enrollment as a student. When the young woman did not respond to him with—by his standards—sufficient enthusiasm, he felt severely injured and ragefully abandoned his academic pursuits. This sequence of events permitted the reconstruction of his abortive childhood experience of the oedipal situation: he had attempted to take revenge on his mother for her continuing loyalty to her husband by frustrating her hopes for his own progress and by making her feel guilty and/or inadequate as a mother by engaging in regressive behaviors.

In the analysis, these issues were also relived during the third year in terms of his competitiveness with me on a phallic level, now focused on my power to analyze patients. In this connection, the central ambitions of his childhood emerged from repression: he disdained scholarly pursuits because his archaic wishes had been far greater; he wished to achieve on a larger scale the omnipotence he had possessed in his daydreams, that of controlling the miniature universe of his toy box. The derivatives of these ambitions that were still operating in adult life had been in the political sphere, and one of the distractions that had originally interfered with his graduate work had been his increasing immersion in student politics. It had only been the growing tendency of the student organization to focus its attacks on the university itself that had stopped his participation: he had come to see that, before he had started his analysis, it had been the various schools he had attended which had more or less provided him with the idealized matrix he had needed to sustain his sense of purpose. Hence, in addition to his other reasons, he could not permit himself to complete his studies because that would in all likelihood have forced him to leave the campus and thus to face disintegration.

The realization that his actions had been primarily determined by a quest for power had a revolutionary impact on the patient's life. It now became clear why he preferred to put in uncounted hours of overtime work on his job: time allegedly needed for the academic pursuits he had always assumed he was most interested in. There had always been time enough for reading whatever gave him pleasure, including difficult treatises on social theory or philosophy; what he had disdained was required work which only led toward his degree. His current role at the university not only paid better than any academic employment was likely to do in the foreseeable future; it also gave him the feeling that the institution was at his mercy: most of its operations depended on the administrative matters over which he had some control. And as he came to appreciate how much of his effort had been invested in making this archaic fantasy of power come true, the patient gradually lost interest in promoting institutional reforms or in improving the budget. He was particularly shocked about having to acknowledge that he was, in fact, identified with his father's and older brother's administrative orientation and shared their disdain for the impotence of academics. He now abandoned the pretense of bohemian heedlessness about the practicalities of life; he began to dress in a rather conservative fashion (quite distinctive on the contemporary campus scene), consistently refused offers of marijuana to smoke, and altered his living arrangements from being a roomer in a Charles Addams household to that of renting an attractive small apartment, which he fitted out with his mother's welcome assistance.

Similar changes also took place in his dealings with women. He acknowledged that he had avoided relationships in which mutuality would have been possible; girls had had to seek him out for some pressing need of theirs while he remained detached and superior. We ended up in characterizing his attitude as that of Baron Ochs in the *Rosenkavalier:* without him, the nights were declared to be long; only by having *him* could a woman avoid unhappiness. He had maintained this fantasy through a system of elaborately rationalized avoidances, which now gave way, leading to a new kind of relation with a woman. Specifically, he once again sought out the girl he had "fallen in love with" the year before and then precipitously dropped because she had not responded to him with wholehearted enthusiasm. He now approached her without demanding any special status, and he found himself, for the first time in his life, experiencing an enthusiasm about the *other* person which was a new way of experiencing love. This feeling, interestingly, did not specifically require sexual consummation, although such gratification had been a routine aspect of his previous relationships with women. He did not become disillusioned or discouraged, in spite of the fact that the woman was scheduled to leave town at the end of summer and refused to change her plans for his sake. His high regard for her survived her departure, and in a somewhat paradoxical way he was gratified about the fact that the whole experience with her had merely added up to having to renounce a person he had come to esteem. Subsequently he had a rather casual affair with a coworker, without feeling trapped in the relationship or humiliated about her lack of extraordinary qualities.

As the archaic ambitions which had determined much of his behavior were uncovered at the end of the third year of the analysis, the patient gradually found himself more interested in getting consensual validation for some of his fertile intellectual preoccupations. He had to admit that pursuing scholarly goals entirely on his own, as he had been doing for some years, had been overly ambitious and the results not entirely satisfactory; i.e., he faced up to the fact that the university had something to offer him academically and was not just requiring him to live up to a set of rigid regulations. Although it provoked storms of resentment in him to give various people (mostly his mother—and the analyst in the mother transference) the satisfaction of *his* success becoming *their* success, he took himself in hand and ascertained that he could clear up most of his unfinished courses by the end of the summer, leaving him only his thesis and one academic year of part-time work to complete for his degree. He succeeded in meeting these requirements during my vacation at the end of the third year of analysis, and in the fall he was readmitted as a student in good standing.

The following academic year constituted a lengthy terminal phase: as graduation was approaching, he made it clearer and clearer that he would consider his analysis to be finished at the same time. He was well able to add the course work he had to take to his usual work load, and he was quite gratified to find that he was really very different, at the age of 28, from most other students in his program. He soon came to the conclusion that the ten years he had spent on various campuses undoubtedly had given him the most splendid liberal education imaginable. What he found even more satisfying was feeling himself to be a member of an older generation: he had now "grown up." His instructors responded to his papers with lavish praise; these writings were the products of research he very deeply enjoyed.

None of this was in the forefront in the analysis, however; what concerned and preoccupied him was his project for a master's thesis. Although his topic sounded quite reasonable both to me and to his advisors, he experienced some difficulty in organizing his presentation, and the whole matter assumed greater significance for him than any single requirement for graduation should do.

When the first draft of the thesis was completed, the patient brought a copy to me with the request that I read it. I agreed to do so, on condition that no specific time limit be imposed on me. As it happened, I finished my reading at about the same time as the official readers of the university did. This turned out to be of some moment, because one of the readers claimed not to understand the paper; the fact that I unequivocally stated that it was clear for me emboldened the patient to stand firm and to become more and more explicit in his claims for the importance of the intellectual content of his work. As it happened, the young professor whose limitations were exposed in this process felt quite humiliated, and retaliated by demanding that the paper be rewritten on a much simpler topic.

In these circumstances, the patient therefore re-experienced the childhood situation in which his father and older brother had been overtly hostile whenever he had shown his creative mentality; the difference in the present was that unlike his mother, who tried to restore peace by getting the patient to diminish the provocation of appearing superior, the analyst responded to the situation by reconstructing the past and thus indirectly confirming the worth of the patient's thinking in the present. It should be noted that I ventured no opinion whatsoever on the merits of the original ideas expressed in the patient's manuscript; on the contrary, after affirming that these were understandable to a well-intentioned nonspecialist reader, I took some trouble to confirm his tentative realization that I was much less knowledgeable in the areas covered by his topic than he had imagined I would be. He was able to tolerate this disappointment without any strong reaction, but henceforth he became much more realistic in his expectations concerning what various authorities might actually know.

In spite of the strong temptation to revert to his old pattern of contemptuous withdrawal, the patient was now able to learn to tolerate the frustration of his need to receive a fair assessment from authority figures. He insisted that his thesis be officially evaluated as he chose to submit it, and he also sought out a number of unofficial opinions about it from eminent thinkers on the campus. On the basis of one of these readings, he was invited to enroll in a doctoral program in a field contiguous to that of his official specialization, with the idea of expanding his paper into a book-length dissertation. In the meantime, however, the official reader did not allow him to graduate in June. Although quite anxious about asserting the possibility that he had made a significant intellectual contribution, for the first time the patient knew what people must have meant in calling him a genius. In the past, to think that he could really be a creative intellectual had made him feel that he was crazy. In his struggle, he was now sustained by the example of his latest hero, a great social scientist who had waited six years for the doctorate a prejudiced faculty had refused to grant him. And when the patient's father started fulminating about the dreadful Jews who were placing obstacles in his son's path, the latter was now able to *refrain* from telling him that in the whole situation the only "Jewish" role had been his own. In other words, he stopped attacking his father by flaunting his identification with the Jews. As for paternal support, he was able to obtain it by identifying with the famous American scholar who had told his own skeptical father that he was not willing to follow him into the banking business because he was not interested in accumulating money. The father had reportedly replied that, in that case, his son was already well off.

As soon as the offended reader had left for the summer, the department assigned a substitute who approved the thesis, and the patient was graduated in August, while I was away on vacation. Everything else in his life was proceeding in an orderly and satisfactory fashion, so that he then decided to terminate the analysis in mid-September, shortly before he would become involved in his doctoral program at the start of the new academic year. The tone of the end of the treatment might be conveyed most succinctly through the dream he reported in the last session. In this he had a sailboat tied up at the Michigan Avenue bridge, a structure he had crossed every time he came for one of his sessions. He had been taking sailing lessons from a pilot-instructor, confining the boat to the Chicago River. The pilot was now leaving the boat; they shook hands to say goodbye, and the patient, on his own, sailed the boat out of the river onto Lake Michigan. The mouth of the river constituted a sharp drop, so that once the boat entered the lake, he could not sail it back to its former mooring. He faced the wide horizons on the lake with the feeling that he could now go in any direction.

There has been a single, chance encounter since termination, although the annual Christmas woodcuts have continued to arrive. When we met each other at a concert, about two-and-a-half years after ending the analysis, he greeted me warmly and asked to have a chat at intermission. He then reported that he felt subjectively pleased with life and with his own performance. He has continued in his job, with appropriate advancement and increased responsibilities, and he had used his improved financial resources to furnish an apartment in a modern high-rise. He had also made satisfactory progress in his doctoral program and was about to take his qualifying examination. He deeply enjoyed intellectual interchange with certain outstanding scholars in his department. With real enthusiasm, he announced that he was engaged to the young woman he had begun to date toward the end of the analysis.

CHAPTER FIVE

Discussion of the First Case

Initial Formulation of First Case

The analysis of this complex character disturbance at first focused on his negativism, which was primarily related to conflict about having been his mother's favorite child. The patient's avoidance of the potential benefits of this relationship seemed to expiate guilt about the misfortunes of his younger sister. Attempts to interpret the regressive episodes that constituted his adaptive failures as part of this pattern of expiation, however, proved to be unproductive. It was the interpretation that these failures were often not desired, but, to the contrary, were in fact consequences of trauma, that led the patient to discover his unconscious wish to be helped to avoid these disasters by the kind of guidance in the transference that his mother had volunteered in the past.

This increment of insight on the basis of accepting the traumatic nature of his regressive episodes seemed to confirm the hypothesis that the latter had not been motivated by wishes to elicit mother's positive response to his pregenital dependency, or by unconscious needs for punishment for such wishes.[1]

[1] I believe this to be an example of an apparent "negative therapeutic reaction" that turned out not to be based on unconscious guilt or even on simple repetition in the service of mastery. Some readers of this case history have, however, disagreed with my interpretation that certain regres-

The maternal transference emerged, at any rate, around the issue of accepting help; it was characterized by anally tinged struggles about commitments, regularity, and obligations. Whenever the patient felt misunderstood, he shifted to a father transference marked by intense hatred and contemptuousness. Gratification within the mother transference, on the other hand, produced regressive episodes—clinical events of the kind Freud designated as actual neuroses (cf. Sadow et al., 1967) and Kohut (1971, p. 229) as the psychoeconomic imbalance often encountered in "narcissistic personalities" because of a defect in the "basic neutralizing structure of the psyche."

Ordinarily, however, the transference took the form of identification and/or competition with mother as a benevolent and self-sacrificing caretaker, with hints of arrogant and grandiose attitudes about his capacities in this regard. This grandiosity broke down with every separation from the analyst, with experiences of disorganization and subjective helplessness; by implication (as well as more explicitly in the latent content of dreams) the maternal transference now reproduced the early childhood idealization of the mother. This aspect of the regression turned out to be a defense against the possibility of reliving the disillusionment with her which had traumatized him when the grandfather had died.

Acknowledgment of mother's limitations as a caretaker was followed by moderation of the patient's own ambitions in that area. In terms of the genesis of the character pathology,

---

sive episodes demonstrated by this patient were incidental consequences of malfunctioning; they have insisted that *all* behaviors *must* be reflections of wishes of some kind. What a comforting view of the human condition that particular vulgarization of psychoanalysis provides! The argument is an echo of the rejection of Freud's concept of "actual neuroses" on the very same grounds. Because there is no way of proving that unconscious wishes are *absent,* the claim that *all* behavior is based on subjective motives is not a scientific hypothesis but an article of faith which cannot be discussed fruitfully.

it now became apparent that he had fallen back on a primitive narcissistic position of grandiosity under the impact of this disruption of the relationship with mother. Contrary to expectations—because the reversal of a regression usually leads to material from a later period—the reversal of this regression led to the recovery of memories from an *earlier* period, that of the third year of life. Repetition in the transference led to reconstruction (and ultimately to recall) of his awe and his competitive envy of the mother's reproductive functions, and this insight removed his avoidance of creative activities. This self-restriction had been based on the dread of narcissistic mortification. He also discovered that this defense had, simultaneously, served as a successful attack on mother by defeating her parental ambitions; he now became aware of this because of his wish to depreciate the analyst by ruining his work. This phallic competitiveness also took the form of a reluctance to acknowledge his need for the continuous availability of analysis in order to maintain his narcissistic equilibrium. Thus he came to realize that his mother had helped him to patch over his "disorder and early sorrow" and had not, in fact, unduly interfered in his life.

Acknowledgment of his pregenital dependency brought the negative maternal transference into focus, specifically his rage about the enforced separations of an analytic schedule. This made it possible to understand that many of his regressive behaviors, albeit not all, *had* been motivated by vengefulness, i.e. they were not always passively experienced. His mother had been unable to cope effectively with these covert attacks upon her because of her own narcissistic vulnerability about her worth as a caretaker. Insight into the destructive significance of lapsing into disorder henceforth enabled the patient to avoid disorganization.

He then began to try himself out in the heterosexual arena, but proved not to be able to tolerate frustration in the sphere of phallic narcissism. His spitefulness when his masculine pride was injured recapitulated the childhood oedipal pattern with his parents. In this context, the crux of his infantile competitiveness with his father emerged from repression: he was uniquely invested in exercising administrative power, especially in a school setting. This realization led to extensive adaptive changes as the patient relinquished these immature ambitions and re-evaluated his current vocational commitments. Similar changes took place in his relations with women; he began to be able to tolerate frustration in the romantic sphere without loss of self-esteem or narcissistic rage. Finally, mastery of his competitive conflicts permitted him to relinquish grandiose attitudes in the intellectual realm, leading to resumption of his studies.

These cumulative successes brought into focus the issue of his resentment about potential exploitation, either by his parents in the past or the analyst within the transference, as a narcissistic extension of another person. As this conflict was gradually mastered, the analysis entered the terminal phase. In this context, he re-experienced his childhood response to envious attacks by males with greater power (father and brother), now re-enacted in the academic arena. The transference significance of this situation turned out to be the gradual deidealization of the analyst, who—unlike the childhood mother—neither claimed expertise in the matter that had provoked the controversy nor tried to create peace by manipulating the participants. At the end, his status had diminished to the modest standing of an instructor, although, to be sure, the regressive pull to return to analysis had to be counteracted by dreaming of insuperable physical obstacles to such a shameful temptation.

In summary, then, this man had several years of untroubled development before being "narcissistically" traumatized by a disillusionment in his mother's perfection. This vicissitude may have been particularly difficult to overcome because the father was quite unsuitable as a replacement for her. At any rate, a regression to pathological grandiosity ensued. The child came to the oedipal phase with this developmental lag; the narcissistic trauma of the parents' sexual superiority reinforced the regressive retreat into grandiosity, and he abandoned the sexual love for the mother in favor of anal-aggressive interactions with her; he also identified with her ambition to be an omnipotent caretaker. An arrest in development had thus come about, affecting certain essential self-regulating functions. Although without the participation of mother or a substitute for her he frequently lapsed into overstimulated states, he continued to disavow his symbiotic needs and grandiosely risked adaptive failure.[2]

For the purpose of comparing the data of this case with those of the others to be presented in subsequent chapters, it may be desirable to reduce the material even further by means of the hierarchical model; the patient's progressive and regressive fluctuations both before and during the analysis may be entered with regard to a series of psychological functions on the general developmental model (see Figure 4).

The presenting clinical picture most closely fits into Mode III of the hierarchical schema. The patient's overt behavior was typically that of a kindly caretaker who resented intrusions upon his own autonomy and held his father's arbitrariness in contempt. This seemingly adequate reality adaptation in terms of his conscious attitudes would be classified as Mode IV in the hierarchy; unfortunately, it did not hold sway at many crucial junctures. More significant and intense features of the personality were disavowed: his separation anxiety, the rage whenever those he depended on failed to live up to his needs for perfection, and his tendency, when he

[2]This case history is particularly illuminating about the issue, so hotly debated in recent years, of the classification of character disturbances in terms of pathology related to object love (and guilt) versus narcissism (and self-realization)—a proposal put forward by Kohut (1971, 1977). In this case, such a schema is clearly unsatisfactory: "narcissistic" fixations rendered the child incapable of tolerating the demands of the oedipal crisis, and the Oedipus complex was decisive in creating the "narcissistic" regression that made it impossible to solve the problem through repetition.

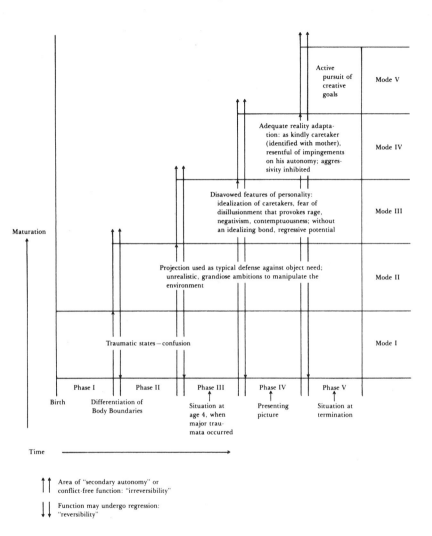

Mode V
Active pursuit of creative goals

Mode IV
Adequate reality adapta-
tion: as kindly caretaker
(identified with mother),
resentful of impingements
on his autonomy; aggres-
sivity inhibited

Mode III
Disavowed features of personality:
idealization of caretakers, fear of
disillusionment that provokes rage,
negativism, contemptuousness; without
an idealizing bond, regressive potential

Mode II
Projection used as typical defense against object need;
unrealistic, grandiose ambitions to manipulate the
environment

Mode I
Traumatic states — confusion

Maturation

Phase I Phase II Phase III Phase IV Phase V
Birth Differentiation of
Body Boundaries
Situation at
age 4, when
major trau-
mata occurred
Presenting
picture
Situation at
termination

Time

↑↑ Area of "secondary autonomy" or
conflict-free function: "irreversibility"

↓↓ Function may undergo regression:
"reversibility"

FIGURE 4
DATA OF CASE 1 IN ACCORD WITH THE HIERARCHICAL SCHEMA

became disillusioned, to regress to more archaic behaviors.
These regressions produced disorganization (classified as
Mode II in the schema), with unrealistic grandiose fantasies

of omnipotent control over various institutions coexisting with states of helplessness. Moreover, on occasion, his incapacity to plan led him into traumatization (Mode I). During treatment, secure idealization of the analyst permitted progression (to Mode IV) and the unprecedented emotional experience of working through the competitive conflicts of the Oedipus complex, including his anxiety about threatened retaliation for his phallic aggressivity. Gradual relinquishment of the idealization of the analyst ushered in functioning for the most part in an expectable adult manner (Mode V).

The foregoing formulations may serve as an optimal example of the power of selected theories of psychoanalysis to organize the observational data obtained in the clinical analytic situation. An impressive range of clinical inferences about functioning in adult life, childhood development, the unfolding of the analytic transference, and the outcome of treatment can be correlated by means of psychoanalytic psychology as a developmental schema. I believe this to be particularly true if we systematically use a set of preselected epigenetic categories, such as the hierarchical model. In this instance, the procedure has permitted the conclusion that psychological development had been arrested by the child's inability to weather the narcissistic frustrations implicit in the oedipal situation; secondary regression had made him symbiotically dependent on others to maintain adaptive equilibrium. Self-esteem could be bolstered through grandiose illusions, but, in the absence of a suitable symbiotic partner, the patient was vulnerable to disorganization and trauma. Because he had a favorable development for at least the first three years of his life, the fixation point for his psychopathology was a relatively late one, and the syndrome can be conceptualized as a narcissistic personality disorder that prevented resolution of the Oedipus complex. Yet, after all this has been said, we cannot be certain that this clinical theory has captured the essence of the patient's human complexity even in this relatively uncomplicated case. Could we, perhaps, do better without resort to the usual psychoanalytic constructs? Let me try.

Reformulation of the First Case

The prevalent negativism with which this man shied away from success turned out to be a manifestation of pervasive rescue fantasies, and it was definitely not self-punitive as part of an expiatory effort. It was the recognition of the fact that, at bottom, the patient was seldom motivated to fail that actually put the analytic work on a secure basis. He was able to confirm that his adaptive disorganization generally came about against his real intentions, as a by-product of his rashness in failing to make adequate plans and his disregard for the actual necessities of life. This realization confronted him with the need to depend on others for rational guidance. As a result, his ambivalence about accepting help was brought directly into the relationship to the analyst because treatment impinged on the patient's need for personal autonomy. Thus, regressive episodes of confusion could also come about if guidance were offered in a less than optimal manner, so that he would have to reject it to safeguard his subjective sense of independence. The most flagrant instances of unempathic interference with his life within the analysis brought his childhood hatred of his paranoid father into current focus.

Whenever uninterrupted and empathic analytic work made it possible to moderate his ambitions to take care of others sufficiently to bring order into his life, the patient experienced the analyst as an omnipotent maternal figure. Through interruptions of the analytic work, he relived the disruption of his early childhood reliance on his mother, who had also failed by undertaking more than was humanly possible. This insight led him to recover earlier memories of awestruck admiration for and attempted imitation of her creative functions, especially that of childbearing. By restricting himself in the creative sphere, he had successfully avoided re-experiencing the childhood feelings of inadequacy in comparison with mother; simultaneously, it had diminished her excellence in her own eyes because of her perfectionistic ambitions as a parent. Episodes of childlike incompetence could therefore be used in the service of this hostile aim, although the hostility was aroused most frequently by another set of issues, that of impingements on his autonomy, or, conversely, by actual failure to meet his needs.

In childhood, as in the present, he had difficulty in achieving intimacy with a woman because he could not tolerate his own imperfection within the relationship—exactly as his mother had been unable to accommodate to her own as a parent. Consequently, at the height of his phallic competitiveness, he had turned away from heterosexual ambitions and had adopted his father's power goals instead. Gradual insight into the perfectionism behind the inability to compete markedly improved his capacity for expectable mutuality in current object relationships. The setting aside of his inhibitions about optimal use of his abilities brought him face to face with hostile responses from the environment similar to those he had endured as a child from his brother and his father. In this context, the meaning of the analytic relationship as a protective matrix like that provided by his childhood mother was understood and relinquished.

In summary, the key to this man's difficulties turned out to be his identification with his mother in her goal of perfection. Because he also absorbed her goodness as a value system, his own competitiveness in any sphere brought him into unavoidable conflict with moral perfectionism. Even more serious was the inability to tolerate personal limits, which caused him to turn away from adaptive solutions in favor of grandiose fantasies,[3] modeled on his parents' activities. The

[3]This case history supports the hypothesis I have elaborated elsewhere (Gedo, 1977b) about the source of subject-centered grandiosity in the child. The grandiose fantasy is a cognitive structure, and its acquisition is prob-

ensuing adaptive deficit made him dependent on the protection of a rational caretaker who could moderate his dangerous rashness without violating his need for autonomy.

Discussion

I do not know to what extent readers will share my judgment that the reformulation of the case material is actually clearer and makes the task of empathy with this person easier than the more traditional manner of summarizing the case did. Perhaps, in this instance, there is no great advantage on either side, and one might make a decision on the basis of personal taste. Yet, it should give us pause that our construct language adds so little to a formulation of case material that it seems to be no more than an irrelevant paraphase of clinical interpretation of the observed data. At any rate, the issue deserves to be investigated through further comparisons of the explanatory range of these two types of formulation. It is quite possible, after all, that my first illustration may happen to have concerned exactly the kind of patient whose psychology lends itself to exposition without resort to familiar clinical theories. On the other side, it might also be noted that I have taken care to use the theories of psychoanalysis in my initial formulation in a manner that minimizes some of their disadvantages. To be precise, I have avoided anthropomorphism and reification; these are the principal dangers, as Grossman

---

ably the result of complex transactions with the familial milieu. In this instance, the child resorted to magical thinking precisely in the same manner as his mother had done—a finding confirmed in my experience with every analysand who has relived such archaic transferences. Although these primitive modes of thought are probably extremely widespread, if not ubiquitous, we may infer that, in principle, appropriate child-rearing practices may minimize or even prevent their development. I believe that these considerations throw severe doubt on Kohut's developmental schema (1966) which attributed the grandiosity to universal vicissitudes of "narcissism."

and Simon (1969) as well as Schafer (1976) have pointed out, for psychological theories cast into the mold of materialist or energeticist epistemological assumptions.

In terms of the treatment process, this case presents existing psychoanalytic theory with a more severe challenge. The analysis was put on a solid footing—as we are now accustomed to say, a "therapeutic alliance" was established—through a series of noninterpretive interventions designed to deal with the disruptive consequences of the patient's inability to establish a consistent and adaptive hierarchy of aims. One example of such an intervention is the set of hints about an acceptable solution for the problem of financing the treatment contained in the analyst's exploration of that dilemma. Certainly the most important of these confrontations was the statement concerning the patient's repetitive failures, i.e., the judgment that they were frequently the unintended by-products of poor planning.

Some observers might look upon the analyst's allusions to the prospective analysand's poor working conditions or to his perplexity in the face of his mother's excessive generosity as technical parameters, adequately accounted for in the theory of treatment of psychoanalytic ego psychology. I do not believe, however, that anyone would regard the clarification of the cognitive deficit that created disorganized behaviors as a parameter, although many analysts would doubtless dispute its validity. Some commentators might classify such a statement as an interpretation, but this usage would reduce the meaning of that term to the designation of any verbal intervention on the part of the analyst. If we agree to preserve the technical specificity of the concept, interpretation must continue to refer only to those statements that translate hitherto unconscious material into discursive language. But this particular explanation did not refer to mental contents at all; it was directed to the understanding of overt behaviors. As such, it is analogous to the judgments analysts are continually called upon to make about matters such as the proper system within which specific sensations reported as associations should be understood: sinus headache or conversion reaction? the aura of migraine or creative imagery? angina pectoris or hypochondriasis?

These reminders about the ubiquitous need for psychobiological judgments in the course of every analytic session should quiet our doubts about the technical propriety of noninterpretive statements about adaptive functions in the nonexperiential realm, e.g., the necessity of making choices among mutually exclusive alternatives. The traditional theory of treatment has completely disregarded analytic activities of this kind, although they form a larger segment of the analyst's actual interventions than do interpretations in the narrow sense. Hence, it has been overlooked that every psychoanalysis is largely concerned with the provision of a holding environment. At the same time, we did not possess any explanation for this phenomenon from the perspective of the patient's intrapsychic world; it has been dealt with exclusively in terms of the various theories of object relations which have of late competed for the attention of psychoanalysts.

In my view, the central task of the analysis in the foregoing case proved to be to provide a convincing demonstration of the patient's need for external assistance both in regulating his propensity for overstimulated states and in organizing his multiplicity of uncoordinated goals into a coherent program of action. By responding to these needs only insofar as the analysand indicated his desire for assistance, it was possible to improve his capacity to regulate tension and to unify his hierarchy of aims by verbal means alone. It did not prove to be necessary to correct the patient's grandiosity through explicit confrontation with the actualities of life—the emergence of grandiose fantasies into consciousness was sufficient for their renunciation. In the terminal phase, however, illusions about the analyst's ideal qualities were relinquished only when he demonstrated in action, in connection with the issue of his alleged expertise about the subject matter of the patient's thesis, that the latter's view of these qualities had been unrealistic. After the analysand learned to create his own holding environment, he became enabled for the first time to tolerate the conflicts of phallic competitiveness through renunciation.

CHAPTER SIX

Second Clinical Illustration: A Case of Fixation upon Archaic Goals and Values

A married woman in her mid-thirties sought analysis because she had developed peptic ulcers after interrupting a relationship with a former psychotherapist. After some years of twice-a-week treatment, this had evolved into an affair consisting of polymorphously perverse behavior which she had experienced as humiliating. Although extremely afraid of becoming dependent on treatment, she accepted a senior consultant's recommendation of analysis because she had not felt content at any time in her life.

The patient was the only daughter and middle child of Methodist missionaries; she was born in the middle of a period of service her parents spent in Lebanon. Her mother, a member of the New England patriciate, had never taken responsibility for child rearing, and so the patient's upbringing had been entrusted to a Maronite nurse. The family was forced out of the Middle East by the outbreak of the Second World War, so that she lost this mothering figure before the age of two. As the outstanding feature of later family life, she recalled the bitter enmity of her older brother. The boy, who was born before the move to Lebanon, was rageful and uncontrolled as a child; he developed into a marginal, though highly gifted person as an adult. Toward her younger brother, born in this country when she was five, the patient had taken a maternal role. She had always remained distant from her father, although he had tried to be very loving with all of the children. Her aloof behavior toward him had apparently begun while he had been away at graduate school for a period of almost a year upon the family's return to this country. In addition, she had bitterly resented his humiliating intrusiveness with regard to her bowel functions. He had checked into her performance in this regard on a daily basis, dosing her with a glass of hot water at breakfast. The parents eventually settled into the life of teachers in small denominational colleges around the South.

When the patient went off to college, she quickly married a foreign student, knowing that she did not love him, but feeling great urgency about having to acquire a man. She had brushed aside her father's hesitant objections to this match, as well as the more tactless remonstrances of certain members of her mother's family; she had felt morally superior in dismissing these warnings as based on ethnic prejudice about her prospective husband's Polish-Jewish background. He became a financially successful but professionally mediocre general practitioner who ruled the house as a tyrant. They had three children, a boy, a girl, and a boy, in the same order as in her family of origin; the youngest was an impulsive, enuretic five-year-old.

By the time the analysis was actually begun, after a few weeks' delay, the ulcer had become asymptomatic. To be more precise, the symptoms that had led to this diagnosis abated gradually, perhaps on the basis of medical management instituted before the patient decided to seek psychological assistance again. The diagnosis had presumably been based on radiological findings; however, this information could not be taken at face value because it was transmitted to the patient through her husband. Her passivity in these matters was striking; she relied on her husband to deal with his circle of medical collaborators concerning her health status as she had had to lean on her father about her bowel functions as a child. She tended to treat the issue of this somatic problem, as well as that of any other danger to her bodily integrity, as a purely mental phenomenon, to be properly dealt with through exclusively psychoanalytic means.

Although it took much effort, over a period of years, to demonstrate that this was essentially a delusional "mind-over-matter" attitude, it is entirely possible that in the specific instance of her gastric symptoms she may in fact have been correct. The "educational pressure" exerted by repeated confrontations with her magical thinking about her body in the analysis finally shook her belief in the possibility of ameliorating certain skin problems which flawed her complexion (a highly prized aspect of her appearance) through "insight." She had expected cure through some kind of magical utterance by the analyst confirming her conviction that she was unconsciously ruining her marvelous peaches-and-cream skin as a self-punitive act. With great reluctance, she finally consulted a dermatologist—if only to prove that no medical measures could overcome her unconscious sense of guilt. Fortunately, a relatively effective medication was prescribed which kept the mortifying problem under control, and this object lesson finally demonstrated to the patient that her "psychosomatic" theories had been untenable rationalizations for a grandiose fantasy.

Subsequently, to my great relief, she accepted a referral to a competent gastroenterologist and was able to cooperate with his efforts. I had found it very difficult to work under the sword of Damocles of having to be concerned about potential gastric hemorrhages or perforation while, in the patient's mind, full "responsibility" for the fate of the "ulcer" was placed on the analytic work. Ironically, no trace of an ulcer was found by the consultant in spite of occasional symptomatic recurrences. The latter were temporally related to periods of emotional withdrawal by the patient, generally under the impetus of some transaction within the analysis which she experienced as a disappointment or humiliation, i.e., they occurred in circumstances analogous to that of her rupture with her former therapist. Eventually, therefore, it began to seem most likely that, at least during the analytic process, the "somatic" symptoms were of a hypochondriacal nature.

To take up a sequential account of the analytic process, initially, the work was mainly concerned with establishing that the analysis was entirely her own. In practice, this meant proving that her husband could not control and manipulate the treatment, especially with regard to schedule and fees. When this effort succeeded (i.e., when I proved that I was willing to face her husband's wrath by insisting on payment for appointments she would have missed if she had accompanied him on a vacation he had scheduled in disregard of her analytic commitment), she began to experience the analysis as a repetition of her father's control over her bowels. This was manifested in the form of her utilizing every cue about my view of reality as a literal prescription for living. In this context, she realized that she had been living a symbiotic life in her marriage because she felt unable to function without feeling connected to a man. (The specifically sexual aspect of this will be discussed shortly.) However hollow and worthless she felt when left to her own devices, grandiose illusions of adequacy coexisted in a split-off part of her personality: she felt herself to be unusually intelligent and beautiful and, above all, socially and morally superior.

After the establishment of a stable transference of this kind, the first major interruption of the analysis revived in her a subjective sense of helplessness which lasted for several weeks. This state was presumably similar to her reaction to the loss of her Lebanese nurse when she had been a toddler. She retreated into haughty aloofness or silence, which I sometimes experienced as spiteful and sometimes as stunned and empty. Although I was not able to formulate the problem in any clear manner at the time, in retrospect (i.e., in the light of transference developments that occurred several years later in the analysis) it seemed that the speed with which such a profound transference reaction had been brought about may have been caused by the success of my firm stand against her husband's attempted interference with the analysis. In the sense of having acted as a rescuer from the incompetence of her former caretakers, I had actually repeated the sequence of events in her early childhood, only to abandon her prematurely, as her nursemaid had done. At the time, however, all I could deal with was the fact that she tried to disavow her needfulness in a grandiose way by focusing all of her concern on her husband or children. This was illustrated by an impressive dream in which she dove into a pool to rescue her oldest, a preadolescent boy who was, as her associations revealed, a champion swimmer. In childhood, she had similarly shown altruistic concern for her brothers, especially the baby whose relative neglect by their mother had deeply troubled her. Insight into the disavowal of her own needs led to some diminution of her "masochistic" behavior in the marriage.

Another aspect of grandiosity which came to light was the formerly disavowed fantasy of perfection as a parent. Demonstration of the connection between her sense of worthlessness and the selective negligence about her youngest child's difficulties (i.e., her identification with the least acceptable aspects of her mother's behavior in her middle childhood) led to the resolution of this paradoxical behavior. As she abandoned the pursuit of two mutually incompatible goals, she initiated getting psychiatric help for her son. In a similar way, behind her complaints about frigidity and her conviction of her own shittiness, there were disavowed fantasies of perfection as a woman. Perhaps most significantly, her fantasies of moral perfection also came into the open. Gradually, as the chronic split between her conflicting aims was slowly overcome, i.e., as she reconciled these mutually contradictory views of her personality, she developed a more realistic assessment of herself, with great pain about her *actual* deficiencies, revealed in the following context. Toward the end of the second year of treatment, with general improvement in her functioning, she expressed wishes that I admire her for her actual qualities, but was deeply humiliated by the characterological handicaps that precluded such appreciation in the analytic setting. This insight, in turn, led to a steady and gradual expansion in the scope of her activities, no matter how much she dreaded potential failure and humiliation.

Unfortunately, her husband could not tolerate this growth; their estrangement deepened, and they discontinued sexual relations. What was worse, his intolerance was not based simply on his characterological problems—to her great dismay, he obviously preferred more active and accomplished women.[1]

The patient's anxiety now began to center on her fantasy that I would interpret her outward improvement as evidence of substantive change and would insist on termination so that she might be deprived of the analytic relationship, which she now experienced as essential for her. Thenceforth, throughout the analysis, there was consistent focus on this separation anxiety. As she increasingly recognized the legitimacy of her needs, she began to express her hitherto disavowed rage and aggression. These feelings were now provoked by any sign of imperfection on the part of the analyst. On the basis of this consistent transference reaction, her disillusionment with her mother, experienced around the age of five to six, could be reconstructed; this disappointment had been especially keen around the issue of the mother's inability to care properly for

[1]It seems probable that he couldn't stand these changes because he interpreted them as products of the success of her analysis. He had tried analysis for himself several times with negative results, and he had adapted to this bitter disappointment by taking the position that psychoanalysis is fraudulent and worthless. Thus his wife's improvement was probably a direct threat to this important bulwark of his self-esteem. An attempt on the part of the patient to encourage him to try analysis once more, with the hope that the management of characterological problems had been improved with recent advances in understanding, foundered when an analyst he consulted prudently discouraged the attempt.

the brother born when the patient was about five. In the transference, the repetition of these reactions of disappointment was alternating with overtly idealizing the analyst's therapeutic capacities.

This propensity for idealization was by no means an unprecedented development in the patient's emotional life: on one occasion before marriage and once afterward she had developed idealizing romantic crushes on men, and she had felt analogously enthusiastic about her college roommate. In each instance, however, the idealization had given way to disappointment. Based on the repetitive nature of this pattern, I attempted the reconstruction that her bitter contempt for her mother had been preceded by a conviction of the latter's perfection. This hypothesis was amply confirmed; in fact, as it turned out, though the disappointment with mother's helplessness with the baby born when the patient was five had been very real (and had set the patient on her defensive course of altruistic surrender through being everyone's good mother which, at the same time, satisfied her ambition to achieve moral superiority) this disillusionment had been by no means complete or lasting, and the surface depreciation of mother still screened a good bit of continuing awe.

Indeed, the mother was in most ways an extraordinary woman. Although she had no aptitude as a parent, as she had discovered to her sorrow with her first child, she had been forthright in facing this and made alternative arrangements for her subsequent children. What seemed so disappointing about her performance with the last child was inherent in the circumstances of a penurious life in the rural South. By contrast, during the patient's infancy, the advantages of Westerners in the Middle East had permitted her to provide very well. In every other respect the mother had seemed well adjusted and competent, indeed quite evidently superior to her husband. Their marriage was harmonious, for both were able to accept themselves and the other as they were.

During the patient's childhood the mother was active as

an instructor of physical education for girls at various colleges where the father taught history. At the same time she was intellectually alert and widely cultured. For instance, not only had she learned to speak Arabic during her residence in Lebanon, she had also managed to acquire unusual expertise about Middle Eastern artifacts and Arabic literature. Of her children, only her intellectual and musically gifted oldest son seemed to have taken after her. The patient and her younger brother were decidedly more like the moderately competent father who had failed in his efforts to gain a Ph.D. after the return to this country.

Undoubtedly the mother also possessed a streak of self-centeredness which was focused on two specific issues: her femininity and her family origins. She was unusually attractive and appealing to men. Not only was the father very devoted to her; when she became widowed, relatively late in life, she was able to make a brilliant second marriage within the exclusive social circles appropriate to her actual origins. She was vain about her appearance, spent a great amount of time and effort on her grooming, and had exhibited her body to her children in a seductive manner which stood in sharp contrast to the father's modesty about his person. The household was organized to pay tribute to these merits, and she was never *expected* to participate in the care of the children (except for the short hiatus between the stay in Lebanon and the beginning of the parents' teaching activities in the South, for much of which she returned to her parental home in New England). Child care was thus the responsibility of the father and of hired help; by implication, children were like the domestic animals kept by the poor Southern towns-people with whom the family did not mix. (Incidentally, it may be of interest that the mother's body narcissism was transmitted by the patient to her sons and not to her daughter. She stimulated each of the boys into impressive athletic accomplishments.)

The matter of family pride was more complex. The

mother's parents were indeed American aristocrats, descended from Mayflower settlers, but the strain had somehow gone to the bad, and their household had had the flavor of Arsenic and Old Lace. In most ways, the patient's mother was the least impaired of the bunch. Most of her siblings never married, and some had crossed the boundary between eccentricity and some form of genteel psychosis. Nevertheless, most of them had decent, if unspectacular, professional careers. Mother's youngest sibling became a physician, married, and was childless for a long time. Many of the patient's childhood summers had been spent at his home, and he was the one male figure in the family who could in some measure compete with mother's glamour. The family had looked upon the mother's marriage to a poor missionary of obscure origins as a *mésalliance* (destined to be outdone only by the patient's *gaffe* with an immigrant Jew!), but it would have been more accurate to see her decision as a logical outcome of the family tradition of Puritan moral commitment. Of course, the mother really had not bargained for the hardships of the penurious life of teachers in obscure denominational schools. Nor was she satisfied, in later years, with the social cachet of the Mayflower: she was spending her old age trying to prove that her first American ancestor was descended from one of the signers of the Magna Carta. Disillusionment with this mother may well have been a prerequisite of sanity!

An unusually long vacation during the third year of treatment once more brought to the fore the patient's paralysis in the face of abandonment. Upon resumption of our work, there were episodes of rageful silence and/or temporary chaos in her thought processes. She felt free to be spiteful because of the suffering the analysis was inflicting upon her. This suffering was also erotized, with elaborate masochistic masturbatory fantasies which warded off feelings of being empty and alone.

It should be added that, at least within the range of her recollection, there was no precedent for her masturbatory self-indulgence. In retrospect, it seemed that the urgency she had felt about getting married in college had been a flight from similar needs to employ autoerotic satisfactions upon being separated from her family. (An additional consideration had been the marriage of her admired roommate, i.e., an identification with an idealized figure.) She had also been frightened of becoming promiscuous with men, but this conflict had not had the intensity of her humiliation about masturbating. There could be no question about the fact that she had only been driven to do this as a last resort by her husband's sexual withdrawal; one reason she could never even contemplate leaving his bed before, no matter how badly he had treated her (and he had at times beaten her in a manner seldom encountered among professional people), had been her fear of being compelled to masturbate. What was so humiliating about this act had nothing to do with the stimuli, physical or mental, she utilized to arouse herself sexually; sexual life with her husband had consisted mostly of the same experiences, albeit less effectively administered by this impotent and ungiving man. What she could not tolerate was the idea of having to do these things for herself instead of having someone else at her disposal to do them for her. This issue was dramatically portrayed in a dream in which she represented herself as a fish, safe in what she associated was her husband's aquarium and then released into a stream where it had to seek its own sustenance.

Although the emergence of masturbation was, in a sense, a by-product of these marital vicissitudes, the patient never wavered in viewing it as the result of strength gained through analysis. Humiliated by the means, she nonetheless found tremendous support in the outcome of masturbation. To be precise, she experienced the capacity to give herself serial orgasms *ad lib* as a firm bulwark of her sense of self, a confirmation of autonomy, of feeling alive and real, and of being competent to pacify herself. The identity that was affirmed in these acts was explicitly bisexual and simultaneously oral, as indicated by the fish symbolism in the dream. (Consideration of the identification with Jesus Christ also implicit for her in this imagery is omitted here.) Phallic and vaginal aims were given focus alternatively in succeeding masturbatory acts, and the greatest satisfaction accrued from her ability to reach orgasm by two entirely different physical methods, one of which had, for her, masculine, the other feminine, significance. The change in her view of herself as a consequence of acquiring the capacity to masturbate was most beautifully illustrated by a dream which followed the establishment of this new pattern. The scene was that of a primaeval swamp, consisting of mushy and slimy vegetable matter in decay, broken trees, etc.—a stagnant mass. Gradually, she began to discern movement; the surface started to break up, more and more running water became visible, the foul compost was washed away; eventually a beautiful and clear river emerged, which she viewed with great emotion. Ironically then, her feeling of shittiness was replaced by one of purity and health when she could move from the emotional position of the asexual and obedient (but anally retentive) child to that of the phallic and vaginal being who had the wherewithal to exclude everyone from this area of her functioning. In other words, although she felt it to be a humiliation to have to do this for herself, she had experienced an even more drastic sense of inadequacy when she had been forced to rely on somebody else for measures necessary to maintain a sense of meaningful participation in life.

The actual focus during masturbation was not on the physical act, however, but on elaborate and conscious fantasies with which she had been preoccupied since childhood. Briefly, these consisted of a fictive world of her own devising, later thinly disguised in ethnographic trappings when she learned about these in the course of her education. In this "primitive society," women, explicitly including herself, were uninterruptedly subjected to various tortures and humiliations by men, generally while being tied to trees or otherwise narrowly confined. There were innumerable monotonous variations on this theme. Although the fantasy was now erotically charged and had been so for decades, in the beginning the excitement it generated had not been clearly genital. If anything, sexuality first entered this private world as a *post hoc* explanation for the men's conduct in tormenting her.

It became quite clear that she had tried to live out this fantasy in her choice of a husband who had initially warned her to avoid him because of his tyrannical disposition. His origins in a patriarchal family had aroused her expectations of being made into a passable approximation of the women in her fantasy. Her husband had, in fact, fallen far short of these hopes, being more detached than sexually rapacious, and irritable about being slighted rather than sadistic. As a result of his relative passivity, he was unable to arouse her sexually, and it was this limitation of her femininity that had led her to seek treatment in the first place. The fact that her therapist then lived out with her a much more vivid and satisfying version of the fantasy testified to the intensity of her wishes (as well as to the degree of his miscarried empathy). She had rationalized the perverse activities between them on the basis of the psychiatrist's statement that it was therapeutically indicated as a rehearsal of what should take place in her marriage. What had finally alerted her to the fatuousness of these proceedings had been the therapist's distressed confession that he was falling in love with her. And her subsequent characterization of the situation as humiliating had nothing to do with the superficially "humiliating" features of the perverse practices which, according to the therapist, were supposed to be (correct enough) action interpretations of her sexual wishes; on the contrary, her early dreams in the analysis indicated that she had felt abused on the basis of her preconscious perception that she had become the medium for an unconscious homosexual transaction between her husband and the therapist, who were close as-sociates in the medical community. For example, she dreamed that she had to drive up a steep hill starting somewhere halfway up the slope. Her husband put a car at her disposal, and she started the engine; when she put the car into gear, however, it unexpectedly moved backward in a wild and terrifying downhill plunge. She awakened in a panic. Her associations led to her feeling that the therapist had been a tool of her husband. She felt particularly humiliated by the fact that the two men continued a friendly professional relationship and, in spite of her overt discomfort, kept promoting social interactions involving their wives. As a matter of fact, her husband had insisted on the choice of this therapist in spite of their knowledge of his deficient qualifications. In general, he made similar arrangements for all of her medical care, always choosing practitioners with minimal qualifications. He then depreciated and second-guessed their efforts until she more or less stopped using their services and turned to him directly as medical advisor. He responded with considerable solicitude to such needs, particularly in the area of her emotional illness. He seemed to have been especially pleased by the failure of her psychotherapy and never intervened to influence her to abandon the obviously hopeless effort. This was in marked contrast to his continuous opposition to her analysis. The pattern of the masochistic ties to her husband and to her former therapist was eventually elucidated through the analysis of her masturbation fantasies.

Understanding the significance of the patient's fantasy world was achieved very slowly; one might say it only became possible when progress in other areas (especially with regard to diminution of her need for moral perfection) had allowed her to alter their manifest content spontaneously. This evolution was in the direction of lesser projection of blame, leading to her realizing ever more clearly that she was not a *victim* in this world of her own devising, constructed according to her own wishes. Ultimately, the unconscious meaning of the fantasy emerged: in her "society," the men were her helpless prisoners, trapped by their infinite sexual need for her, unable to leave her for a single moment, and held exclusively by the force of her desirability and perfection. The acme of her triumph was provided by the detail of her being tied up: like a Houdini, she did not need to lift a finger to achieve a miraculous result.

Resort to this private world continued in frustrating circumstances throughout the analysis as part of the process of mastering her conflicts, although it occurred with diminishing frequency and less and less pleasure. In the terminal phase, when she reported such an incident, it was in a tone of defiance, as if to indicate that she was rejecting the rationality of the analytic point of view wholesale; by implication, she was no longer able to lose herself uncritically in a universe of personal omnipotence.

After the summer vacation of the third year of treatment, the sessions were characterized by the expression of overt feelings of entitlement to absolute control over the analyst, i.e., the unconscious wishes of her lifelong grandiose fantasies had now become conscious within the transference setting. This was the issue that proved to present the greatest technical dilemma in the treatment. The clearest illustration of the emotional pitfalls involved can be described in terms of one concrete example, that of the patient's reaction to the illumination of the analytic office. This would come up in the associations whenever the lights were turned on. The patient felt that a floor lamp, placed behind the head of the couch, was purposefully designed to shine into her eyes, in the manner of lamps at police stations where prisoners were being subjected to the third degree. The connection to her masochistic fantasies was pointed out to her, but she would not accept having these complaints treated as associations, i.e., as statements requiring no action in response. My initial attempts to deal with the issue in this way promptly led to her lapsing into angry silence which, at other times, she freely characterized as overtly defiant. The intensity of her conviction of being wronged and the attribution of malicious motives to the analyst raised the possibility of a paranoid decompensation.

Partly as a way of testing the intactness of her reality sense, some explanations were offered for my decision to investigate the meaning of her complaint, instead of complying with the demand implicit within it. No other patient had found the light to be objectionable, so that she needed to understand her distress in psychological terms instead of insisting that it was an expectable response to the realities. She contemptuously dismissed this statement as a rationalization and, reassuringly with regard to my concern about her reality testing, as an irrelevance. She made it clear that the principal point was to comply with her demand not to have the light shine upon her. The exhibitionistic conflict implicit in this demand could never be clarified in this context because she was never able to acknowledge that her expectation involved an idiosyncratic psychological need. On the other hand, my conviction that yielding to her infantile demand would preclude the successful analysis of her exhibitionism did turn out to be a groundless rationalization. It appeared, in fact, that she could only become aware of her wishes to be in the spotlight when she placed herself in such a situation of her own volition, and she proceeded to do this not very long after the mobilization of the exhibitionistic conflict had been heralded by her objections to the analytic "spotlight." The actual circumstances she arranged were those of a part-time teaching appointment in a large municipal junior college. She found the experience of lecturing to her classes excruciatingly frightening, in spite of the generally low scholastic aptitudes of the students. At first she was able to rationalize her discomfort on the ground of her lack of previous teaching experience and minimal formal background in her subject matter. As she made no effort to compensate for these deficiencies in preparation, it gradually became clear that she wanted to deliver perfect lectures, fit for the most erudite and sophisticated audiences, and that she wanted to score a personal success with each and every student in addition. It took several years of consistent analytic confrontation to moderate these senseless ambitions, to accept the inevitability of not being able to please everyone and the desirability of turning to fellow-teachers for advice about the techniques of instruction, etc.

At the time these exhibitionistic concerns first cropped up in the analysis, however, the matter of the illumination of my office was well on its way to becoming a power struggle. My countertransference response was the growth of a conviction that the opportunity to observe the patient's facial expressions, the actual "reason" for having the illumination, should not be sacrificed, and that it would jeopardize the analysis to give in to the patient's infantile demand. There things stood for a number of months, without great consequences as long as there were not too many dark days! As time went on, whenever she found the lights on when she came into the office, she refused to lie on the couch, either sitting on it in scowling silence or stomping out altogether. No attempt to talk about the issue was acceptable to her as long as she did not get her way.

It took me some time to realize that the dispute was no longer motivated by her exhibitionistic conflict alone—or by my analytic requirements. On her side, the issue had become that of being entitled to impose her subjective needs on our transactions without being made to feel unreasonable as a consequence. On mine, it was an attempt to safeguard my own boundaries; the demand that I conduct an analysis in a dark room (or acknowledge bizarre motivations for my manner of lighting it) had made me feel that I was being absorbed into the patient's system of volition against my will. This realization then permitted me to try to resolve the impasse by initiating a reluctant compromise, i.e., turning off the light but specifying that this was done as a therapeutic concession.

I first did this one day when the need for illumination was, in actuality, marginal. I stated that I was making this concession as the lesser of two evils and that the necessity for it would have to be understood at a later time. Such an opportunity did not arise immediately, however, because the patient treated the whole matter as *non arrivé* as soon as she got her way. Subsequently, if the light were on, she was not quite as virulently angry as before, particularly after the analysis of her exhibitionistic conflict, accomplished in the context of her teaching activities, helped to reduce her actual discomfort about being in a spotlight. What did emerge directly from the transaction concerning the light was the meaning of her deliberate withholding of her associations in reaction to not having her way in the analytic setting.

Confrontation with this negativism within the transference led to associations about lifelong manifestations of silent, stubborn, passive resistance. Ultimately these memories led to recall of the story of her departure from Lebanon from which she retained only some dim fragments as actual recollections. The shattering sense of loss of control over her milieu which she had experienced once again in the analysis as a result of the long vacation and then expressed in connection with the issue of the light had apparently occurred for the first time when she had been forcibly separated from her nurse in Beirut harbor. The moving and pathetic scene of mutual desolation as nurse and toddler lost contact with each other had become a family legend. The competence and devotion of the nurse were not only recalled from the days of the patient's infancy; this woman had subsequently made a career of raising Westerners' children throughout the Middle East and was uniformly praised by postwar returnees from there who brought news of her. It may not be superfluous to note that one factor in the patient's willingness to resign herself to a male analyst, after having been told by a senior female consultant that she would do better with a woman, had been the fact that she had heard rumors to the effect that I had once lived in an Arabic country within the French empire, and she had jumped to the conclusion that this must have been Lebanon.

The displacement of concern to the peripheral issue of the lights seemed to be based on similar defenses in the childhood situation. On the ship bringing the family back to this country, there had been two incidents of striking significance. On the one hand, the patient would not move her bowels; on the other, in the parents' absence at dinner, her brother stole and swallowed a bottleful of toxic medication. Upon finding evidence of this, unable to determine which of the children was in danger, the parents had gastric lavage performed on both. As the patient continued to retain her feces, she became impacted, and this alarming assertion of self-control was once again forcefully overcome amidst violent struggles. Ever after, the patient was outwardly submissive, but inwardly she was filled with resentment and rebelliousness, especially whenever anyone infringed upon her autonomy. This was particularly true with regard to her father's later custom of making her drink warm water for laxative purposes upon arising. In childhood, she could preserve the air of submissiveness and "goodness" while secretly enjoying or even promoting her older brother's wild rebelliousness; in the recent past, she had similarly submitted with docility to her husband and vicariously shared her younger son's expressions of negativism. The unsuitable marriage she had rushed into over her family's objections had also had this rebellious flavor, perhaps with one difference: in that instance, by showing their ethnic prejudice, her family had abandoned the position of moral superiority, so that she could be rebellious *and* good at the same time.

At any rate, my relative tolerance of her negativism during the sessions and the successful interpretation of its genetic roots as the assertion of her integrity when she had been overwhelmed by losing her nurse were the therapeutic achievements that made her feel most meaningfully understood. The recollection of this piece of analytic work safeguarded the analysis against the disruptive effects of later failures in empathy and injuries to her self-esteem. What it did *not* accomplish was any substantial modification of the feeling of entitlement to control over the analyst. However, it did permit the handling of this issue in purely verbal fashion when it once again came into focus, late in the analysis.

The specific incident that finally led to the interpretation of the childhood need behind the transference manifestations involved, once again, the physical environment. On a particularly torrid day, the air-conditioning system proved to be insufficient, so that for the first time in the patient's experience the window was open when she arrived. Her reaction was to ask, "How would you feel if I closed the window?" Because it was understood between us by this time that she was, in fact, free to make such minor adjustments on her own initiative, I chose to respond to the literal meaning of her question: "I would feel very hot." There followed the most impressive outburst of rage this wrathful woman ever demonstrated, lasting through the whole session. Its purport was to refute the possibility that one could feel hot in such circumstances; any such claim had to be the result of malice. The stream of profanity and abuse issuing from this formerly excessively polite and etiquette-conscious lady was astonishing. She was still in a rage the next day, but it was by then possible to point out that what was intolerable for her was my insistence on the *fact* that I constituted an independent source of volition, instead of experiencing the world in a manner identical to her own. She grasped the fact that this illusion of reacting in the same way was something she really required; she had needed her mother to be capable of this in childhood, as her nurse had seemingly been able to be during her infancy.

By the end of the third year of analysis, the patient was behaving more adequately in every area of living, as shown by her getting a teaching job at the college level. Fears that these improvements would lead to her dismissal as a patient continued. At the same time, frustration of her needs for admiration from me for these achievements led to repeated retreats into more unrealistic grandiose attitudes. At first I attempted to interpret these unfavorable developments as self-punitive behaviors, based on unconscious guilt about her successes. Although there was much confirmatory evidence about her feeling guilt whenever she failed to behave in a selfless manner, these interpretations were entirely ineffective in altering the pattern of "negative therapeutic reactions."

On the other hand, there was no way of preventing narcissistic injury whenever she wanted admiration: no matter what my actual response was, whether explicit or unspoken, she was delusionally certain that I was filled with contempt for her. In one way this was a vicissitude of the mother transference: she assumed that, like her childhood mother, I was filled with a sense of my own unique value and regarded anyone *different* from myself in any dimension whatever as *inferior* on that account. This was particularly true with regard to her sexual fantasies. She could not imagine that either I or her mother could view masochism as anything but disgusting and infrahuman.

In addition, her conviction about my private opinion of her constituted a projection of her own hostility, i.e., of her intolerance of my being different from her. This attitude was understood as a childhood identification with her mother's assumption that her own attributes were the only worthwhile ones. In another sense, this hostility was a manifestation of the need that my reactions parallel her own. Early in the analysis, the same need had been demonstrated by way of her sexual jealousy of her husband, which was based on her automatic assumption, during the period of her affair with her previous therapist, that her husband had to be interested in an extramarital involvement, as she was.

Her hostility in the transference took the form of wishing to cut down my effectiveness as her analyst and thereby humiliate me. As indicated earlier, she felt free to act on this impulse through defiant uncooperativeness whenever she felt herself injured and/or humiliated. Without this kind of "justification" (with which, of course, she was able to supply herself because of her continuous conviction of being held in contempt), the emergence of her hostile, castrating fantasies made her look upon herself as a very bad person who was beyond therapeutic help—and whom everyone naturally despised! Focus upon this judgment as a transference from the childhood past permitted her to understand that she had identified with the parents' (especially the father's) attitude toward her older brother's hostile misbehavior. In a paradoxical way, then, her largely conscious penis envy (mainly directed at her brother and his many talents and professional opportunities) was, on one level, a reaction formation.

During the period of her early childhood, extending back into the Lebanese interlude and up to the time of her puberty, it was, in fact, her brother who had been underprivileged. His behavior was particularly unacceptable to their father, but he was also *persona non grata* at the home of the admired maternal uncle. Moreover, the family atmosphere was unmistakably one in which being a woman, i.e., in mother's position, was most advantageous. Envy of the brother's phallic attributes (and actual competition in physical pursuits during the years when the faster growth rate of a girl made this more or less feasible) had been one way of disavowing the chronic feeling of guilt about having had "unfair" advantages over him. In adult life, she was very upset by the serious consequences of his psychopathology and continued to be extremely solicitous and helpful to him, in spite of his extraordinary arrogance and ingratitude.

In the analysis, it was gradually possible to discern the emergence of a similar attitude toward her husband, brought about by the realization that fate had once more given her something of value, a meaningful and potentially successful treatment, of which he had been deprived. The more fortunate she felt herself to be, the more important it became to her that she too was one of the underprivileged, especially in comparison to the analyst, and the more she had to erect defenses against the temptation to gloat over the defeat of her persecutors, her brother and her husband.

Thus it became clear that regressive swings into grandiosity simultaneously served two functions: they represented reactions to the frustration of her wish to be admired; at the same time, insofar as they involved her commitment to the ideals of self-sacrifice and saintliness, they also served to avoid her guilt about competitive hostility. It was possible to attribute her major ambition in the direction of goodness to an identification with her father, both in terms of his explicit Puritan righteousness and because of his selfless behavior within the family. In addition, her lifelong behavior in conformity with this standard had, indeed, earned her positive recognition from him.

Her guilt was also caused by her wish to destroy the analyst's work through her regressive behavior. From transference manifestations of envy about the creativeness of therapeutic endeavors, it was possible to reconstruct her competitive hostility toward her mother concerning the birth of her younger sibling and her rage at her father for being able to give the baby to mother. Thus her phallic competitiveness was related to both male and female sexual functions and was not merely a reaction formation to ward off guilt about being less unfortunate than her older brother.

In the fourth year of analysis, she became aware that she had covertly acted out her destructiveness through the unconscious encouragement of her son's impulsive behavior; this outcome was supposed to disgrace the analyst because her son's psychiatric consultant had declared that the boy's behavior disorder would respond *pari passu* with the success of the patient's analysis. In childhood, she had done the same kind of acting out by provoking her older brother into delinquent activities, thus proving that the parents were not adequate. Mastery of this aspect of her competitive hostility and of the resultant guilt brought about real change in her moral masochism, i.e., it ended her overvaluation of saintli-ness. Even the vacation separation that summer passed with-out trauma, and she no longer feared that I would seize on her external success as an excuse to undermine her by inter-rupting the analysis prematurely. In other words, this fear had been based on the projection of her own hostile competi-tiveness about my analytic competence and her impulse to destroy it by sabotaging my work.

The fourth year of treatment drew to a close with the in-sight that another motive for opposing change had been a need to maintain her idealization of me by perpetuating a gap between us through clinging to feeling like a child. She realized that she had always tried to buttress her parents and her husband through similar self-abasement. In this connec-tion, her infantile erotic impulses toward her mother were in-tensely re-experienced in the transference, leading to detailed analysis of a second aspect of her phallic competitiveness. This had been based on the early realization that, in addition to her own person, the mother had appreciated only the male genitals. Much of the patient's defect in self-esteem had resulted from hopeless attempts to monopolize her mother and to gain her favor by becoming as masculine as possible.

In the fifth year of analysis, occasional signs of heterosex-ual evolution began to emerge. Every indication pointed in the direction that her enduring enthusiasm about men in general (or for myself as a man specifically) had had no pre-cedent in her emotional life, but constituted a new develop-mental experience. In this context, she gained insight into the fact that her own narcissistic vulnerability about any fai-lure to elicit admiration had precluded investment of her father as an oedipal object. In this setting, in spite of the frustration of her wishes for the reciprocation of her love within the transference, correct understanding of her di-lemma made the analytic sessions into supremely desirable experiences for her.

The intensity of this feeling attained a degree that transcended my empathic capacities and led to the single most serious failure of understanding on my part. During this period of the treatment, the patient had to drive for almost an hour (each way) to my office, and her obligations to her children prevented her from leaving home early enough to allow for unexpected delays in transit. On the day preceding a long weekend which was to include Christmas, she failed to arrive, but telephoned about fifteen minutes after the scheduled starting time, announcing with some distress that she had been held up by a traffic bottleneck. She was now past this obstacle and estimated that she could not get to the office for more than five minutes of the session. I misread the purport of this message, despite some awareness of the special significance Christmas had for her. I thought that she was seeking confirmation for a decision to return home directly so as to avoid having to do about an hour's driving in order to make a pro forma appearance for her session. I told her that I understood how much she would regret having missed the last visit before Christmas and how painful it was for her whenever external obstacles defeated her best efforts. She responded with appropriate holiday sentiments and rang off.

Although this holiday period proved to be a very difficult one for her, the seriousness of her reaction to this misunderstanding did not become clear for some time. A pattern of chronic lateness for her sessions, which now developed, was the clue that led to the revelation of her bitterness about my failure to grasp that no amount of effort and trouble was too great for the sake of making even the briefest contact with me possible. Of course, this state of affairs held sway only during the brief periods of perfect empathy on my part; when I failed her, as on the occasion of the traffic bottleneck, she felt that the relationship was forever spoiled. By this time, however, she no longer ascribed my failure to malice; she accepted it as the inevitable limitation of a mere man who could not be expected to know anything about mothering!

By contrast, a similar incident early in the analysis had created a grudge which lasted for years. This came about as a result of the only encounter outside of the analytic setting which took place in the course of the six years of treatment. It occurred at a Christmas party (!) at the home of a mutual friend (more accurately, a physician who was a good friend of mine and a professional acquaintance of the patient's husband. He had been the source of the personal information about my exposure to Arabic culture which had facilitated her acceptance of the referral to me). The patient eagerly rushed up to me and introduced me to her husband. Proceeding on the assumption that in these matters the Miesian motto, "Less is more," is applicable, I withdrew after complying with the demands of politeness; I spent the rest of the party in a quiet conversation with an old friend. This alleged snub persisted as a source of pain for the patient, although she realized that any other course of action on my part would have led to unacceptable difficulties, e.g., to betrayal to a large circle of acquaintances of the fact that she had started analysis with me. In the transference, of course, she required me to shout from the rooftops my pride about having her in treatment!

Concomitantly with the emergence of her positive feelings, the patient began to be able to express her frustration and rage in words alone. Her behavior at home had changed so radically that, around the end of the fifth year of analysis, her husband tried to disrupt the work by refusing to finance it. His stand eventually led her into leaving the home, with her children, and initiating divorce proceedings. The analysis now entered a lengthy terminal phase in which disappointed rage about any lack of perfection in my empathic capacities alternated with blissful alliance with me as a reincarnation of the Lebanese nurse. She was murderously jealous about my relationships with anyone else, and we were able to grasp that it had been in similar circumstances of frustration with her childhood mother (particularly during the period of her father's absence at graduate school) that the regression into various positions of grandiosity had arisen. She re-experienced these primitive fantasies in the course of the sixth and last year of treatment.

Parallel to the gradual emergence of various aspects of archaic grandiosity, she made the decision to terminate the analysis at the start of my winter vacation. Her plans for the postanalytic future assumed ever more realistic configurations. She obtained her divorce, reassumed her maiden name, rejoined the faith of her forbears (with the assumption that she was thereby also differentiating herself from the agnostic analyst), bought herself a modest but suitable home, and made arrangements for advanced training in her field. In the meantime, the material of the sessions often consisted of fantasies of pre-eminence by way of religious salvation or through sharing the extraordinary excellence she attributed to me.

Perhaps the most interesting instance of the second of these issues involved her use of language in general and her efforts to master French conversation in particular. Partly in emulation of her mother's command of French—*souvenir du Liban!*—she had for many years been taking lessons in that language. It had been something of a shock to me to discover, when I had used some very common gallicism in my speech with her, that she had made practically no progress in these studies. She assumed, on the other hand, that I must have retained a perfect command of French from my supposed residence in the Levant. As I grew to know her better, I came to realize that her use of English was also rather stilted and primitive. Her syntax contained many of the characteristics of that of poor rural folk from the South; her use of words verged on concreteness, with a paucity of metaphors, and her vocabulary, although superficially adequate, seemed impoverished in terms of what one could expect from a person of her intelligence. (Her better than average endowment could be inferred from such accomplishments as her discriminating taste in music and mastery of playing the piano.) Although she was easily humiliated about these limitations, it became possible gradually to include these functional characteristics among those of her handicaps that could be understood psychologically and, it was hoped, eventually mastered. These archaicisms of speech turned out to be related to most of the conflicts which emerged in the course of the analysis, but this developmental arrestation was not undone until the terminal phase.

Briefly, progress in increasing her language skills began after we realized that she regarded English as if it had not been her mother tongue; to be sure, she could not recall a single word of the latter, i.e., of Arabic. In many ways, she held onto the childish language of the Southern rednecks with whom she had been raised and resisted the cultivated speech of her parents—as she had rejected them as substitutes for her nurse in so many other ways. In the transference, she was willing to compromise by making Lebanon's second language, French, serve as a shared matrix between us. A scattering of words and phrases were sufficient to establish this, and my willingness to adapt my speech to her preference soon led her to seek out a French tutor who was successful in instructing her in the context of an informal relationship. During the final summer of the analysis, the patient went on a pilgrimage to France (with her daughter) and wrote me a letter of gratitude—in French—from there. This was, in fact, the only communication from her that was not in English! We came to understand her gradual mastery of "my language" (French) as the reversal of her regression to a grandiose attitude about verbal communication, that of insisting on her current language skills as perfect. By way of idealizing a tongue she regarded as mine, she was able to learn it; afterward, the same sequence took place about my use of English. At first, her idealization of my speech had unrealistic dimensions; later, as her own archaicisms were given up, she was able to perceive that my use of English was actually limited by a slight foreign accent, if nothing more.

In the final three months of the analysis, the patient became aware of a series of magical rituals to which her omnipotent illusions had been attached, and she gave these up with much anxiety. This was another instance in which interpretation alone did not suffice to loosen a system of rationalizations which concealed the magical ideation behind the overt behavior. Relying for leverage on the great practical importance that adhering to the planned termination schedule had for the patient, I exerted pressure for alteration in this behavior by stating with emphasis my opinion that the rituals protected her against certain anxieties and that to avoid facing these in the period still available for analytic work would seriously jeopardize the outcome.

Reluctantly, the patient then yielded, first giving up a midafternoon nap which had been a lifelong habit whenever circumstances permitted. Forgoing this made her realize that she had been encouraged to resort to this measure by her mother who had also utilized it for herself as a magical preservative of her health. Aside from the feeling of protection afforded by placing her trust in mother's omniscience, the naps had the advantage of making her feel like a special person *like* her mother (and unlike ordinary people such as the Southern townsfolk who could not afford that kind of leisure).

She found it much more difficult to abandon the other part of her ritual, namely, the secret ceremonial consumption of an aperitif before dinner and of a glass of wine with the meal. The great anxiety generated by giving up this addiction was intense enough to shake her belief in her capacity to relinquish the analysis. Thus, the rituals had been in the nature of transitional phenomena, i.e., alternatives to analytic treatment, unconsciously experienced as the real guarantors of her stability and of her affective self-control. The last two months of the work were characterized by expressions of grief and rage about giving up fantasied mergers with all maternal figures, i.e., even the illusion of the analyst's omniscience.

The first subsequent contact between us occurred about three years after termination, when the patient called for a referral for her daughter, now in late adolescence, who was experiencing some psychological discomfort. She reported having completed her work for an advanced degree in her field and working full-time in her profession. She was subjectively satisfied with her progress, including some recent efforts to form social relationships with men. She also recounted that, as a graduation present, her mother had taken her on a joint visit to Lebanon where they had found her nurse, now an octogenarian, in an old-age home. She sent me a photograph of their joyful reunion, which had apparently been deeply meaningful for all three participants.

Several months later, she came to see me on her own behalf, ostensibly in connection with a serious threat to her health that called for a decision on her part that she found difficult to make. She was able to resolve this ambivalence almost immediately, however; nor did she require my assistance with the anxiety generated by the uncertainties of her somatic condition. She realized very soon that she had in fact returned because she had been resentful about having had to terminate her analysis in a hurried fashion, because of financial pressures. She had at first experienced this necessity as a failure on my part, and she had been very angry for some time, although not without insight into the irrationality of her reactions. These wounds had gradually healed, but she continued to think of me as her caretaker, as shown by her return when she was faced by an emergency of sorts. She now reported a dream that recapitulated her sense of helpless longing for the exclusive possession of an ideal mother. This was followed by a whole series of dreams in which she gradually overcame her distress about taking leave of me. She discontinued this series of visits on her own initiative within a few weeks.

CHAPTER SEVEN

Discussion of the Second Case

Initial Formulation of Second Case

It was clear from the first that this patient had always managed herself by entering into symbiotic relationships in which she took a largely passive position. She had sought psychotherapy because of her husband's inadequacy in the sadistic role she required of him, and she entered analysis because of similar disappointment in her former therapist. Left to her own devices, she had developed a psychosomatic illness (or perhaps hypochondriasis). A bond similar to those in her previous significant relationships was rapidly established within the analytic transference. With the achievement of narcissistic equilibrium, a multiplicity of disavowed grandiose fantasies became apparent.

Separation from the analyst produced a traumatic state, and reintegration took place by way of very primitive grandiose attitudes and archaic reversals, akin to altruistic surrender. Interpretation of the defensive disavowals led to the acknowledgment of the significance of her archaic ideation and experience of the full extent of her frustration about her real limitations, i.e., her actual need to depend on others for guidance. In the present, she was now quite explicit in her statements of continuing need for the analyst and anxiety about his potential lack of availability. Relative security in the relationship allowed her to show her rage about the limits of the analyst's perfection and commitment, and this reaction was seen as a repetition of her latency-age disillusionment with her mother. There were recurrent attempts to ward off these reactions through defensive idealization of the analyst.

The vacation separation during the third year of analysis was again traumatic; this time however, she was able to describe her emergency measures during the actual period of difficulty—namely, her novel resort to perverse masturbatory fantasies. This ideation failed to satisfy her as long as it did not actually involve another person in fulfilling her needs. Her newly found freedom to achieve orgasm by self-stimulation proved to be an unprecedented bulwark for the maintenance of her sense of continuity and meaningfulness. The content of the perversion had, however, preoccupied her for decades, and she had arranged her life so as to bring about such experiences in the world of actuality. With gradual diminution of her commitment to "goodness" as a result of the analytic work, she was able to get beyond the manifest masochism of her lifelong schema to see it as a demand for unconditional adoration.

Expressions of entitlement to absolute control over the analyst characterized the middle phase of treatment; at times, this attitude was experienced with delusional conviction, i.e., the analyst was seen as malicious for refusing to comply with her wishes. The therapeutic impasse was overcome by means of token compliance with one of her demands as a way of acknowledging in action the legitimacy of establishing her own ground rules if the customary ones were unbearable to her. This "parameter" led to the successful analysis of other aspects of her negativism, ultimately traced to their origins in the traumatic loss of her whole infantile milieu at the age of eighteen months. Her skillful maneuvers to conceal her rebelliousness or to provoke others to act it out for her were now identified. More essential for progress, however, was her insight into the need to be *understood* rather than gratified if she was to achieve actual autonomy. The "parameter" was resolved late in the analysis by means of interpretation of her need for the experience of the analyst as an alter ego; this capacity to share her point of view had been lacking in her mother, but had been amply supplied during infancy by the Lebanese nurse.

Between episodes of rage about the analyst's independent system of volition, the transference turned to the patient's wishes to be admired. These developments always eventuated in regressive episodes, based on an aspect of the maternal transference, namely, the conviction that the analyst would only be able to value someone to the extent that the other person could serve as an "alter ego" for him. Another aspect of this childhood gestalt was her competitive hostility toward the analyst as transference mother, acted out by means of defeating the joint effort but rationalized on the ground that he was allegedly humiliating her. Acknowledgment of her own hostility filled the patient with guilt, which she attempted to expiate through the very same "negative therapeutic reactions," i.e., the regressive behaviors. Similarly, she had tried to expiate guilt about having been favored over her brother as a child, and this dynamic was now being relived in relation to her husband: by sabotaging the analysis through her competitiveness with the analyst, she could diminish her sense of privilege vis-à-vis this sick man.

The expiatory need was related to the patient's absolute commitment to an ethic of goodness (probably in identification with her father), the only value shared by her entire family. In the context of analyzing the unrealistic aspect of this ambition, the patient was able to connect her hostility to her childhood envy of the mother about the birth of her younger sibling. This insight permitted her to stop the current acting out, via her son, which echoed the childhood attacks on mother through provoking her older brother's misbehavior. Simultaneously, she lost the fear, based on projection, that the analyst would ruin her treatment by dismissing her prematurely.

Working through the phallic competitive conflicts of early childhood led to the emergence of the Oedipus complex in the transference. This took the form of reliving her intense erotic attachment to her mother, and her hopelessness about competing for the latter with phallic beings was understood as the major source of her sense of inadequacy. Empathic understanding of this dilemma turned the analysis into a supremely desirable experience for her, as she gradually accommodated to the frustration of her absolutarian demands. She was now able to do this in the context of an idealizing transference which was generally silent—i.e., its presence could only be inferred on the basis of her rage about the slightest break in the analyst's empathy.

In the lengthy terminal phase, she worked through the reactions to the inevitable disappointments of her need for perfection in the analyst. These reactions had always been regressive moves to positions of archaic grandiosity—e.g., primitive religious attitudes involving personal salvation. The reversal of this regressive propensity was signaled by her newfound capacity to accept the language of the adult world: in the transference, the analyst's second language, as well as his manner of using English. In similar fashion, a series of magical rituals, which had had the function of transitional experiences (in the sense of Winnicott), were now given up.

This case history might be summed up in the following way: development was originally interrupted by traumatic loss of the infantile environment, followed by a period of confusion and lack of empathy for her need for emotional resonance from her caretakers. The resultant fixation on primitive goals made it impossible for her to tolerate the confrontation of her competitive limitations in the phallic stage—particularly her incapacity to compete with males for admiration from her mother. These narcissistic blows reinforced the regression to grandiose ambitions, thus creating an arrest in her development. The consequent adaptive deficits forced her into symbiotic dependence, usually in a sadomasochistic relationship with a man.

If we attempt to enter this summary on the hierarchical

model (see Figure 5), we encounter a diagram of greater complexity than we did in the first illustrative case, in line with the more primitive cast to the personality organization

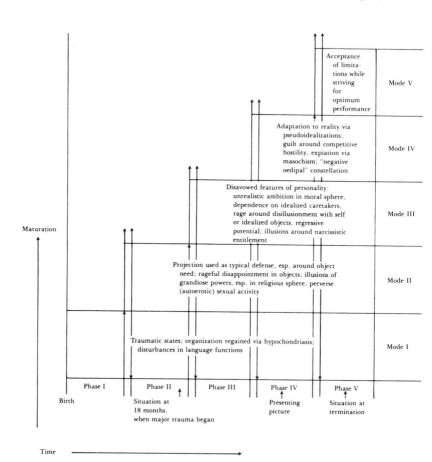

FIGURE 5

DATA OF CASE 2 IN ACCORD WITH THE HIERARCHICAL SCHEMA

in this second patient. The conscious self-image she had when she sought assistance was one of passivity and masochism; she expiated her guilt about competitive hostility through these behaviors. Typically, her relationships with significant people were characterized by thin pseudo-idealizations.[1] The foregoing features of personality organization in Mode IV were relatively sparse; her functioning had much more to do with Mode III, and all of those features were disavowed: her idealizing needs and the rage about their recurrent frustration, her grandiose attitudes (especially in the realm of morality and in that of phallic competition with men), and her feelings of entitlement to control over her objects in narcissistic merger. Even the maintenance of organization in Mode III was insecure; any disruption of her symbiotic adaptation led to regression into Mode II. In such circumstances she projected her sense of badness and helplessness into others; at the same time, she attributed her needs for symbiosis to everyone else. Her split-off illusions of personal salvation and other transitional experiences, such as rituals or perverse behaviors, also belonged to Mode II. Further regression to traumatic states (Mode I) also occurred at times, sometimes heralded by hypochondriacal symptoms.

The analytic process met her idealizing needs and, in a

---

[1] In a previous communication (Gedo, 1975a), I made an attempt to differentiate the various types of idealizing relationships encountered within the analytic transference. I proposed that we reserve the term "idealization" for instances in which belief in the perfection of another reflects similar attitudes from earliest childhood. In most instances, conscious idealizing attitudes actually screen negative feelings; for these circumstances, I urged use of the term "pseudo-idealization." This generally constitutes a defense against disappointment in a previously idealized object. Although genuine idealizing transferences may occasionally be available to consciousness, more often they are unconscious, so that they operate more or less silently in the analytic situation. It should also be noted that the converse of pseudo-idealization is also quite common: manifest attitudes of contempt and devaluation of others may be used defensively against idealizing propensities. In sum, we can never rely on manifest behavior to assess the human depths.

more limited way, led to insight into the nature of her requirement for narcissistic merger. On the basis of this unprecedented kind of relationship, she was able gradually to work through the conflicts concerning her oedipal wishes and anxieties (Mode IV). This progress, in turn, led to the reversal of her regressive propensities, with relinquishment of her needs for archaic narcissistic positions. Expectable adult functioning (Mode V) was achieved gradually as her idealization of the analyst was given up; this process seems to have reached its conclusion several years after the official termination of treatment.

Let us compare the formulation of the two case protocols on the basis of the summaries in terms of the hierarchical model. As we would expect in the case of individuals who seek psychoanalytic assistance, both patients achieved expectable adult functioning only as a result of the success of their analyses. Before treatment, both typically functioned in accord with several less adaptive modes of organization, mostly in the range usually referable to neurotic and/or narcissistic personality disturbances. Both patients were forced to resort to various emergency measures because of tendencies to get disorganized, even to succumb to traumatic states. Nonetheless, specific permutations of the Oedipus complex had left their mark on each of these personalities; yet no solution of the oedipal conflicts was possible without prior correction of the pathological legacy of earlier developmental crises.

Another way to state this conclusion is that, in both cases, the vicissitudes of the oedipal triangle had caused an arrest in psychological development because the child, who had not been able to overcome infantile narcissistic attitudes before entering this new phase of emotional life, had been unable to tolerate the mortification of having to acknowledge the superiority of any rival. As a consequence of the resultant regression, both patients had become symbiotically dependent on others to maintain adaptive equilibrium; simultaneously, they maintained a spurious sense of self-esteem through resort to grandiose illusions. These regressive qualities amounted to a retreat to the major fixation points of their prior developmental history. The two patients differed from each other with regard to the emergency measures they used to avoid disorganization upon separation from their symbiotic partners. The most marked of these differences was the inability of the second patient to tolerate temporary states of traumatization without immediate resort to primitive and potentially dangerous adaptive measures.

In general, my first effort to formulate this second case is even less satisfactory than was the initial employment of a similar schema in the first case example. Diagnostically, the patient might be seen as a "narcissistic personality disturbance" (cf. Kohut, 1971) with perverse and hypochondriacal features. Existing clinical theory fails us, however, in illuminating the significance of the specific syndrome in this case. What explanation does it offer for the "choice of symptom"—either the hypochondriasis (or, for that matter, the psychosomatic illness originally postulated) or the masochistic perversion? The formulation is notably weak with regard to explaining the reasons for the inability of this person to have adjusted, in early childhood, to the changes in the circumstances of her family; after all, many children are able to develop without such catastrophic consequences in spite of similar changes of personnel among those who nurture them.

Let us see whether a reformulation of the case material in a manner that focuses on the patient's self-organization will yield better results.

Reformulation of the Second Case

The second patient's characteristic role as the masochistic partner in a symbiosis with a tyrannical man who humiliated her is best understood as insistence on her part upon enlisting someone else as the executor of her volition without offending the ideals of goodness she had acquired as a young child. These ideals included the need to be virtuously humble, necessitating the disavowal of a host of fantasies of arrogant pre-eminence. When nobody had been available to play the role of omnipotent caretaker at her behest, the patient had, in all probability, regressed into hypochondriasis. She had thus preserved her personality integration through the medium of being preoccupied with painful digestive disturbances, i.e., by focusing on the goal of appetitive satisfactions.

When she committed herself to the analysis at the cost of alienating her envious husband, interruption of our work caused a more profound disruption into confusion and aimlessness. She was able to reintegrate around the aim of taking care of other people in need—the pattern she had consolidated at age five after the birth of her younger brother. This fantasy came into conflict with her ambition to see herself as a successful parent; in fact, it led to the acknowledgment of her embarrassing failure with her own son. This turned out to be only one among numerous examples of disavowed limitations which she had been unable to correct until she had overcome the defensive distortions in her assessments of her own performance.

The most striking instance of such a distortion was her projection into me of her wish to see herself as perfect, a defense which created anxiety about the possibility of a premature termination. Conversely, she also demanded perfection from me and re-experienced her childhood anger about the disillusionment with her mother. She attempted to ward off this disappointment by means of distorted assessments of my performance which echoed the childhood aim of pleasing her self-centered mother through expressions of admiration for her.

During the disruptive separation caused by my vacation in the third year of treatment, the patient discovered a more satisfactory solution for safeguarding her integrity than hypochondriasis had been: she now became able to seek the satisfaction of her sexual appetite through masturbation. This change was a measure of new-found freedom, in part based on clearer understanding of her past relationships as equivalent measures to shore up her shaky adaptation in perverse ways, rather than through healthy companionships. In any case, her humiliation about not being able to command a lover to satisfy her sexually had decreased sufficiently to permit her to resort to perverse fantasies for masturbatory gratification. This ideation was eventually understood as an assertion of her irresistible sexual attractiveness, such as the seductiveness she had attributed to her mother as a child. The ambition to equal the latter's success with men had screened the patient's underlying striving for autonomy, i.e., her need to acquire the ability to pacify herself. Conversely, as long as she had not been able to manage this without turning to other people, she had fallen back on fantasies of omnipotence, especially in the realms of beauty, knowledge, and goodness.

In relation to the analyst, these strivings for absolute power were now relived in terms of claims of being entitled to control our transactions within very wide limits; implicitly, omnipotence was also being attributed to me because she assumed that my refusal to go along with her demands was dictated purely by malice, that it did not exceed my powers to comply. Subjectively, I experienced this pressure as moral blackmail to surrender the independence of my own volitional system. In other words, the veneer of the patient's commitment to goodness, acquired from her father in middle childhood, had now been stripped away—it had not formed part of her internalized morality, after all, but only one of her series of immoderate ambitions. A token concession to the *infantile* legitimacy of her need to control her caretakers was sufficient, however, to restore a working alliance; she was now able to focus on her lifelong negativism, initiated by the traumatic events which had disrupted her life as a toddler. The outcome of those assaults upon *her* autonomous volition had been to place the goal of averting such intrusion[2] at the very top of her hierarchy of motivations; her seeming avidity for symbiotic relationships was part of a pattern of repeating the potentially disruptive circumstances in order to master them. Central to this issue was the demand that her caretakers experience the world affectively exactly as she did, as her Lebanese nurse had apparently been able to do.

The patient's demand that the analyst respond with an outlook identical to her own was also based on her conviction that her mother had only been able to appreciate others insofar as they were like herself, an attitude she now attributed to me in the transference. Hence she was once again turning a passive experience into its active counterpart in requiring me to echo her reactions; at the same time, she was directly projecting her own intolerance into me. Thus life had turned into a competitive struggle for her about which of two people could humiliate the other, although she had to justify her hostile behavior on the ground of the injustices she had suffered. In other words, her acceptance of her father's striving for goodness had put her into insoluble conflict about her need to triumph over other people, rivals such as her husband or her brothers. To be more exact, she could only triumph by being more saintly than they were, i.e., by sacrificing her potential advantages over them. In turn, she felt more defeated by my therapeutic skills, current analogs for her mother's capacity to bear a child during the patient's oed-

---

[2]This statement has borrowed terminology selected by Robert Gardner for his tentative classification of character types. He has developed three major categories of behavior: the assertive, the accommodative, and the aversive (1976). According to Gardner's observations, these qualities suffuse behavior at every level from the observable surface to the mental depths, but the actualities of specific personal activity should be described in accord with a series of qualifiers for each of these major categories. I believe that Gardner's schema may be one workable manner of characterizing what I have called "goals"; it remains to be seen whether his work will eventuate in a list of qualifiers for these fundamental aims which might be correlated with what I have called "values."

ipal period. We could infer that the patient's phallic competitiveness had also been fed by the sense of her mother's tendency to gloat narcissistically about her own excellence as well as by her marked preference for phallic beings. The patient was now able to relive her oedipal ambition to gain her mother's love through masculine performances, and this understanding of her dilemma was sufficient to transform the transference experience into an intensely meaningful and favorable one from her vantage point—hence, one she could gradually integrate and master. By contrast, any failure of empathy in the analysis reawakened the childhood rage about her mother's self-absorption and lack of genuine concern about the child's frustrations.

In the terminal phase, the patient re-experienced the frustration of her needs for exclusive possession of her caretakers and the resultant regressive resort to illusions of religious salvation. This also turned out to be an assertion of her need to differentiate herself from me, since she considered me to be an agnostic. Because this self-assertion did not arouse my intolerance, as analogous moves had done with her mother, she was simultaneously able to learn on the basis of my example with regard to some of my attributes that she looked upon as more desirable, i.e., my use of words for the purpose of maximal communication or my refusal to accept the usefulness of magical rituals.

Comments on the Advantages of the Reformulation

The foregoing reformulation makes it apparent, I believe, that both the separation from her nurse and the parents' subsequent handling of the child's reaction to it had constituted severe assaults on the need for autonomy. Much of the patient's maladaptive behavior must be understood as a series of regressive evasions of this issue or attempts to master it through repetition. To put this in another way, the only traditional construct referable to the crucial features of her pathology is that of the repetition compulsion. As I try to demonstrate in Chapter 15, this construct fits into the overall framework of psychoanalytic theory only if we resort to an unacceptable conceptualization, that of an instinct of primary masochism.

My reformulation focused on the self-organization illuminates the same issues in a more direct way. Although the actual outcome in each instance was invariably painful, the patient came for analysis presenting two sets of behaviors. Whenever possible, she strove for intimacy with a man whom she could implicitly idealize; if this goal became unattainable, she became preoccupied with her digestive processes. Her main defense upon reintegrating after such regressive episodes was an "altruistic surrender," i.e., a displacement of concern to other people in need, in which she actively did for them what she had been unable to secure for herself. A complicating factor, probably based on similar distortions concerning her mother in childhood, was her propensity to give credence to illusions of excellence in various endeavors, prominently including that of saintliness. These false idealizations were repeated in the transference relationship; in part they seemed to have been encouraged by the mother's high valuation of the child's efforts to please her. Systematic correction of these distortions led to sufficient diminution of her false pride to enable the patient to substitute a better method of appetite satisfaction for her former somatic preoccupations, namely, that of masturbation with perverse ideation.

The choice of perverse sexual gratification in circumstances that call for buttressing the sense of self is one of the issues that has been least satisfactorily handled by the traditional theory of psychoanalysis. A theory that attempts to explain all behavior as the expression of one or more instinctual drives, however modulated by discharge thresholds, is necessarily unsatisfactory when it comes to clarifying what is unique to behaviors in which inappropriate sexual gratification is the *central* feature. In the context of a psychology focused on a hierarchy of goals and values, this particular conceptual problem dissolves—*only* "sexual" gratifications (in the broader sense) are seen in terms of the goal of appetite satisfaction, and that aim is clearly one of the most fundamental and probably comes into the infant's awareness earlier than any others. The question to be answered in any specific instance thus narrows down to the meaning of the particular "perverse" fantasy that accompanies the erotic act.

To put this in another way, what is puzzling about the perversions is the fact that expectable adult genital acts do *not* affirm the self sufficiently, as they do in better adapted individuals. Perverts require transactions in which they are essentially in control of transitional objects; hence I am in agreement with Bak's dictum (1974) that the basic perversion is fetishism—i.e., that all other forms can be conceptually reduced to variations on the theme of manipulating an infantile fetish.

To return to the specific instance of this analysis, the patient's new-found capacity to masturbate clarified her lifelong ambition to equal her mother in the sexual sphere. It also led to the insight that this competitive aim had to be sacrificed because it threatened another goal, which had higher priority, that of safeguarding personal autonomy. In interpersonal relationships, such as the analytic transference, this autonomy could only be guaranteed through the power to command the other person—in spite of the concurrent attribution of perfection to the latter. Lacking *this* power, the patient had always resorted to covert negativism, i.e., evasive maneuvers designed to thwart the influence of others upon her—unless they could respond to the world in a manner identical to her own.

The patient's need to exercise control over other people had created insoluble conflict for her when, in middle childhood, she had accepted her father's value system of goodness and altruism; she had tried to resolve this dilemma by focusing her ambitions within the realm of saintliness. Analytic insight enabled her to return to the childhood ambition of winning the competition for intimacy with mother, a goal she was gradually enabled to relinquish in the context of empathetic concern about its frustration. She was thus able to grasp the reason for her original retreat into grandiose fantasies of pre-eminence, especially in religious terms, in the lack of parental understanding for her needs for intimacy. The patient then gained the ability to accept certain attributes she had seen as desirable in me and to differentiate herself from me by rejecting others which did not suit her.

Reduced to its essentials, analytic treatment can be understood to have altered the patient's propensity, acquired from her mother, to accept illusory convictions of pre-eminence. More accurate assessments of her actual levels of performance brought her face to face with the dilemma that she could not compete successfully in the interpersonal sphere as long as she had to safeguard her autonomy by exercising her absolute veto over the potential influence of others upon her. During the treatment, she attempted to solve this dilemma through her usual methods of adaptation, such as certain secret rituals. At the same time, she automatically made the analysis into a "holding environment" through a silent idealization of the analyst as soon as he prevented external interference with the joint effort. Disruptions of the genuine idealizing transference caused the patient to become disorganized, but her rage against the analyst at these times precluded turning to him for assistance with the resulting handicaps; restoration of function could take place only when the idealization was re-established by actual alteration of the circumstances. Hence, most of the analytic work concerned the grandiose illusions through which she denied her objective need for a symbiosis. The success of these interventions in producing "optimal disillusionment" led, late in the analysis, to the patient's discovering her symbiotic needs for herself. This insight, in turn, began the second stage of her relinquishment of illusions, that of the gradual renunciation of her idealization of the analyst.

In terms of the definition of psychoanalytic technique introduced by Eissler (1953), a "parameter" was introduced when the illumination of the office was adjusted, in spite of the analyst's conviction that the patient's expectation in this matter had no valid rationale. The parameter was later resolved in connection with the incident concerning the open window, in which the demands for total control over the volition of another person were confronted as unrealistic, i.e., based on the illusion that others could completely share her responses.[3] I am willing to classify this event as a "parameter" because it involved an actual, involuntary compliance with a demand on the part of the patient to alter the psychoanalytic setting to her specifications. In my clinical experience with persons whom I have analyzed with success, this was the sole instance in which I was unable to deal with such a situation through verbal means alone.

Through most of this analysis, it was also possible to maintain a satisfactory holding environment through the provision of the standard psychoanalytic situation. The most essential ingredient for establishing this silent, idealizing transference was simply the continuing availability of the analyst. As the material from the follow-up visits several years after termination shows, even explicit efforts to undermine the illusions upon which this relationship was based had not succeeded entirely in helping this patient to renounce her view of the analyst as a magical caretaker. In this matter, as in that of the illumination of the analytic room, it seemed that only an actual event, the occurrence of a somatic illness, could finally convince her that I did not possess the powers of a healer.

In the meantime, however, it had been necessary repeatedly to intervene directly to prevent dangerous consequences when the patient conducted herself in ways dictated by

---

[3]More detailed discussion of the appropriate management of such archaic transferences will have to be undertaken in separate publications (but see Gedo, 1975a, 1977b, in press).

her illusions—e.g., in failing to get adequate medical care for her "ulcer" and her skin condition, or refusing to make adequate preparations for her teaching job. It required consistent attention to these irrationalities over a period of years to "disillusion" her about her own magical powers.

CHAPTER EIGHT

Third Clinical Illustration: A Case of Conflicting Systems of Values

A 35-year-old writer called me for a consultation on the recommendation of a colleague whose analytic books had come to his notice in the course of his work for a local publication. He explained that he wished to make a decision between two courses of action which seemed available to him: whether to undertake psychoanalytic treatment and thereby attempt to find some meaning in life, or to go into the Arizona desert in order to let himself die of dehydration.

He went on to say that he was considering the first alternative only for the sake of a young woman whom he loved, because he knew that she would be profoundly grieved by losing him. On the other hand, one reason for his longing for death was his inability to offer her the conditions she needed: they could not marry because of his responsibility toward his wife, and he could not even support a woman because he had given up his job some six months ago. He had been married for over a decade before he left an increasingly frustrating and barren relationship upon discovering the mutual love between himself and a young co-worker. Even then, he considered his action the consequence of a sapping of his strength and determination rather than an active decision. Not long afterward, he completed in a successful manner a major work assignment which had required that he be away from the office. On returning to his usual routines, he found he could no longer tolerate what he felt to be the shoddiness, selfishness, and dishonesty of the world of the communications media. Although he had actually found himself unable to go to work, he had not regarded this condition as an emotional disability and had allowed himself to be furloughed without compensation.

Paradoxically, this chain of events had unrolled in spite of the fact that the patient had been in regular psychiatric therapy for about four years. Initially, he had insisted on his wife's need for such assistance; after she had complied with his demand to accept it, her therapist had urged him to enter treatment as well in order to salvage the marriage. He had found the regime of weekly individual sessions complemented by regular group therapy to be bewilderingly irrelevant to his concerns, and he had concluded, on the basis of the enthusiasm of the other members of the group and of the therapist's evident sincerity and good will, that it was he himself who was lacking in the usual human capacity to communicate with others. Only the ease and directness of his interchanges with his new friend had permitted him to preserve some hope that the failure of treatment had not been entirely his own fault, and he had dropped out of therapy after he had read certain psychoanalytic works which implied that there might be more to life than sharing one's affects with one's neighbors. In addition, his new friend turned out to be in therapy with an analyst and encouraged his interest in these analytic ideas.

He had spent the last six months in keeping house for her, desperately trying to present her with a normal façade. Indeed, while they were together, he even felt more or less intact, although never for a moment could he forget that his overall situation was a hopeless one. In his friend's absence, he could mechanically go through the motions of the household chores, or he sat immobile, either oblivious to his surroundings and the passage of time or filled with anguish and a feeling of chaos. He had felt impelled to write descriptions of his various feeling states, and he brought a sheaf of these for my consideration. They turned out to be gripping and pitiless introspective pictures of a welter of simultaneous affects, written in a powerful, direct style which I found moving and impressive. The patient was able to recall that he had often felt these unbearable emotions since early in his childhood, and many of his verbal self-portraits referred to past feeling states rather than one in the immediate present.

Upon inquiry, this man was able to give a concise and coherent account of his biography. His origins lay in a small city of the upper Midwest which had already become something of a backwater when he was born. His parents, children of the Anglo-Saxon small bourgeoisie, had been high school sweethearts and are still remembered as the ideal couple of their generation in the town. His father had been an athlete of great promise who had given up his professional ambitions in that sphere for the sake of family life. He had then thrown himself into a career as an independent businessman; he won increasing success and was currently heading into old age as the wealthy head of a printing company on the West Coast. His mother, an outstandingly beautiful girl with musical gifts, became incapacitated with tuberculosis in the course of her only pregnancy. As a result, the patient had been raised from birth by his maternal grandmother. As far as he could recall, mother had been confined to her bed in the back room and was not to be disturbed, but she had been unfailingly loving, soothing, and interested in him whenever he had been permitted to have any contact with her. When he was four years old, she had abruptly died as a result of an unexpected intercurrent infection.

For two years after his mother's death, his bereaved father had largely been absent, apparently trying to reorganize his life by establishing his business in a larger community. Although this pattern may actually have been instituted earlier, it is certain that during these years, at any rate, the care of the patient was divided between the two sets of grandparents. The arrangement called for his spending alternate fortnights in each household. He remembered these years as a time of some confusion because of the widely differing atmospheres of the two settings. He was able to describe these only in terms of external criteria, however. He volunteered no psychological portrayal of any member of his complex family, and I did not press him for this. Briefly, the maternal family was warm, quiet, and pious, while that of the father was distant, rigid, demanding, and moralistic. The women were dominant in both settings, and there were several uncles and aunts in each but no children aside from the patient. He led a solitary life, preferring to daydream inside old abandoned buildings or in his grandmother's attic. Although he did not learn of this during childhood, the observable pall over his father's family had been present since the suicide of the paternal grandfather. The latter had supposedly killed himself because of his wife's allegations that he had been a poor provider.

Although the patient was quite open about describing this early period of his life, he laid much greater emphasis on the one that followed it. When he was almost seven years old, his father suddenly reappeared with a new wife and reclaimed the child. He was taken to live in a strange city; as he recalled, he had been eager to rejoin his father and gratified by the latter's acknowledgment of parental responsibility. As matters turned out, however, his father was unaccountably passive in leaving all decisions about the child to his new wife, who embarked on a campaign to reform the boy from the ground up. This effort involved a literal attempt to reshape every aspect of the child, from outward behaviors through basic attitudes to the very fabric of his body, upon which she insisted on having performed all of the feasible "corrective" surgical procedures, such as tonsillectomy and circumcision. The child at first defended himself with lively anger; however, overt expressions of this reaction were severely punished, and even his father regarded them as evidence that his wife was justified in her view that the child was bad. The patient's helpless rage sometimes surfaced, nonetheless, in certain dramatic episodes: on one occasion, he stole a loaded revolver from the home of a friendly policeman in order to shoot his stepmother and was only restrained from carrying out this resolve by the last-minute thought that he would be causing his father the same kind of enduring grief that his mother's death had brought about. Another time, when his stepmother had unjustly accused him of some sexual crime, he determined to prove his innocence by starting to cut off his own penis—which she detected and stopped. Much of the time, he tried to comply with her instructions, but could find no way to satisfy her because her expectations seemed to shift in an unpredictable manner. What he found most difficult in all this was her firm and insistent disagreement with him about the basic *facts* of what had transpired between them. He never quite abandoned his own sense of the realities, and he concluded that his stepmother must be a habitual liar. Because his father seemed always to take her side, without passion, to be sure, the patient did not push these disputes very far.

By the time he was eight, the patient was living for the day when he would be able to get away from home, and he repeatedly tried to gain permission to live elsewhere. His stepmother determinedly opposed these plans and succeeded in obtaining the father's veto until the boy reached the age of thirteen. At that time, he took matters into his own hands by running away and making his own living arrangements. He went back to the town where his grandparents lived, enrolled in school there, and tried to conceal himself from the family. When, inevitably, he was discovered, his father consented to the *fait accompli,* only insisting that he submit to the grandparents' supervision. Thus he lived alone for the year and was able to manage quite well, and he had his most productive experience from the scholastic point of view. Of course he had always been an outstanding student—he had learned to read, apparently without instruction, at the age of three —but until this last year in grammar school, he had remained socially isolated.

From then on, with negligible exceptions, the patient remained on his own. He was still eager enough for his father's approval to attend an Eastern prep school for a year. He became a successful quarterback there, although he had no enthusiasm for football and was subjected to repeated injuries because of his small size. His father did come to see him play but was unimpressed; the patient stated dispassionately that, by his father's standards, he had indeed been an ordinary player. His father wanted him to join him in the printing business and could neither understand nor value his son's intellectual bent. He was not pleased by the boy's decision to finish high school in the old home town, nor did he alter his feelings merely because, by the time he graduated, the patient had also managed to accomplish more than two years of course work at a nearby small college.

The patient's teenage years were clearly marked by a prodigious outburst of enthusiasm directed toward preparing himself for a productive life. At the same time he became sexually active, forming his first long-term liaison with a young divorcée who was explicitly maternal toward him while she taught him how to please adult women. At the age of eighteen, he left behind him his family and his small-town world to come to Chicago to attend a famous university. Although he was already quite certain of his intention to become a writer—specifically one who would help people by alerting them to the truths society tends to disavow!—he wanted the best possible education on which to base this activity, instead of training in journalism. The university did not disappoint him, and he underwent an intoxicating period of growth and learning. This became so exciting that he could hardly eat or sleep in his continuous quest for more knowledge. He drove himself into exhaustion and was briefly thought to have Addison's disease in the middle of his college career. What he could not manage to integrate was the consensus of the faculty that he possessed a major literary talent, and upon graduation he entered the workaday world of Chicago journalism.

Although he found many facets of his various jobs exciting and continued to be committed to the primary importance of a free press for our society, in none of the numerous work settings in which he functioned in the next decade and a half did the patient feel at home. The standards of his co-workers generally struck him as shockingly low, and he could not accustom himself to the commercial ethos which seldom allowed for the kind of public service he was interested in. Management always recognized his outstanding competence and gave him all the responsibility he wanted, but because he asked for neither money nor status for himself, his accomplishments were known only to his immediate collaborators. For the past several years he had worked directly under a man who tried to appropriate for himself all the rewards and credit in the department; for the patient this person had come to symbolize the evil nature of mankind. He had never complained, however, nor did he ever dispute his boss's version of events. He wouldn't even claim that his own view of the profession was necessarily more accurate or valid than that of his venial supervisor.

The patient did not deny that there were many exceptions to his judgment of the unworthiness of his colleagues; however, he was too shy to approach those august people who did meet his ideal standards. The one departure from this rule had been his relationship to his wife. She was an artist he had met while they both worked for a trade magazine. In spite of the failure of their marriage, he was still firmly convinced of her superior worth and talent. He had married her because he had admired her work, and he had devoted considerable energy to furthering her career, encouraging her to obtain the highest qualifications in her field and supporting her through her chronic depression to reach the top of her profession.

The marriage had failed because these external signs of

progress had not altered her chronic depressive mood, and the patient felt increasingly frustrated in his absolute need to make her happy. He often thought of the problem mainly in sexual terms; although he had never had trouble in achieving mutual satisfaction with other women, his wife's unalterable frigidity made him feel that he was a failure as a husband. Indeed, he felt acute remorse about having finally given up on the marriage when the unsought-for love affair with his new friend had presented him with an alternative which had relieved his burden. In turn, his wife's reaction to the separation was one of boundless bitterness about his "betrayal." He did not agree with the accusation she was hurling at him, knowing full well that he had only left after his strength had given out. He also felt relieved of the burden of doing professional work he could not believe in; as a consequence, he was no longer obliged to rely on amphetamines to produce artifically the enthusiasm he had experienced spontaneously as a student. On the other hand, he had concluded that there was no place for him in the real world, nor could he much longer bear the suffering, he thought, that had afflicted him for almost 30 years, without feeling that he was living for some higher purpose. He had hesitated to end his life only because his young friend valued him, and all of her many acquaintances seemed to find him pleasant, interesting, and even wise—a fact he could integrate as little as he had been able to absorb his teachers' positive evaluation long ago.

My major intervention in the course of a series of exploratory interviews which revealed the foregoing history was to communicate the conjecture that the patient's desire to end his life might have been a reaction to the unresponsiveness of his environment—starting with his stepmother and continuing through his wife to his most recent employers—to his heroic efforts to achieve perfection. I wondered whether his specific plan to bring about his own death might not have been a last defiant affirmation of the power to arrange a flawless event without outside interference, an event characterized by grandeur and purity, a work of art involving a fantasy of psychic fusion with Nature. He responded with thoughtful reserve, agreeing that what he could no longer tolerate was the malicious depreciation of his accomplishments and the absence of even a single person who would share his goals. When I questioned whether the woman who loved him also failed in this regard, he said he was not sure; his uncertainty seemed to be based on a set of interpretations of her attachment to him made by her therapist. According to these, her relation to him was unrealistic, based on the acting out of her oedipal conflicts with a person who would always remain unavailable to her. Implicitly, she was under pressure to leave him and, because he could no longer present her with continuing proofs of his professional skills, she seemed disappointed and half inclined to give him up.

I also inquired about his potential sources of financial support if we were to undertake an analytic procedure. He explained that his resources would be sufficient for a period which he hoped would restore his work capacity—provided he could continue to live with his friend. I wondered whether additional support could be mobilized should his own funds run out before he was once more able to earn his expenses. He thought he could discuss the matter with his father, whose resources were ample enough. I urged him to ascertain whether everyone concerned was willing to cooperate in order to enable us to make realistic plans for treatment, adding that I certainly thought this should be attempted before he decided that there was no hope for establishing bearable conditions for his existence.

The results of the direct questions he then addressed to the crucial people turned out to be reassuring. His willingness to seek help was clearly sufficient to restore his friend's hopes about their future, and she declared herself ready to make sacrifices for his sake. His father found the situation most bewildering, but he promised to provide the requisite money if things had really reached a danger point. The patient reacted to these proofs of loyalty with sufficient relief to convince me of the feasibility of attempting an analysis. I made this recommendation with the proviso that, before he once again considered a plan of suicide, he give our common effort an adequate opportunity to get to the bottom of the problem—a stipulation to which he agreed as a matter of course. As things turned out, my offer to perform the analytic treatment had an immediate and unforeseeable beneficial result: it caused his girl's therapist, who was a former student of mine, to revise his pessimistic estimate of her chances in the relationship. He evidently began to support her commitment to my patient, and her therapy soon came to a satisfactory conclusion. As a result, she soon became able to be much more forthright in her expressions of affection and admiration, so that the patient never again felt as isolated as he had been before he began the analysis.

The psychoanalysis proceeded with surprising ease and was brought to a satisfactory termination within a period of barely fourteen months. The work involved a more restricted segment of the personality than lengthier analyses generally do, but the outcome left no room for hesitation about stopping. The patient brought a decided talent for introspection to the task, and he was able to accept interpretations about his resistances without feeling injured or criticized. On the contrary, shortly before termination, he stated that throughout the analysis he had never felt misunderstood, an assessment which formed a complement to my impression that, although I had often been baffled by his associations, no serious failures of empathy had interfered with the work. The specific flavor of this collaboration was already foreshadowed by the first dream reported in the analysis. In its expressiveness, transparency of texture, and wealth of associative connections, this dream proved to be quite typical of the patient's productions:

> The patient was a nonhuman creature, an "android," and the only one of his kind on earth. For reasons beyond his com-

prehension, all humans were hostile to him. He was a persecuted fugitive, ever in danger of being killed. After countless narrow escapes, he came upon another android. With immense relief, he joined his fellow; their substance merged into one being, a "superandroid" impervious to human persecution.

His associations immediately led to the interpretation that the dream expressed his hope to be strengthened by the analysis so that he could tolerate human relationships.[1] Other aspects of the dream were clarified in the course of the next several weeks. Here, I shall only mention that the science-fiction setting was connected to decades of fantasies in that mode; in many of these, he had indulged in orgies of "justified" destruction against those who had interfered with his idealistic plans. Thus it became possible to interpret that much of the

---

[1] Within the confines of this brief report, I have not been able to include all of the detailed evidence which had given me the confidence to venture this seemingly conjectural interpretation. I can only assert here that its cogency was subsequently confirmed in a variety of ways. Moreover, this patient, in his lengthy previous exposure to interpretive psychotherapy, had demonstrated no tendency whatsoever to accept the arbitrary conjectures of authorities. I am inclined to believe, to the contrary, that he had sought me out as a prospective analyst because he knew about my long-standing and more than casual interest in the problem of creativity. Although he had repressed the fact that he was acquainted with some of my work, we discovered after some months of analysis that he had attended a symposium on psychoanalysis and the humanities in which I had been prominently featured as a participant.

I therefore infer that my response to the patient's initial communications was probably very much in the nature of what he had anticipated from me. To put this more emphatically, his analysis as a whole was just as much of a perfected happening as the scenario alternative to it, that of the spotless suicide, would have been—and it was just as carefully prepared and staged by the patient. Analytic treatment may only be feasible in those instances in which the patient's scenario (a set of unconscious expectations brought to the encounter by every potential analysand) does not happen to clash too drastically with the requirements of Freud's procedure!

I trust, therefore, that the clinical data of this treatment will not be lightly dismissed as "nonanalytic" because of this early transaction. It is true that the nature of the archaic transference bond it established was never subjected to verbal interpretation, so that the analysis must be judged to have remained incomplete.

hostility he encountered was reactive to his anger and contempt toward those who did not share his values, and this
line of inquiry led him to memories of his childhood wars
against his stepmother.

We were now able to reconstruct the fact that she must
have been reacting to his shock and disapproval of her "selfishness"; her savage intolerance seems to have been a manifestation of her need to merge with people, in the manner of
the androids in his dream, but to retain absolute control over
the volition of the resultant team. On one level, the creation
of the superandroid in the dream signified his identification
with the stepmother's aggression. She had insisted on break-
ing his will, and he had only been able to fight back covertly:
by urinating in a closet while he was "sleepwalking," for
example. Under the circumstances, he was able to retain positive regard for his father because the latter, although he
never contradicted his wife, certainly respected the boy's autonomy.

His more recent inability to fight back against his parasitic
superior on his last job seemed to have come about because
he had a need to overlook the deficiencies of all male authority figures, as he had needed to disavow those of his father
during the period of the stepmother's reign. In fact, it was
only in the course of the analysis that he became enabled to
examine his father's persisting passivity in the face of his
wife's poisonous sarcasm and depreciation. The patient now
grasped that, in spite of his outward success as a man of affairs and a sportsman, the old man was essentially dependent
on a woman's tyranny. He realized that his father had never
been able to manage independently, i.e., he had been a pup-
pet of his own mother throughout his first marriage and had
merely substituted the second wife's régime for the earlier
one. It was in this context that the motives for maintaining a
false belief in the adequacy of his "superiors" rose to consciousness. The issues might best be highlighted by means of
one of his most striking dreams:

He had written an encyclopedic work on the defects of the Nixon administration, a twelve-volume compendium detailing not only what was wrong but also specifying the exact remedies to be applied. The books had gone to press and were being distributed to the public. He joyfully opened his advance copy, to discover to his horror that the printers had totally jumbled everything—the entire text was unintelligible. He awoke in rage and panic.

The ruin of his own ambitions was directly attributed to the inadequacy of people on whose support he had every right to count, and these individuals were in the same business as was his father. It had been precisely in this manner that his supervisor had sabotaged all of his efforts to use their publication in the interest of the community, and he had been unable to do anything about it because of his own anxiety whenever he had been confronted with the other man's limitations. He had preferred to view the boss as malevolent and powerful, instead of facing the fact that he was weak and timid. It had been the very likelihood of prevailing against the man in any confrontation that had been frightening and had caused the patient to collapse into confusion. He generally became inhibited by the thought that his own plans must have been unrealistically ambitious, like the absurd twelve-volume exposé in his dream. In order to function at his best, he needed continuous external confirmation of the value and feasibility of his goals; this is what he had received in abundance at the university, leading to the great creative outburst of his student years.

Insight into the sources of his frustration at work soon led the patient to the conclusion that he would never resign himself to the gross imperfections of the communications media. The very thought of having to go back to work in such a job when his financial reserves were exhausted filled him with despair and fantasies of suicide. He realized that he derived satisfaction only from working toward the highest standards, and he knew that these were not feasible in the commercial world. In associating to this dilemma, he began to refer to the manner in which he passed many of the solitary hours when, in his vocabulary, he was "doing nothing." He was actually haunted by verbal images related to his emotional states. The descriptions he had brought me had been efforts to report this ideation as a journalist should; in its raw form, however, what he was obsessed with came nearer to lyric poetry. He had had similar experiences, particularly when he was alone, since early childhood, probably starting with efforts to put into words whatever he saw when he was three.

The most convincing illustration of the patient's absolute need for outside intervention to allow him to pursue his own goals was provided by his response to my inquiry about the reason for transforming his poetic inspirations into journalism. It had simply not occurred to him that he could more fruitfully write poetry than produce clinical reports about himself, but when my question alerted him to this possibility, he began to experiment in the alternative direction, and his formerly endless, empty days were transformed, with truly surprising speed, into the feverish activities of a creative artist. It must not be supposed that he was in any way satisfied with what he began to produce. He felt he was technically an amateur, and he estimated that it would take years of study and practice to gain mastery of this unfamiliar medium. More central still was his conviction that the abstruse and hermetic verses he was creating were of no use to anyone but himself, and therefore could not be regarded as anything more than a self-indulgence—therapeutic, to be sure, and therefore permissible in the present emergency.

In this way, we learned of the patient's commitment to his father's ethic of utilitarianism which had impelled him to make use of his talent in the area where he thought it could be of maximal public benefit. It now became clear to him why he had been unable to respond to his teachers' estimates of his superior literary endowment: he could not regard literature as an acceptable vocation for a decent person. In this regard, writing poetry was the most reprehensible of literary alternatives, because there is no real prospect of earning a living from it—his father had dutifully renounced an athletic career for the sake of his family, although the chances of substantial remuneration in that field had been tangible even in his youth. As it turned out, the effects of this ethical imperative were by no means confined to the patient's vocational choice; they pervaded his entire range of activities. For instance, he was able to behave in a pleasant and companionable manner when other people were present (but could not recall how that felt when he was later left to himself) because this activity was justified by his duties as a social being. By contrast, when he was alone, he felt obligated to refrain from entertaining or soothing himself. Sexual activity could be enjoyed as long as its aim was to give to the partner; this is why he had found his wife's frigidity unendurable: there was no way of justifying any intimacy on the basis of *her* needs. He had busied himself with making himself useful to her in all sorts of other ways, even to the extent of writing some of her papers while she had been in school. In fact, as it gradually emerged, he must have been rather obtuse in failing to see that some of her dissatisfaction had probably stemmed from his refusal to let her do anything for *him*. This realization quickly led to alterations in his relations to his current companion, who was then able to verbalize how much happier she had become as a result of being allowed to do more for him. One practical result of this tipping of the balance was the patient's decision to accept more financial help from her and to devote most of his savings to paying for a divorce. The legal details were attended to in due course; in about six months he was divorced, and about three months later he married this woman who was so easily made happy.

It should be noted that these desirable behavioral changes did not reflect any alteration in the patient's ethical position: he had merely discovered a superior method of making himself useful to others. With regard to his creative work, his attitude of disapproval persisted, so much so that, when writing made him feel sufficiently better to permit it, he often stopped because it was no longer justified by the therapeutic need to continue. In examining the self-imposed states of aimlessness and suffering that resulted, we were gradually led to memories of the usual behavior of the patient's paternal grandmother. Whenever she had completed her household duties, she had sat immobile, with a blank expression on her face; the child's intrusions on her self-absorbed withdrawal had been met with angry disapproval. It became possible to reconstruct that the patient's ethical position, so much more stringent and fanatical than the morality behind his father's Babbitry, had only acquired a veneer of the latter's utilitarian rhetoric; in fact, both father and son had adhered to the standards of the pitiless matriarch whose husband had sacrificed his life so that she could collect his insurance.

On the one hand, this acceptance of the grandmother's values entailed placing responsibility for taking care of women at the summit of a man's hierarchy of goals. In this regard, both the patient and his father had unquestioningly followed the family prescription. The realization that his father had responded to the same influences that had shaped him helped the patient to accept the former's neutrality at the time of the wars with his stepmother. Previously, he had rationalized the lack of support from his father through fantasies that, in some way that had escaped his notice, he might, after all, have been in the wrong in defending himself. The new insight also helped him to go through his divorce without giving in to his first wife's unreasonable demands, claiming literally every scrap of their joint property. At the time of their separation, he had left with only the clothes on his back; he was now able to retrieve most of his personal effects.

On the other hand, there had also been some differences between the influence the grandmother had exerted on her own sons and that on her grandchild, based on her own emotional states during the widely separated periods of her life when she had raised them. As a middle-aged widow, her outward behavior, as the patient remembered it, suggested the demeanor of someone suffering from melancholia—with one exception: she directed her continous stream of reproaches not against herself but against anyone who interfered with her. In other words, she vehemently asserted that her own immobility and lack of interest in her surroundings constituted the only morally correct line of conduct. In lapsing from time to time into similar behaviors in the present, the patient was demonstrating his intermittent acceptance of her example.

The waxing and waning of this identification could not be correlated with the schedule of analytic sessions or with any other events in the present. Consequently, we had to assume that they reflected the alternating sequence of the influence of the two grandmothers during that period of the patient's childhood when he had been shuttled between their households on a more or less regular basis. The manner in which the childhood reactions to the constant need to adapt himself to sharply contrasting requirements were being relived in the present was most dramatically illustrated through the analysis of another vivid dream:

> The world had been taken over by a totalitarian regime which imposed uneventful order and work on society; all activities related to the spirit had been proscribed. The patient had gone underground as a rebel against this system; he fled into a region of remote mountains. In his wanderings, he came upon a lost city that formed a complete contrast to the prevailing world order: there, total preoccupation with matters of the spirit prevailed. He found the best products of human creativity in intoxicating profusion, but the city was entirely depopulated. He wanted to stay there forever, but he could not tolerate permanent isolation. Reluctantly, he left again, but not far from this haven he encountered his fiancée who came to live with him in his secret city. Moreover, she had the privilege of free passage from his world to that of common humanity.

Aside from the direct representation of his creative work as the sole escape from a humdrum tyranny he could not bear, the patient's associations connected this dream with his desperate longing for his mother and for her family when, at his paternal grandmother's, he felt disapproved of for feeling enthusiasm for anything. After his father had taken him away from both grandmothers, he had been hopelessly trapped in the totalitarian world, but the memory of the realm of the spirit had sustained him. As an adult, however, he had not received the necessary reinforcement to recapture the creative Paradise Lost of his early childhood until these insights in the analysis permitted him to turn to his fiancée with the direct question whether she would be willing to plan a joint life if he were to devote himself permanently to the vocation of a poet. Her unhesitating agreement, which seemed to be based on complete confidence in the magnitude of his talent, henceforth served as an antidote to the aftereffects of his grandmother's disapproval.[2]

The likelihood that his reluctance to commit himself to creative work had had other determinants came to light in

[2] It is entirely probable that the extremely rapid adaptive improvement that brought this treatment to its unusually speedy conclusion was in fact contingent on the availability of this relationship as a partial symbiosis. In this second sense too, the analysis can only be regarded as incomplete. However, I did not see any possibility of undoing the effects of this splitting of the transference in the foreseeable future, so that I would not have opposed the patient's decision to terminate even if certain reality considerations had made continuation of the work more feasible than it was in actuality. The same consideration foreclosed the possibility of interpreting the idealizing grandmother-transference prior to the interruption of the collaborative effort. The holding environment was established in the initial consultation, when I did not disappoint the fantasy that had brought the patient to my office—the hope for a fusion of creative personalities. In that context, he was enabled to face his disillusionment with some of the important figures in his life, especially his father and his wife. When the analysis brought his grandiose fantasies out of repression, he was able to renounce these spontaneously, and he was able to dispense with the analytic situation as a holding environment. The fate of the idealizing transference remains uncertain.

connection with his discovery of memories about the paternal grandmother's attitude toward his sexuality. He now recalled that he had slept in her bed, a circumstance made possible by her widowhood, and unthinkable in the intact family of the maternal grandmother. Sometime in his fifth or sixth year, he had become so sexually stimulated by this body contact that he had actually mounted the woman. She stopped him with so much disgust and scorn that he was overcome with remorse. He accepted her sexual prohibitions to the extent of never challenging his stepmother's premises in accusing him of evil on the ground that he was sexually responsive to her. His attempt at self-castration on one such occasion had merely been aimed at proving that he had been innocent of the specific sexual intentions she was attributing to him at the moment. In spite of this, by the time he reached the age of eight, he was fully determined to have intercourse with women at the earliest opportunity, and he was completely aware of the fact that sexual partners who would approve of his phallic masculinity would not be difficult to find. He never had the least disturbance of potency, nor was there any inhibition about establishing an active sexual life with women, starting in his early teens. In other words, his grandmother's moral influence did not persist into his adolescence, and it could not by itself account for his lifelong avoidance of the pleasurable creative activities his literary gifts would make possible for him.

Moreover, the explanation of this avoidance on the ground that he was committed to a life of public service turned out to be a rationalization. To be more precise, he was indeed wholeheartedly committed to the moral elevation of mankind, but we discovered that his ideal predecessors in this quest were the supreme artists of our civilization: such secular prophets as Shakespeare, Euripides, Bach, Rembrandt, or Dostoievsky. It gradually came to light that he had been afraid to embark on a poetic career because of the limitlessness of his own ambitions in this area. He was frightened by the austerity and ruthlessness of his judgments in aesthetic matters, of his contempt for triviality or the handling of less than tragic themes. If he allowed himself to take his poetry seriously, as he was beginning to do as a result of our work, he experienced states of mounting excitement in which he often lost track of time and even forgot to eat and to sleep. On a few occasions, he had only regained his bearings on the following morning, with no memory of the external events of the previous day, although, as in his childhood "sleepwalking," he had clearly gone through a series of routine activities in an automatized manner.

After approximately ten months of analytic work (in the course of which there had been two vacation interruptions of several weeks' duration, which had not created any perceptible change in the patient's overall emotional state) he announced that he was feeling much better; in fact, he estimated that the analytic task might have been about half accomplished. Around this time he had to turn to his father for a loan to continue financing the analysis; because the patient could no longer claim to be suicidal, however, his father yielded to the stepmother's opposition to granting this request. As a result, pending the outcome of his efforts to mobilize some other source of funds, we had to face the possibility that the analysis might have to be interrupted. He briefly considered the possibility of taking some job in order to earn enough to be able to continue paying my fees, but he came to the conclusion that such a course of action would reverse the progress he had made just as surely as giving up the analysis would do. He felt that without my explicit or tacit confirmation of his discoveries about himself, he might still be unable to cast aside the moral judgments of his paternal family consistently enough to persist in his literary goals.

In this context, he was able to realize that his father had always been ready to listen to the attacks his wife was making on the patient because he was chronically envious of what he had seen as the latter's freedom to pursue higher ambitions: a university education, glamorous jobs in Chicago, beautiful and sophisticated women, etc. His current determination to become a serious poet had brought the father's attitude of depreciation and envious interference into the open with the refusal of the promised loan, but the unspoken reproach, "Who do you think you are?" had never been too far from being articulated. The patient was thus by no means surprised by his father's refusal to attend his wedding, a rather elaborate affair arranged by his bride's socially prominent family in the Southern city where they lived. He was quite certain now that the old man could not stand any unfavorable comparisons between his own status and that of his future in-laws, but this attitude was covered with sanctimonious disapproval of the patient's divorce, the expenses of the wedding, and the like.

In reviewing his past relations with his father, the patient now realized that he had been aware of similar attitudes for a long time, perhaps extending all the way back to the mother's death, when the father became homeless but the child continued to have the gratifying relationship with his maternal grandmother. It was not possible to determine whether this envy had a role to play in establishing the disruptive routine of alternating residence with both sets of grandparents that then followed. What did come into the open was the fact that, in spite of his awareness of his father's hostile envy, the patient had always felt guilty toward the latter. He had the underlying attitude that he was totally responsible for setting up a good relationship with his father—indeed, with everyone. Hence, his stepmother's or his first wife's paranoid characteristics had given him no excuse, in his own eyes, for not being able to get along with them in complete concord.

In response to this material, I made the first far-reaching intervention in the analysis since my comments about his motives for suicide during the initial consultation. This consisted in summarizing his account of his system of morality as a private religion characterized by mystical union with nature and a conviction of ethical perfectibility, akin to certain forms of Buddhism. In association to this description, the patient began to give details of the religious atmosphere of his mother's family and, more specifically, about the private convictions of his maternal grandmother. She had been a person of shining goodness and unfailing kindness who had devoted herself to the care of her family and to religious meditation and reading. She had abandoned her Protestant background long before the patient's birth and had evolved an original system of beliefs which had, indeed, drawn heavily on Theravada Buddhism. She had been entirely uninterested in converting anyone else to her point of view, and probably only the children she had raised could infer these facts about her, mostly on the basis of her spontaneous responses to the vicissitudes of everyday life. It was not clear to the patient whether she had believed in reincarnation, but he *was* completely certain that her moral ambitions did not stop at the comparatively modest goal of those Buddhist believers who strive to be good in order to gain a better chance in the next life. She had been engaged in the quest of Buddhist saints who seek to gain Nirvana. All her efforts had been directed at moral self-improvement, at that elimination of self which is purported to confer absolute moral power on the mystic. In her view, if one achieved sufficient goodness, one gained the capacity to stop an attacking tiger in midleap. Wrongs had to be remedied, not through action, but exclusively through the exercise of such moral influence.

The patient now arrived at the realization that much of his puzzling behavior throughout his lifetime could be understood as the result of an identification with these outstanding and admirable qualities of his grandmother. For one thing, he had tried to emulate her because of his enthusiasm for her charisma; for another, she had failed to teach him the same kind of humility and moderation in the moral sphere that she had counseled in all other enterprises. On the contrary, she had rewarded and encouraged his efforts to be good, self-sacrificing, unaggressive—to influence people by personal example alone, instead of criticizing or opposing their transgressions. These so-called "passive" behaviors had already become the patient's characteristic style in his relation to his paternal grandmother; his total and immediate acceptance of her condemnation of his sexual response to her was only the most dramatic of many incidents in which the burden for right conduct had been unfairly put on him alone, with his own concurrence. Although he could not contain his indignation in reaction to the steady barrage of unreasonable blame emanating from his stepmother, he had been overwhelmed with the conviction of his own moral failure through this evidence of his angry nature—in his grandmother's world view, a taint of constitutional evil, of an excess of native aggressivity.

It did not prove to be necessary to review in detail the countless repetitions of his pattern of irrational otherworldliness in his dealings with everyone he had encountered in adult life, although numerous examples from his domestic and professional life did occur to him in the course of his analytic sessions. The moderation of his ambitions for sainthood could be observed almost immediately; as one instance, he was now able to apply for and obtain disability compensation for having been unable to work for almost two years—one concrete result of his abandonment of reliance on the power of magical goodness.

Approximately a year after the start of the analysis, the patient began to report feelings of unprecedented well-being which were seldom interrupted by relapses into the states of emptiness and inner pain he had formerly experienced. He was now able to pinpoint the proximate cause of each of these unfavorable reactions in terms of fresh disappointments in the people around him and/or in his power to elevate them into perfection through his own example. He found that the ability to identify these sequences of subjective experience had given him the power to regain his own psychic equilibrium. More and more of his sessions were characterized by stretches of contented silence or by preoccupation with the latest poem he was polishing. With some surprise, the patient now came to the conclusion that he felt he would be able to dispense with my services in the near future.

The termination phase lasted for only about six weeks and did not reveal any fresh material. He gave up the personal contact of the analytic relationship with appropriate sadness and expressions of appreciation. At last report, almost two years after termination, he sent word for Christmas that he continued to feel well and to work productively.

CHAPTER NINE

Discussion of the Third Case

Initial Formulation of Third Case

Although the patient's suicidal plans appeared to be in deadly earnest, analysis was attempted on the assumption that mitigation of his grandiose perfectionism might allow for a tolerable adaptation. Hope for such relief was based on the calculation that the grandiosity would prove to be a regressive response to disillusionments with important figures, most recently with his former therapist. Optimism was also justified by the patient's response to the deep intervention during the diagnostic period, that of interpreting the contemplated fantasy of suicide as a last desperate effort to create an unspoiled work of art. This response had consisted of his statement that he needed at least one person who would look upon his efforts with approval.

The actual start of analytic treatment meant that three persons (his mistress, his father, and the analyst) shared his goal of achieving some tolerable emotional state, and the patient reacted to this immediately (as shown in his initial dream) with a hopeful expectation of being strengthened through a fantasied psychic merger with a like-minded person. Presumably this "alter ego" transference repeated the childhood relationship to his maternal grandmother. This sense of support permitted him to face his destructive rage toward those who had been blocking his plans and his contempt for those who did not share his system of values. In this sense, he gained insight into his own contribution to the constant hostility of his stepmother and into his identification with her savage intolerance. By contrast, he had erected a reaction formation against his disappointment in his father and other male authority figures; the analytic work permitted him to acknowledge their limitations for the first time.

It now became possible to understand the collapse of his self-esteem on the basis of his continuing dependence on adequate assistance from such paternal transference figures. Among other things, they were needed to confirm the feasibility of his projects because of his propensity to engage in unrealistically ambitious enterprises. Simultaneously, he realized that the commercial world could never live up to his requirements; only in the solitary realm of his secret poetic endeavors was it possible to strive for perfection. The analyst's questions about the necessity to avoid commitment to poetic activity now brought to light the moral prohibition against "selfishness" in the form of self-improvement without utilitarian overtones.

This utilitarian ethic had been adopted from his father and was ultimately seen to be derived from the moral demands of the paternal grandmother. In her system, only the pleasure in pleasing was acceptable; it was this set of expectations that the patient had attributed to every woman. This insight permitted him to be more empathic with his mistress, who preferred mutuality, with a notable gain in the harmony of their relationship—as well as a sense of having improved his capacity to please! Part of his sense of aimlessness and suffering when he had finished discharging his duties toward others was now understood as an identification with his paternal grandmother and her unusual melancholia. In relinquishing this identification, the patient was able to shed his need to sacrifice himself for his psychotic wife, so that he was able to obtain a divorce.

Intermittent shifts in the patient's emotional state, unre-

lated to current events, led to the reconstruction of his childhood experience of having been subjected to the alternating
influence of the two sets of grandparents; dream material
suggested that the role of the analysis in the present dupli-
cated that of the maternal grandmother in childhood and
that his fiancée now served as a bridge helping him to integrate the conflicting value systems represented by analysis
and the commercial world. He was able to recall his frustrated longing for his grandmother during the period of
subjection to the attacks of the stepmother and, earlier,
whenever his enthusiasm had aroused the disapproval of his
paternal relatives. In this connection, he recalled his oedipal
sexual wishes and their prohibition by the paternal grandmother and realized that he had accepted her moral condemnation without giving up his phallic strivings.

Consequently, he was stimulated to explore the reasons
for his morally determined avoidance of the gratifying creative activities that later became possible for him. He realized
that he viewed Art as supreme among the instruments for
the moral elevation of mankind; thus, he was opposed to his
own creativity not on grounds of principle but, as he now
discovered, because of disapproval of his infantile ambitions
in this area. His fear of his own grandiosity now disappeared,
and the capacity to invest himself in creative work brought
about an unprecedented state of well-being that lasted even
through the disappointment of his father's failure to honor
the commitment he had made to help with the expenses of
the analysis.

The resultant threat that the treatment might have to be
interrupted led him to the explicit realization that he was
using the analyst as an auxiliary ego in order to neutralize
the persisting effects of his childhood morality on his current
behavior. In this context, he was able to see his father's
sabotage of the analysis as the continuation of a persistent
pattern, that of destructively acting out his chronic fraternal
envy toward the patient, usually by subjecting him to the rule

of despotic women. He could now acknowledge that he had been aware of this attitude on the part of his father for a very long time, but had nonetheless felt guilty about the difficulties in their relationship, as if the responsibility for concord had been entirely his own.

The analyst's reconstruction of the patient's deepest moral convictions in terms of a Buddhist-derived private religion, in response to this information, brought into focus the patient's childhood acceptance of such a set of beliefs from his admired maternal grandmother. He now realized that his moral strivings, modeled on hers, amounted to a grandiose quest of sainthood. He began to view his wish to alter people through moral influence alone as a lack of humility and common sense on his part—starting with his attitude toward the tyranny of members of his own family in childhood. His conviction of his own badness stemmed from his inability to refrain from responding to ill-treatment with anger.[1]

In summary, psychological development seems to have been unusually fortuitous until the child was overburdened with the necessity to adapt in rapid and repetitive fashion to

[1]This clinical example seriously calls into question the wisdom of Kernberg's technical recommendations (1975) for the treatment of character disturbances with archaic fixations. Kernberg advocates emphasis on the patient's innate destructiveness in interpreting his difficulties in object relations. Although it is certainly true that most such patients are indeed full of hostility, and this destructiveness is clearly an innate human potential (whether or not we choose to conceptualize it as a drive), to stress the nature of the patient's activity without regard for the context in which it occurs is to place him under exactly the kind of impossible moral burden that the child I have described in this case history was expected to carry. The usual consequence is reactive outrage and its expectable complications. Contrary to Kernberg's claims, the alternative to his recommendation is not to pour soothing syrup over the patient (an irrational procedure in which some analysts may occasionally indulge, but one that nobody would defend in principle). The appropriate analytic stance is to examine in detail the particular circumstances to which the patient responds with inappropriate rage. In the great majority of instances that are unjustified in actuality, these behaviors are found to be transference reactions, i.e., perfectly understandable and more or less appropriate in a *childhood* context.

the alternation of conflicting demands on the part of the two families who shared his custody from the age of four until he reached six. In accordance with an already established identification with one grandmother's moral values, he tried to assume responsibility for this burden. In latency, the pressure was increased through exposure to psychotic demands; he succeeded in adapting to these by repressing and/or disavowing his personal ambitions, erecting reaction formations against his contempt and disillusionment with his destructive caretakers, and adopting their utilitarian rhetoric as an ethical imperative. The resultant character structure rendered him completely dependent on the good will of his environment and eventually sapped his capacity to tolerate its exploitativeness.

In contrast to the previous cases I have discussed, this patient turned out to have a much better differentiated personality, almost invariably organized in Mode IV (see Figure 6). His greatest conflict revolved around his moral taboo against selfishness, which, according to the utilitarian ethic he had absorbed from his paternal relatives, included his personal ambitions in the creative sphere. He had erected reaction formations against his intolerance and contempt toward those who did not live up to his moral values, reserving condemnation for his own failures. His disavowal of earlier modes of functioning was completely effective. Only in analysis did he discover his disillusioned anger with the imperfections of others, his own grandiose perfectionism (especially with regard to sainthood), and his archaic need for merger with like-minded and accepting caretakers. Similarly, his split-off transitional experiences in the realms of poetry and religion were only unified with the rest of his personality in the course of treatment. The unrealistic religiosity was rapidly renounced, while the creation of idealized artistic products assumed a dominant role in his adult personality. With the resolution of the conflict between his personal ambitions and his morality, he was able to renounce the narcissistic merger within the

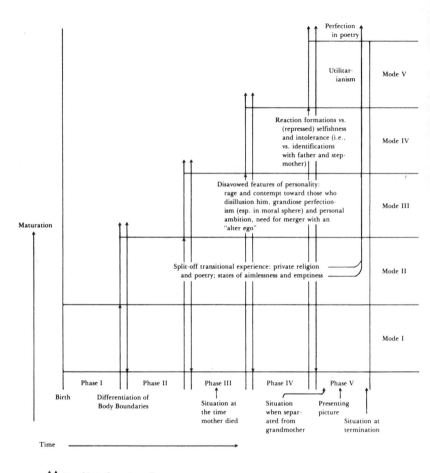

FIGURE 6
DATA OF CASE 3 IN ACCORD WITH THE HIERARCHICAL SCHEMA

transference and spontaneously attained the expectable adult mode of functioning.

Psychoanalytic theory has sometimes been misused as an a

priori description of universals (rather in the manner of an atlas of anatomy): data that do not fit into its categories are then dismissed as epiphenomenal, and the observer who reports them is accused of having overlooked the real issues, usually because of some flaw in his psychoanalytic technique. The only defense against such a challenge is to assert that one's technique in most cases is beyond reproach—i.e., whenever the Oedipus complex is relevant in pathogenesis, one has been able to assist the analysand in reliving it in the transference. I trust I may have demonstrated as much in my account of the analyses of the other two patients I have described. I should add at this point that my technique in the particular treatment at issue here was indeed marked by innovations; I would claim that these were required by the nature of the actual problems—much as the distinctive techniques of child analysis are necessitated by the actualities of the child's personality organization. Use of the technique appropriate for conventional neurotic characters with persons whose difficulties lie elsewhere can only lead to therapeutic failure. This principle has always been recognized by analysts who use stringent criteria of analyzability in selecting their patients. Unfortunately, there are some analysts who are less discriminating but prefer to sink with the traditional dogma rather than to face that there are more things in heaven and on earth than the theoretical models of yesteryear.

This has been a roundabout way of stating that, in my judgment, the foregoing formulation in terms of existing psychoanalytic theory barely serves to organize the observed behaviors into understandable propositions using a shared vocabulary. Neither the reasons for this patient's serious maladaptation nor those for the effectiveness of the unorthodox analytic interventions can be grasped through this conceptual schema. In other words, I consider this set of familiar formulations to be the least satisfactory among those I have offered. More detailed explanations for this view will be offered in the course of the reformulation in terms of a psychology of goals and values I shall now present.

Reformulation of the Third Case

The patient's presenting statement concerned his sense that the only avenue left to him to pursue his ambition of improving the world was that of removing himself from it while causing a minimum of pollution. He could think of no alternative purpose that he could approve, although his profound affection for his mistress obviously constituted an active striving for personal intimacy. His deep sense of failure about his inability to support this girl financially and/or to sustain his psychotic wife emotionally betrayed his absolute commitment to a utilitarian value system. In turn, he had a need for people who shared his ideals, but he could no more condone his goal of intimacy in this regard than in the realm of romantic love. In the absence of activities of which he could approve, he condemned himself to aimless immobility, which he experienced as a profound frustration. This state was presumably similar to the mixture of outrage and humiliation he had experienced in middle childhood about his father's failure to protect him from the attacks of the stepmother. However, the patient's commitment to rationality had greatly increased in the intervening three decades (this was one of the ideals he had acquired at the university in late adolescence), so that as an adult he no longer rebelled against his persecutors, either in action or in fantasy—not against a venial boss, an exploitative wife, or a fatuous psychotherapist. To the contrary, he had become confirmed in the striving to make everyone in contact with him maximally happy; hence, he was free to approach only those who were obviously in need, so that he seldom had contact with persons who could offer him very much. His affair with a young woman whose greatest expectation was to find him admirable was therefore an unprecedented circumstance in his life, and her confirmation of his viewpoint about the differences with his antagonists had, because of her rationality, forced him to re-evaluate his investments in hopeless causes.

My intention in offering a deep interpretation about the meaning of the patient's fantasy of an apotheosis was to test out whether he had the capacity to accept the offer of an intimacy based on sharing the ideal of perfection.[2] In combination with his obligation not to cause grief to his beloved, my implicit offer to join him in his search for a way to achieve such goals proved to be sufficient to tip the balance in favor of the analytic attempt. This impression was confirmed by his early dream about the merger of the androids. The latent meaning of this visual metaphor proved to be that he hoped to be able to resist the utilitarian ethic inculcated in him by his father and thus to commit himself to efforts to create perfection; in order to do this, he needed confirmation of the value of his creative aims from a respected person who shared them.

By tacitly allowing myself to be used to accommodate this need as if I had been a transitional object in a child's world of play, I reawakened the patient's childhood outrage about his father's failure to do so. In the present, therefore, he became conscious of his counterhostility toward those who interfered with his creative efforts and his contempt for people with differing ideals. In this manner, he became aware of his own role in provoking holy wars because of the intolerance he had learned from his caretakers. His struggles with his stepmother had become desperate efforts to ward off her insistence that he adopt her ambitions and ideals as his own,

---

[2]It may avoid potential misunderstanding to specify that I was well aware that neither the patient nor the two of us together could ever hope to *achieve* perfection, nor did I ever imply to him that our efforts could have that as *their* goal. I was trying to convey a basic attitude about perfection as an abstract aim, i.e., my personal conviction that *perstare et praestare*—to persist and to prevail—is as legitimate and valuable a goal as any other. In this regard, we may do well to recollect Freud's letter to his fiancée (Jones, 1952, p. 175) expressing his identification with Don Quixote as a "noble knight, passing through the world" (see also Gedo and Wolf, 1973). In other words, the ideal of perfection is grandiose only if one cannot tolerate falling short of it.

i.e., a determined defense of his need for autonomy. Under maximal pressure, the lonely child had consciously accepted the validity of the parents' viewpoint, but his self-organization remained essentially unaltered and expressed itself in complex acts of defiance in the absence of consciousness, i.e., while "sleepwalking."[3]

The second major insight achieved in the analysis concerned the need to disavow his father's collusion with the stepmother's attacks on the patient, echoed in adult life by his unrealistic difficulties in making reliable assessments about male authority figures. He was now able to grasp that he had falsely idealized his father (see p. 107n, above). His dream about an exposé of Nixon showed the nature of the problem in its basic theme of a supreme authority who had betrayed his trust; it also conveyed the insight that the patient's own performance still depended on the adequacy of silent collaborators. He had thus been trapped in a vicious circle: he could not acknowledge the limitations of people as long as his own integration depended on being able to see them as better than adequate. They were needed, specifically, to stop the patient from embarking on unrealistically ambitious, i.e., overtly grandiose, projects. Left to his own devices, he was truly incapable of curbing an unconscious propensity to attempt the impossible. Hence, the loss of confidence in his father's judgment (or that of a current superior on a job) threw him into panic or confusion. By contrast, his rapid sub-

---

[3]In a discussion of this case material in another connection, (Gedo, 1976) I have tried to conceptualize such altered states of consciousness as regressive returns to an infantile mode of organization, i.e., to one before the secure establishment of self-awareness. This state corresponds to Mode II of the hierarchical schema (see Figure 11, p. 195); in this mode, certain subsets of personal goals may be acted on in disregard of other subsets, without foresight or planning. In this particular instance, the child had acted out one side of his ambivalence, in jarring contrast to his affectionate submissiveness toward his father. The example may be prototypical for dissociative states in general (cf. the patient's loss of consciousness during the height of his creative frenzies).

jective improvement in the analysis signified his confidence in my reliability as an umpire.[4]

Insight into his need to foster illusions about authoritative superiors led the patient to realize that the commercial world would forever clash with his value system. In this context, I was able to focus his attention on his avoidance of poetic activity, an ongoing process that was never far from his awareness, but which he treated as an alien intrusion because of its lack of congruence with his utilitarian ethic. In tracing this pattern to its childhood origins, the patient now reviewed his relationship to his paternal grandmother. After this, he was enabled to differentiate the value systems of the various individuals in his current environment, most significantly those of the women in his life, permitting him to improve his empathic capacity toward them. This did not change his conviction that he had to choose a vocation which would help him to support a woman or his feeling that engaging in art for art's sake was only permissible as a kind of occupational therapy for the duration of his illness. Only when he had grasped the fact that his choice of lapsing into apathetic states after discharging his duties had been a global identification with his paternal grandmother did he realize that all of his personal goals had become subjected to the veto of a maximally exploitive person—most recently in the form of his parasitic wife, whom he was now able to divorce as a result of this insight.

[4] I have devoted a separate paper to the discussion of the psychoanalytic management of archaic transferences which require the analyst to respond to the patient's grandiosity (see Gedo, 1977b). Nonetheless, I should like to underscore one important inference which can be made on the basis of even this single case: it is by no means true that confronting a grandiose patient with the irrationality of his behavior must inevitably produce "narcissistic rage" (cf. Kohut, 1972). The person under discussion here urgently wanted, even *required,* such a restraining influence. One of the more undesirable side-effects of the popularization of Kohut's work has been the spread of the simplistic notion that people with self-cohesion disturbances require "mirroring," i.e., continuous confirmation of the alleged legitimacy of their infantile claims.

Alerted by alternations between acceptance of the fruits of the analytic work and their rejection, we were able to reconstruct the influence of the experience of having repeatedly been subjected to the melancholic grandmother at intermittent intervals. The patient's dream of a Shangri-la of creativity also alluded to such an alternation, experienced on his behalf in the present by his fiancée. Moreover, this dream betrayed the fact that creative work had always constituted one of his fundamental aims, although the influence of his paternal relatives had hedged in this commitment with innumerable oppressive contingencies. When the patient decisively rejected these conditions by turning to his fiancée for agreement to a shared life which would permit him to devote himself entirely to his poetry, he realized that in certain other matters, notably that of sexuality, he had needed no external assistance to reject the oppressive standards of his family. It thus became clear that his reluctance to pursue the path of creativity had had further determinants.

The patient's acknowledgment of the fact that he valued Art above all other avenues to the moral elevation of mankind removed the rationalization that he had avoided creative pursuits principally on utilitarian grounds. This realization led him back to the theme of his frightening fantasies of grandiosity, and he reached the insight that he had nothing to fear on that score when it came to his creative work. As he reviewed his aesthetic judgments, he was able to modify his former absolutism and lack of tolerance in these matters. Moreover, he gradually became used to the experience of loss of self-awareness in the midst of creative spells, ceasing to regard this contingency as a dangerous threat. The possibility that the analysis might have to be interrupted for financial reasons focused his attention on the specific need which continued to be fulfilled by his contact with me: he still could not withstand the pull of his childhood value system without external confirmation of his rational judgments.

The persistence of the influence of his paternal family came to an end at this time as a result of the patient's insight into his father's unconscious motives for refusing to help with the analytic expenses. He was able to see the moral precepts he had been taught in historical perspective, as one tool in a steady campaign to rob him of his capacity to enjoy life, attacks based on the envy of a whole generation of depressive personalities. As a consequence, it became clear that he had understood his father's hostile behavior even as a child but had felt the obligation to overcome his father's attitude through his own efforts.

It was this evidence that led me to conclude that the patient's life could only be understood in terms of the prevailing influence of an unconscious value system, already established prior to the time he had been subjected to the supervision of his paternal family. In trying to raise these ideas to the level of explicit awareness, both in their childhood concreteness and in more abstract terms suitable in the present,[5] I took care not to betray any disagreement with these beliefs—although the patient was, of course, quite aware that I did not share them. But then, as far as his conscious awareness went, neither did he! He was quite able to sort out by himself the unrealistic aspects of the quest for sainthood from the admirable qualities of his maternal grandmother. In other words, he did not discard his lifelong ideals; he merely corrected his childish literalness and concreteness about them, bringing them into harmony with his commitment to rationality. Among the most important proximate results of this shift was the moderation of his guilt about reacting with anger to being mistreated in various ways.

The manner in which I summarized this case history in

[5]Basch (1978) has written a seminal paper about the rationale of psychoanalytic interpretation which reviews in detail the cognitive task the analyst must perform when repressed or disavowed mental contents emerge in this manner.

the initial formulation could also serve to cap my account here. As a matter of fact, that statement was already made in terms of the competing systems of moral values the patient had acquired at various stages of his childhood and might well be considered to fit into the usual framework of psychoanalytic psychology only in the loosest way. The case material was pulled together in that formulation under the rubric of the concept of "narcissistic merger." Although this term graphically conveys the subjective sense of certain early experiences by means of a biological metaphor (that of the conjunction of paramecia, a specie of one-celled organisms), it is actually a recent addition to the conceptual armamentarium of psychoanalysis and has never been adequately defined in theoretical terms.[6] Moreover, in the context of our traditional concepts, we are confronted with something of a paradox by this case: that of the necessity of using constructs referable to very primitive stages of development in the presence of a well-differentiated personality.

I should now like to attempt to review and condense the reformulation I have offered in terms of a psychology of goals and values. The patient consistently presented himself as a person whose sole ambition was to improve the world for mankind. He had a number of other goals, such as that of personal intimacy or that of the creation of perfected works, but these were given scope only if they could conform to his

[6]Perhaps the most acceptable use of this term has been as a designation of those archaic transference manifestations which presuppose a loss of differentiation between the volition of the patient and that of the analyst (see Kohut, 1971). It has not been emphasized sufficiently that, at least in persons who can profit from psychoanalytic treatment, such a "merger" does not involve any actual difficulty in differentiating one's own person from others. Kohut's delineation of "merger transferences" has been obscured in an unfortunate manner by his adherence to the libidinal conception of narcissism. The fact that these patients are creating an illusion of merging with someone else was made clearer in the terminology advocated by Winnicott (1951), who called this type of relatedness "transitional"—i.e., a way-station between failure to recognize separateness and its acknowledgment.

primary ideals. His invariable preference for actions based on his inconvenient morality showed that his underlying central goal was the conservation of his autonomy. His acceptance of the value of reason had constituted the transformation of his self-organization that marked his adolescence. This change had failed, however, to alter his childhood commitment to making other people happy; it had merely extended this ambition into the wider social arena in his professional career. Contact with another rational person, his second wife-to-be, had undone the web of defensive denial and rationalization which had been required to make him blind to the hopelessness of his efforts to improve the lot of the sick people he had collected around himself. He was then able to accept analytic assistance from a person who showed willingness to share his quest for perfection.

We discovered that he had succeeded in preserving his early childhood self-schema throughout the oppressive regime of his paternal relatives; his adherence to their utilitarianism turned out to have been a compliant maneuver designed to keep *them* happy, in line with the earliest version of his lifelong ambition, that of altering others by the sheer force of his own goodness. In this specific area, his early upbringing had been deficient in common sense; he had been turned into a Daniel thrust into a den of lions armed only with a private religion according to which his failure to tame the beasts only proved his own shortcomings. The analytic work consisted of making this set of repressed fantasies available for integration into his conscious thinking. It should be noted that the treatment did not alter any of his goals or values. By bringing to his attention an area of thought that had not been subjected to rational control, it changed the specific ambitions which had arisen out of that basic self-schema. He abandoned the attempt to change people by magical means in favor of doing so as a secular prophet, through the productions of a tragic poet.

Discussion

To turn now to the issues of therapeutic technique illustrated by this analysis, it is perhaps most notable that only two major interpretations were offered in the course of the entire treatment, and one of these was made during the consultation preceding the patient's decision to commit himself to the analysis. Both interpretations, moreover, described hitherto unconscious aspects of the patient's value system. With regard to his previously unacceptable impulses, both sexual and aggressive, this analysand proved to be uniformly capable of attaining self-knowledge through introspection. He was quite able to arrive at these insights on his own, between his appointments, although my presence as an empathic witness tended to assist him in this self-analysis.

It must not be supposed that the fact that few interpretations needed to be made meant that the analyst could afford to be inactive. Although this patient had actually reached a large degree of expectable adult functioning before he had begun treatment, the success of his analysis was dependent to an extraordinary extent on the quality of the psychoanalytic setting as a holding environment. One way to paraphrase this point is to repeat the fact that his relationship to the analyst silently recapitulated his childhood idealization of his maternal grandmother. The crucial role of noninterpretive interventions can best be exemplified by the manner in which my question about the patient's need to transform his poetic inspirations into prose reports alerted him to the possibility of engaging in creative activities of a more meaningful kind than the journalistic work he had chosen as a compromise between his need to express himself as an artist and his utilitarian ethic. I had been extremely careful not to influence him to change his behavior through any statement that might be taken as advice; nonetheless, the patient immediately understood that I viewed his self-restriction as an excessive burden he had chosen to shoulder, i.e., as still another aspect of his general propensity to engage in quixotic behaviors. At other times, of course, it was he who explicitly demanded that I confirm his rational judgments and/or stop him from acting on the basis of the irrational childhood versions of his value system.

I believe it is quite instructive to reflect on the fact that this patient, who appeared to be so desperately ill when he first consulted me, rarely lapsed into disorganization (into either Mode I or II) and only for the briefest periods. Moreover, these regressions turned out to be actively sought by him, for moral reasons. In other words, in terms of the criteria proposed by Kohut (1971) to distinguish patients with insecure self-cohesion (in Kohut's terminology, persons with "narcissistic personality disturbances"), this individual had definitely achieved a firm self-organization. At the same time, it is reasonably clear that he was not troubled by the usual type of neurotic conflict either. His intrapsychic tension might best be described as a conflict between an earlier value system, impregnated with magical illusions about the potential consequences of personal virtue, and a later one which seemed to be quite conventional. It is important to note that the earlier of these value systems had been relegated to an aspect of the personality that was entirely disavowed. As a consequence, its continued influence on behavior was not comprehensible (either to the patient or to nonanalytic observers); in other words, it had all of the qualities Freud (1923) attributed to the id.

CHAPTER TEN

Orientation for Theoretical Section

> As a rule ... theoretical controversy is unfruitful. No sooner has one begun to depart from the material on which one ought to be relying, than one runs the risk of becoming intoxicated with one's own assertions and, in the end, of supporting opinions which any observation would have contradicted. For this reason it seems to me to be incomparably more useful to combat dissentient interpretations by testing them upon particular cases and problems.
>
> —Freud, "From the History of an Infantile Neurosis"

The most recent period in the evolution of psychoanalytic theory, the era of "ego psychology," was inaugurated by Hartmann's work on adaptation (1939), and it was elaborated with maximal distinction in his subsequent writings (1964; Hartmann, Kris, and Loewenstein, 1946). This school of thought within psychoanalysis probably reached its culmination well over a decade ago: Rapaport's (1959) monograph on *The Structure of Psychoanalytic Theory*, Gill's re-examination of Freud's topographic and structural hypotheses (1963), and their joint essay on "The Points of View and Assumptions of Metapsychology" (1959) may add up to the most explicit and most complete statement of the ego psychological viewpoint. The end of that era may have begun with warnings about the potential abuse of structural concepts through reification (Beres, 1965) and the illegitimate anthropomorphism of numerous psychoanalytic concepts (Grossman and Simon, 1969). Most recently, the methodological shortcomings of the traditional viewpoint have been powerfully argued by Schafer (1970a, 1973).

Throughout this period in the recent history of psychoanalysis, little attention has been given to the multiplicity of clinical theories within the field and their seeming lack of congruence with each other. Rapaport (1960b) was probably the first to express misgivings about the inner coherence of our theoretical framework: he specified that our complacency about simultaneous use of Freud's drive psychology and of more recent theories of object relations is ill-founded.

In my clinical efforts over the past decade and more, as well as in the course of supervising psychoanalytic candidates, I have been confronted with an increasing discrepancy between the traditional theories of psychoanalytic psychology and the actualities of current experience. This lack of congruence has seemed especially glaring in connection with nosological categories devised by Freud while he was forging the psychoanalytic method. Attempts to improve our theories of psychopathology have foundered as long as they have had to be squeezed into the mold of the traditional framework of psychoanalysis, because the latter had developed out of and could therefore only reflect Freud's original nosology.

Scientific need has, in consequence, propelled me into the daunting realm of psychoanalytic theory. In order to prepare the ground for future work, I began these studies with a re-examination of the congruence of the several major theories of the mind within psychoanalytic psychology (Gedo & Goldberg, 1973).

The majority of psychoanalytic clinicians probably have not experienced much discomfort about the loose fit between their theoretical tools and their patients' associations. Loewald (Panel, 1976) cited one reason for this complacency in his telling summary of the fate of scientific ideas: if a theory has served well as a convincing explanation for a body of material, in the course of time its users tend to blur the distinction between the concepts of the theory and observational data. In this manner, novel configurations may easily be overlooked in the course of organizing clinical data too cavalierly in terms of familiar generalizations at inappropriately high levels of abstraction (see also Waelder, 1962). These expectable abuses of scientific theory were indelibly impressed on the young Freud by Charcot, his mentor of 1885 (Miller et al., 1969); in reply to Freud's preference for clinging to the assumptions of a traditional theory, Charcot delivered his famous aphorism: *La théorie c'est bon, mais ça n'empêche pas d'exister!*—theory is good, but it doesn't prevent things from existing. Clearly, old theories have always formed obstacles to the perception of hitherto unrecognized actualities.

It is reasonably certain that most people choose among alternative theories in accord with a number of criteria—congruence with clinical observations being only one among these. In fact, it is safe to assume that psychoanalytic theories which have gained some degree of acceptance will prove to be more or less adequate in that regard, at least on casual inspection. Aside from essentially irrational, personal considerations—unfortunately, by no means negligible factors in the fate of psychoanalytic hypotheses!—probably the most important factor with regard to theoretical preferences may be the contemporary intellectual climate.

Freud's physicalistic theories have endured within psychoanalysis for 80 years, while the philosophy of science—in part under the impact of the Freudian discoveries concerning the limitations of rationality—has left behind the inadequate epistemology on which they rest (Polanyi, 1974). In recent years, psychoanalytic clinical experience has increasingly focused on man's existential problems—his concern about who he is and what he is about, his goals, in other words. This is illustrated by the three case histories I have provided for this book. *Pari passu,* a number of voices within the psychoanalytic community have begun to express dissatisfaction with the gap between clinical interpretation of the meanings of behavior and theoretical explanations in terms of presumed forces and energies fueling an apparatus.

We must remember that the entire edifice of Freud's metapsychology rests on an axiomatic assumption with which he opened his psychological work in 1892: *"The nervous system endeavors to keep constant something in its functional relations that we may describe as the 'sum of excitation'"* (1888-1892, p. 153). In spite of his shift from a neurological to a psychological level of discourse, Freud retained this assumption throughout his theoretical writings. In his very last statement of theory, in "The Outline of Psycho-Analysis," he was most explicit about this: "We assume, as other natural sciences have led us to expect, that in mental life some kind of energy is at work. . . ." although he added an apology about the difficulty of coming "nearer to a knowledge of it. . ." (1940a, p. 163). This axiom has continued to characterize the traditional metapsychology of psychoanalysis.

If Freud initially chose to cast psychoanalytic psychology into an energeticist mold in order to remain within the context of his own scientific *Zeitgeist,* at the present time psychoanalytic theory is bound to move, for parallel reasons, in the direction of stressing stability and change in mental processes. Although I am in essential sympathy with those who are demanding that psychoanalysis retain scientific respectability by adopting the conclusions of contemporary philosophy of science (e.g., Basch, 1975c, 1976b, 1977; Rosenblatt and Thickstun, 1970; Rubinstein, 1965, 1967, 1976), in this work I have chosen not to focus my presentation on the epistemological shortcomings of our traditional metapsychology. Indeed, previous writers have accomplished that task with distinction, most recently in the volume edited

by Gill and Holzman (1976). My critique stems from the opposite end of the spectrum from that of philosophy, namely,
from the empirical finding that the natural-science concepts
of the traditional theory have only very limited relevance for
illuminating the clinical problems that have increasingly occupied the forefront in psychoanalytic practice.

My collaboration with Goldberg was a maximally conservative stand, an effort to salvage as much of the Freudian
paradigm of mental functioning as possible half a century
after its last reformulation by its inventor. Perhaps expecta-
bly, the book has received a friendly welcome. Were
psychoanalysts relieved by the body of familiar constructs we
were able to retain? Did they fail to notice how much of their
familiar baggage we had jettisoned? Although *Models of the
Mind* was notably influenced by the cogent criticisms of the
physicalistic concepts of Freud's metapsychology enunciated
during the 1960's by a number of authors, it certainly fell
short of the drastic theoretical revolutions advocated by
some, such as George Klein (1976), Benjamin Rubinstein
(1967, 1974, 1976), or Roy Schafer (1976). The only overt
concession we made in the direction of radical change was
the omission of the concept of psychic energy from our own
hypotheses (and a decided underemphasis of this aspect of
the theories we were considering from the historical point of
view). Only one commentator (Zaleznik, 1975) has responded
to the fact that we had deprived Freud's metapsychology of
its energic cathexis: he noted that we had only succeeded in
reconciling various fragments of analytic theory by abandon-
ing the principle of parsimony, one of the usual pillars of
theory construction. This was, of course, the price we had to
pay for continued adherence to Freud's specific propositions
while we refused to accept the unifying framework he had
provided for them, that of his energy hypothesis.

Except for matters of detail which will be corrected in the
present work, I still stand behind the views we articulated in
Models of the Mind. However, I am no longer satisfied with

the uneasy compromise between traditional metapsychology and the viewpoint of its critics we employed in 1973. On the one hand, I have become persuaded that neither a literal nor a metaphorical interpretation of the concept of psychic energy is epistemologically tenable; in other words, to retain scientific respectability, psychoanalysis must decisively reject all of the constructs within its theory based (even in part) on energy assumptions. On the other hand, I wish to keep in mind the necessity of scientific thrift and to repair the breach of optimal methodology we perpetrated in *Models of the Mind* by articulating a simpler, more elegant, a more *beautiful* theory of human mental life which will, at the same time, have maximal relevance for the purpose of illuminating the observational data we now obtain in the clinical setting of psychoanalysis.

The traditional metapsychology has been under attack not only for its inadequacy when measured by the criteria of contemporary philosophy of science; it has also been accused (Swanson, 1977) of providing only a redundant paraphrase of our clinical generalizations or interpretations. This failure of relevance has become increasingly apparent with the gradual shift in our focus of attention from isolated neurotic compromise formations to those patterns of human adaptation we have designated as *character*. In the early 1970's, when we wrote *Models of the Mind,* I shared the conviction of my co-author that psychoanalysis would develop in a radically new direction as a result of a series of clinical discoveries such as the ones Kohut was then in the process of making public (Kohut, 1968, 1971, 1972). His proposed revisions of developmental psychology were incorporated into our work, although they were then clearly too recent to have been thoroughly tested.

In the interval, it has become apparent that Kohut has chosen to anchor his increasingly divergent clinical hypotheses within the confines of traditional metapsychology (see Kohut, 1977). He has understood his novel findings as supplements to the body of observational data previously accumulated by psychoanalysis, presumably congruent with the overall framework of psychoanalytic psychology (provided we accept a slight modification Kohut proposed in 1966, that of assuming separate lines of development for narcissism and object libido). Loewald (1973) and Schafer (1973) were the first to point out that Kohut's clinical propositions are, in fact, at variance with the traditional constructs he has continued to employ—a point of view I also share (see Panel, 1976). In my judgment, recent clinical discoveries, including the valid aspects of Kohut's hypotheses, have greatly worsened the disarray of post-Freudian psychoanalytic psychology.

It is my impression that the widespread tendency to reject modifications of clinical theory (by no means confined to those of Kohut) stems from analysts' implicit awareness of the threat posed by a shift of focus to the psychological vicissitudes of the first three years of life for the overall fabric of the theoretical framework that has guided us. Incidentally, Kohut has clearly declined to explore the discrepancy between his clinical generalizations and the metapsychology he has continued to use because he has consciously decided that he does not wish to tamper with such cherished guideposts (see Gedo, 1975b). There are other authors, among whom Otto Kernberg (1975) may be the most influential, who also stress the importance of early childhood transactions for personality development, but dispute with considerable heat the need for radical theoretical revisions. For instance, Kernberg categorically rules out clinical theories that do not assume that pathological transactions between the infant and its caretakers (what Kernberg calls early "object relations") are consequences of "pathological narcissism," i.e., basically to be seen as disturbances in drive organization. [1]

At any rate, in the present fluid state of psychoanalytic

[1] In this sense, Kernberg's role in contemporary psychoanalysis is that of the last-ditch defender of the old order who has confused its hypotheses with matters of fact.

psychology, I clearly cannot rely on anyone else to fit my clinical experiences to a tenable and relevant theoretical position. Because I no longer espouse Freud's metapsychology and the developmental propositions borrowed from Kohut in *Models of the Mind*, the time has come once again to embark on a major attempt to redefine my views about the optimal manner of organizing the observational data of psychoanalysis. But I wish to repeat my opening statement: my *primary* aim in this book is to present the full range of observational material I now obtain within the clinical setting of psychoanalysis. Explanations for much of this data base are difficult to develop out of existing psychoanalytic theory, as I have tried to show in my formulations of case material in this book. The proposals of the major critics of traditional theory, excellent as these are in many ways, have not been adequate to the task I have in mind because none of these critics has tried to encompass a range of clinical material broader than Freud's—that is, they have confined themselves to the field of the neuroses proper where the material can legitimately be understood in terms of our familiar constructs.

In therapeutic disciplines such as psychoanalysis, an antitheoretical bias is particularly tempting because it seems to be possible to conduct therapy in a pragmatic fashion, on the basis of empirical rules of thumb. Aside from the high probability that intuitive practitioners who operate in this manner will obtain only indifferent results, such pragmatism is unacceptable on two counts. First, it is bound progressively to impoverish and ultimately to destroy the integration of psychoanalysis into the overall fabric of human knowledge, an integration that can only take place on the level of theoretical abstractions. Second, the absence of theory in this pragmatic approach is more apparent than real; as Loewald (Panel, 1976) has noted, it depends on a collapse of the distinction between abstract theories and concrete data.

All of this is an elaboration of the simple fact that the choice among competing theories unavoidably leads to weighty practical consequences. To cite only the most familiar of examples from the contemporary analytic scene, witness the several alternative approaches to the emergence in the course of psychoanalytic treatment of archaic grandiose fantasies (Panel, 1973; see also Gedo, 1977b).

Viewed in terms of intellectual history, Freud's greatest accomplishment may have been the successful reintegration of the tradition of humanism into Western science. He achieved the description of the effects of unconscious conflicts on human behavior in a systematized manner; his clinical accounts concerned sentient beings struggling with the profound dilemmas previously portrayed by such artists as Sophocles, Shakespeare, or Dostoievski. However, in the materialist and positivist atmosphere of late nineteenth-century scientific thought, Freud felt obliged to buttress his conceptualizations with a "metapsychology" based on contemporary natural-science assumptions (cf. Toulmin, 1978).[2]

Although Gill (1976) may well be correct in arguing that by "metapsychology" Freud consistently meant biological and, more specifically, neurophysiological propositions, I do not think that we need to be constrained by such precedents at the present time. In my view, the term "metapsychology" is most conveniently employed to refer to any psychoanalytic theory that cannot be derived from clinical observations by a process of induction. Moreover, in my judgment, it is impossible to construct purely "clinical" theories without reliance on deductive propositions which reflect our presuppositions about the nature of the human organism. Although my proposals in this work are formulated on the basis of the inductive method, they are therefore also congruent with a set of general concepts borrowed from contemporary science.

Naturally enough, practitioners of psychoanalysis are

---

[2]This explanation for his scientific strategy is confirmed by Freud's statements in his correspondence with Jung (McGuire, 1974) about the function of the libido theory as an anchor against the dangers of sliding into vitalism—or worse, into occultism!

much more concerned with the pragmatic clinical applications of its theories than with the latter's scientific standing. Hence, repeated demonstrations of the scientific inadequacy of traditional metapsychology (e.g., Applegarth, 1971; Holt, 1965, 1967a, 1976; G. Klein, 1969, 1973; Rosenblatt and Thickstun, 1970; Swanson, 1977) have scarcely loosened its grip on the loyalty of psychoanalysts in the absence of a viable alternative.

I am painfully aware that the theoretical program I have in mind here is exceedingly ambitious. Psychoanalysts who have not as yet reached the conclusion that traditional metapsychology has begun to obstruct their capacity to make significant clinical observations have little patience with proposals for theoretical reform which dispense with that metapsychology; such proposals are regularly met by objections which assume the continuing necessity of the familiar overall framework of psychoanalytic psychology, often on an a priori basis. On the other hand, global indictments of the scientific and philosophical shortcomings of traditional metapsychology also have not been given very much weight. Moreover, a large number of essential psychoanalytic concepts seem so inextricably embedded within that framework that any general call for its abandonment will possibly be seen as an invitation to leave behind all theoretical guidelines. Needless to say, I believe the last problem to be soluble through careful revision of these subsidiary concepts in line with any new consensus about the metapsychological approach to our data.

CHAPTER ELEVEN

The Theoretical Yield

In order to perceive the gain in clarity obtained by the new way of formulating the case histories I have illustrated, it may be instructive to present a summary of these generalizations, once again, for purposes of comparison. Simultaneously, I should like to offer the same material in tabular form (see Table 1). The table lists each analysand's concrete ambitions, the more abstract goals that seemed to underlie these, and his major value systems, as observed in the course of treatment. I have tried to arrange these personal aims into some rough order or hierarchy in terms of the relative importance they seemed to have had in the mental life of each individual.

The categories I have included in this classification are extremely tentative; it should be obvious that the complex process of reducing the data of my clinical observations into such skeletal schemata without prior guidelines to follow was bound to produce somewhat idiosyncratic results. In other words, other judges might well have arrived at a different set of categories on the basis of the same behavioral data.

The most important feature of the schema is the very great variety of personal ambitions appearing within it. This recognition of the multiplicity of human strivings stands in marked contrast to the emphasis of early psychoanalysis on

TABLE 1
THE SELF-ORGANIZATION IN CASES 1 THROUGH 3

Case	Concrete Ambitions	Goals	Values
1	Rescue the needful CONTROL THE MILIEU Create works	Autonomy PERFECTION Intimacy	Helpfulness Goodness Justice
2	Pre-eminence as: 　wise caretaker 　*seductress* 　exemplar of virtue *Masochistic personal* *relations* RELIGIOUS SALVATION	AUTONOMY Intimacy PERFECTION APPETITE SATIS- 　FACTION	Goodness Humility
3	Improve the world Make people happy Affection for all Sharing ideals *Create works* Sexual satisfaction	AUTONOMY PERFECTION Pleasure in 　pleasing Intimacy linked 　with appetite 　satisfaction	SAINTLINESS Usefulness Rationality

Items in capitals have been repressed; items in italics have been disavowed; items printed in regular type represent the ego.

the duality of incest and patricide as the truly significant ambitions of man. These motivations occupied so low a place in the hierarchy of the third patient's ambitions, for example, that a narrow focus on them would have overlooked all of the more significant issues causing his personal difficulties.

The list of ambitions in the schema is also much broader than that yielded by recent efforts within psychoanalysis to complement these prototypical wishes in the spheres of love and hate within the family matrix with a set of "narcissistic" aims, such as strivings for excellence in the realms of beauty, knowledge, or power (see Kohut, 1971). To be sure, these familiar categories of human ambitions are all represented within Table 1, although none of these patients was significantly committed to them all.

For each of the illustrative cases, Table 1 indicates what has been relegated to the id through repression and disavowal. For the first patient the id consisted of his insistence on perfection and his commitment to control his milieu. For the second, it consisted of her ambition to gain religious salvation and her disavowed strivings for success as a seductress and as a person who was to be mistreated. Her goals of autonomy, perfection, and appetite satisfaction were also mostly unconscious. In the third patient, the id consisted of disavowed creative ambitions and repressed saintliness; the goals of autonomy and of perfection were also repressed. The summation of these qualities comes very close to certain character types described by Robert Gardner (1976) as the aversive, the assertive, and the accommodative, respectively.

It should also be noted that in each case there was at least one major ambition that had been essentially repressed (Cases 1 and 2) or disavowed (Cases 2 and 3). Table 1 does not show the manner in which psychoanalytic intervention altered each patient's hierarchy of ambitions, although such a rearrangement of priorities was, in actuality, the major outcome of these treatments. Insofar as I could judge, there was a radical shift in the direction of creative ambitions in every case and a corresponding diminution of commitment to influencing other people or the environment. In Case 1 the wish to control the environment disappeared, and that of rescuing needful people was greatly mitigated. In Case 2, the masochistic relationships were given up, and the ambition to care for others and to set them a personal example lost its flavor of self-aggrandizement by becoming embodied in a professional ideal. At follow-up, the patient no longer seemed to be committed to her former strivings for religious salvation. In the third case, none of the ambitions were entirely given up, but each of the others became a subordinate aspect of the governing creative wishes.

In contrast to the list of concrete ambitions, the variety of abstract goals I was able to infer from them was, in this limited sample, quite restricted. Three of the items are repeated in every case, although they occur with slight variations with regard to their sequence within the hierarchy and with even greater variability with regard to their accessibility to consciousness. These three goals are those of autonomy, perfection, and intimacy. Except for the fact that two of these analysands happen to have been highly unusual individuals in certain respects, the lists of abstract goals might well have turned out to be identical, suggesting that they come close to describing certain human universals. The first patient was of a rare human type, the kind for whom the satisfaction of appetites seemed to have no great meaning. Perhaps this circumstance had much to do with the all but universal recognition by his milieu that he might be a genius. And the third patient had a most unusual investment in the pleasure of pleasing (see G. Klein, 1976); this aim therefore constituted an addition to the quartet of goals that may well be characteristic of most people. It is this set of four aims that appeared in the second patient.

In each instance, the goal of personal autonomy occupied the summit of the hierarchy of aims. I expect that this finding will turn out to be absolutely invariable, a prediction based on the assumption that the goal of personal autonomy is actually a restatement, in language shorn of implications about psychic energies, of one of the basic principles of behavior regulation; in Gedo and Goldberg, (1973, Chapter 12) this principle was called "self-definition." This is probably a supraordinate goal, in the sense that it involves the maintenance of the integrity of the whole hierarchy of goals and values.

In a more tentative way, I wish to raise the possibility that the goal of appetite satisfaction may also correspond to one of the principles of behavior regulation we designated as a universal in *Models of the Mind*. This is the principle, first proposed by Schur (1966), of the avoidance of unpleasure; it regulates behavior in the prepsychological mode of functioning. Similarly, we might attempt to correlate strivings for perfection with the central behavioral issues of Mode III, those having to do with the persistence of illusions.[1]

In Freud's psychological system, the goal of appetite satisfaction occupied a role of pre-eminence; clearly, it was the only human aim that Freud regarded as significant in pathogenesis. The listing of goals and values I have offered here is similarly noninclusive, i.e., it covers only those aims which came into focus in the psychoanalytic treatment of these individuals because they had bearing on the psychopathology. The absence of the goal of appetite satisfaction from the list in the case of the first patient is not to be taken, therefore, to mean that he was an ascetic. Quite the contrary was actually true: this man gratified his appetites with complete casualness. It was, in part, this matter-of-fact quality in his approach to living within his own body that suggested that these satisfactions were not terribly important for him. This state of affairs stands in total contrast to the manner in which the issue of appetite satisfactions figured in the life of the second patient. For her, somatic experiences appeared to have had enormous significance much of the time, but appetite satisfaction was, until the middle phases of her analytic treatment, not one of her conscious goals. The hypochondriacal symptoms, which constituted a large segment of the appetite satisfactions which this woman strove for but was never conscious about, persisted as such even

---

[1]The goal of intimacy and that of the pleasure in pleasing cut across the categories suggested by the modes of psychic organization. Further detailed studies of case material will doubtless add to the list other goals which also cannot be correlated so closely with particular modes of functioning.

after she had acquired other appetitive aims about which she was aware.

To put this another way, some of these somatic strivings never had had and never could gain mental representation. They were handled by "primary repression"—Frank's (1969) "unrememberable and unforgettable" repetitions. They are not merely unconscious—they lie outside the realm of subjectivity altogether. It is true that in the course of psychoanalytic treatment we may attempt to assign meanings to the patient's perceptions about these somatic happenings, but it is never possible to validate these attributions in the way that interpretations of unconscious subjective motives are validated, namely, through the spontaneous emergence of confirmatory material in the associations. It is the claim of psychoanalytic psychology to explain events lying beyond the boundaries of subjectivity that obligates us to broaden the clinical theories of psychoanalysis beyond the realm of symbolic meanings, i.e., to devise what Freud called a metapsychology.

Thus my clinical findings support Rubinstein's (1976) philosophical position about the needs of psychoanalytic theory. Rubinstein has rejected the claim of many thoughtful critics of Freud's physicalistic theories (e.g., Gill, 1976; G. Klein, 1976; Schafer, 1976) that psychoanalysis may, at least for its internal purposes, dispense with a theory that goes beyond the realm of subjectivity. Rubinstein justified his view on the ground that theories based exclusively on the data of introspection cannot account for unconscious mental activities. I agree with that argument. I believe that my clinical data also demonstrate that such theories cannot adequately encompass the continuing influence of the prepsychological (sensorimotor) patterning of behavior characteristic of the earliest phases of life.

The values I have singled out for listing in Table 1 are, once again, only those that were found to be significant for the patients' principal conflicts. Because of the paucity of material on this issue, I have made no effort, as I did in the instance

of goals, to differentiate the concrete expression of values in
the form of ideals from a more abstract level. In principle,
however, such a distinction would be useful. The relative
scarcity of information about these matters is probably the
result of insufficient attention on my part to this aspect of
mental life at the time these analyses were performed. In retrospect, I have the impression that deeply significant insights
would have been gained had I been more alert to such matters as the commitment of the first and third patient to the
value of complexity and that of the second patient to its polar
opposite, one we might designate as simplicity. The significance of these and similar issues awaits elucidation through
empirical research.

A New Psychology Centered on a Hierarchy of Personal Aims

The goals and values I have listed in these schemata of
my patients' discernible motivations comprise all of the varieties of motive, both conscious and unconscious, that were
covered in the traditional theory by the concepts of instinctual drives, ego interests, and superego standards. The resulting schema of the self-organization is able to do justice to the
accumulated clinical knowledge of the past; at the same time,
it illuminates the hitherto poorly understood maladaptive behaviors described by a succession of recent observers, such as
Winnicott (1954), Erikson (1959), Lichtenstein (1963, 1964),
and Kohut (1971), all of whom have referred the pathological adaptations in question to certain mental dispositions acquired in earliest childhood. They have termed the structures
responsible for the patterns of behavior they have highlighted in a variety of ways: "the self," "basic core," "identity," or
"self-cohesion." I believe all of these concepts attempt to describe what I have defined as the hierarchy of personal aims.

Each of the terms proposed for this hierarchy seems to
have certain shortcomings. My preference would be for the
simple term self, were it not for the difficulty of differentiat-

ing this usage from references to the person as such, in the sense of being opposed to "not-me." Unfortunately, both Hartmann (1964) and Jacobson (1964) have used the term self in just this sense in their psychoanalytic writings. Such a competing nonpsychological definition has probably precluded continuing to use the same word as a psychoanalytic concept. Sandler and Rosenblatt (1962) have introduced an intermediate usage through their concept of "self-representation." This refers to aspects of the system of memories, specifically of past transactions between the person and his environment. Although "self" in the term self-representation continues to refer to one's own person, the idea of memories of oneself in action as enduring representations comes close to G. Klein's (1976) recent proposal to center psychoanalytic theory on the concept of a "self-schema."[2]

Klein's term has the advantage of having no confusing additional meanings, but it is also unsatisfactory because it is entirely lacking in the connotation of a motivating factor. As stated previously (Gedo and Goldberg, 1973, pp. 63-64), we need a concept that will convey with unmistakable emphasis the enduring dynamic importance of the overall organization of the personality. Definitions of the self that focus on its aspects as mental *content* (e.g., Kohut, 1970) explicitly disavow what I consider to be the cardinal importance of the concept, the epigenesis of human motivations, i.e., of mental structure itself (see Sapirstein and Gaines, 1973). I trust the terminological problem will be obviated if we compromise on

[2]Because of his premature death while he was working on that book, Klein did not have access to recent publications dealing with these issues. His own conceptualization was clearly reached independently. The editors of his manuscript have unfortunately tried to minimize the importance of this aspect of Klein's thinking, even asserting erroneously that for Klein the term "self" had the connotation of "person" (see Klein, 1976, p. 8n). Contrary to the editors' claim, Klein obviously had in mind an apparatus or cognitive schema rather than an individual (see Klein, 1976, pp. 8, 265-266, 268).

the term "self-organization" as a new paradigm for psycho-analytic psychology.[3]

Mental life begins with a phase of uncoordinated, discrete goals, which may be viewed as separate nuclei of function (Gedo and Goldberg, 1973, Chapter 5). From these subsets, the cohesive hierarchy of personal aims I call the self-organization is gradually integrated. In this sense, the cohesiveness of the self-organization means the relatively permanent structuring of goals and values into potentials for action. This is the phase of the unification of the personality that Lichtenstein called the formation of a "primary identity." During this phase, the main issues of psychic life can be conceptualized as those of self-definition (see Figure 7).

The definition of the self-organization is thus a basic psychobiological phenomenon, a process incapable of detection through reflexive self-awareness and not to be confused with a development characterized by motivation. It is only after the accomplishment of psychobiological integration or self-cohesion that we can begin to view behavior as regulated by the principle of seeking satisfactions on the basis of purposeful choices—conditions Freud summed up in the concept of the "pleasure principle." Those phenomena of the repetition compulsion (i.e., "beyond the pleasure principle") which are not directly related to the avoidance of unpleasure, including certain negative fluctuations during treatment, may therefore be understood as manifestations of the overriding need to restore self-cohesion, at no matter what cost.

In this regard, the most important implications follow for psychopathology and the strategies of treatment. The primacy of the formation of a unified hierarchy of aims, which accounts for the phenomena of the repetition compulsion,

[3]The hierarchical model of mental functioning we developed in *Models of the Mind* is actually a developmental record of changes in the self-organization. The emergence of a psychology of the self was explicitly predicted in *Models of the Mind* (in Chapter 5), although we did not then foresee that it would deal with a hierarchy of personal aims.

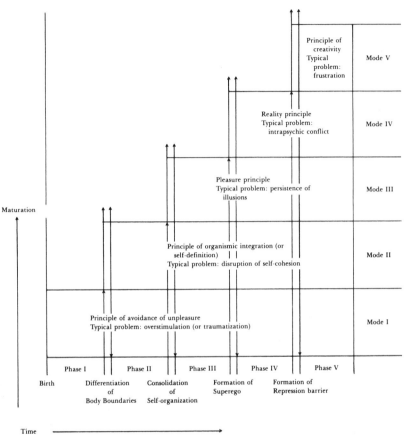

Maturation

Mode V
Principle of creativity
Typical problem: frustration

Mode IV
Reality principle
Typical problem: intrapsychic conflict

Mode III
Pleasure principle
Typical problem: persistence of illusions

Mode II
Principle of organismic integration (or self-definition)
Typical problem: disruption of self-cohesion

Mode I
Principle of avoidance of unpleasure
Typical problem: overstimulation (or traumatization)

| Phase I | Phase II | Phase III | Phase IV | Phase V |

Birth | Differentiation of Body Boundaries | Consolidation of Self-organization | Formation of Superego | Formation of Repression barrier

Time

↑↑ Area of "secondary autonomy" or conflict-free function: "irreversibility"

↓↓ Function may undergo regression: "reversibility"

FIGURE 7

HIERARCHICAL SCHEMA OF PRINCIPLES OF BEHAVIOR REGULA-
TION AND PROBLEMS TYPICAL FOR SPECIFIC MODES OF FUNCTIONING

should also be recognized in clinical theory as it attempts to deal with states of disorganization, impending or actual, acute or chronic. In other words, the defense of an endangered self-organization or restoration of one that has become disrupted has to be understood as a significant need, both in the course of analytic treatment and in other circumstances. In a large category of clinical contingencies, our therapeutic strategies should be oriented to re-establishing coherence in the hierarchy of personal aims (see Chapter 2). An illustration of such vicissitudes in analytic treatment is provided in the case history in Chapter 6, especially with regard to the patient's reactions to lengthy interruptions of the analysis.

The severity of subjective anxiety experienced whenever the individual cannot maintain the integration of his various goals, i.e., when the self-organization is threatened with fragmentation, is a clinical finding familiar to therapists of patients with a vulnerability to psychotic reactions to stress. Even in analyzable cases, such as the first illustrative history in this book (Chapter 4), the dread of loss of "autonomy" often leads to a struggle against "identification" or "fusion" with the analyst, seen in the transference as the mother of early childhood. This struggle might well be summed up in the motto, *"Nego, ergo sum!"*—I resist alien goals, therefore I am. Lichtenstein (1971) has called this attitude "the malignant no"; but the idea was already expressed by Camus in his novel *The Rebel* (see Panel, 1970). In introducing a distinction between the true and the false self, Winnicott (1954) was also referring, it would seem, to subsets of goals that are authentically one's own versus others that are provisionally accepted under external pressure.

The enduring dynamic effect of the organization of a cohesive hierarchy of personal goals was not completely neglected in the earlier literature of psychoanalysis. It was dealt with in terms of an *a priori* function of the ego, called the "synthetic function" (Nunberg, 1932). This formulation is both teleological and illegitimately reified, for it merely gives a name to the discrete function being conceptualized and regards that as an explanation. In contrast, the hypothesis of a necessity for maintenance of the specific manner of self-organization is a natural reflection of the general propensity of the human nervous system to create order.

The synthesis of a stable hierarchy of personal aims, like all other developmental achievements, is at first vulnerable to regression in situations of stress. The young child's capacity to continue to pursue his characteristic goals may require the availability of an empathic caretaker because he may need assistance with disorganizing experiences. I have tried to furnish examples of corresponding transference situations from the analyses of adult patients, especially in the case report in Chapter 4. I share the judgment of Loewald (1973) that the most valuable aspect of Kohut's clinical contributions (1968, 1971) was his insistence that we look upon the analysand's subjective experience in such circumstances in terms of a one-person psychology. In other words, what the outside observer sees as a transaction between two people is actually experienced by the patient (and presumably by a small child organized in this mode) as taking place within the boundaries of his own self; the "other" cannot be conceived of as an independent source of volition in these mental states—at least on the unconscious level.

The child's hierarchy of goals and values becomes sufficiently stabilized to guide his actions more or less irrespective of immediate environmental influences only through the structuralization of the superego. We know, of course, that even this statement is only valid within certain specific limits for any given person. Nonetheless, superego formation, i.e., the addition of a set of moral values to the hierarchy of personal aims, is a decisive advance in behavior regulation in the direction of personal autonomy. Subsequently, so-called "narcissistic injuries" are much less likely to disrupt behavior by impelling the individual to adopt *ad hoc* measures alien to his characteristic aims (e.g., lapses into perverse activities or into addiction) in order to restore self-esteem in the short run.

At any rate, after the superego has been established, men-

tal life may conveniently be conceptualized in terms of intrapsychic conflicts, as Freud (1923) postulated in his structural theory. It should be noted that the attainment of this
new mode of mental organization does not necessarily mean
that there has been any change in mental *content*, aside from
the adoption of previously alien moral standards as one's
own. In its new mode of organization (Mode IV within the
hierarchical schema), the organization of personality may be
described as whole, albeit conflicted—in spite of unresolved
conflicts, the person does not become disorganized in carrying out his aims. Compromise formations are therefore characteristic for this stage of self-organization.

The epigenesis of the self-organization may be concluded
by considering a mode of optimal adaptive success, i.e., an
area of mental life in which personal aims may be har-
monized so as to minimize conflict. In such conditions, the
metaphor Freud (1923) borrowed from Plato to describe intrapsychic conflict, that of a horse and rider, has to be replaced by the image of a centaur, one that combines the qualities of man and beast in one creature.

Placing the epigenesis of the self-organization at the
center of the theories of psychoanalytic psychology entails the
abandonment of drive theory as the *universal* explanatory
framework underlying psychoanalytic views of mental life.
Freud made explicit that role of his libido concept in a section he added in 1915 to his "Three Essays on the Theory of
Sexuality" (1905b, pp. 217-219). If drive theory is no longer
to serve that function, we may leave open the question of its
usefulness as a special clinical hypothesis assisting our understanding of numerous intrapsychic conflicts. Nothing in my
proposals should be taken to indicate that the importance of
sexual and aggressive wishes in human mental life can be
downgraded. As George Klein (1969) has convincingly
shown, the drive conception of sexuality is not to be confused
with Freud's empirical discoveries about the importance of
infantile sexuality for human development.

Klein's conclusion clarifies for us that man's appetitive

behaviors cannot be presumed to be drive regulated as a matter of course. It is true that, whatever symbolic significance the behavior leading to such gratifications may have, once it has been put into action, it will subsume within itself the biological drive pattern upon which it is based. However, to reduce it on that account to an episode of drive discharge is truly to fall into the "genetic fallacy" so often decried as one major pitfall of psychoanalytic conceptualizations.

In the realm of sexual behavior—central in the psychoanalytic view of instinctual drives—the biological drive pattern probably becomes the primary regulator of action only when orgasm has actually begun, and symbolic, i.e., psychological, considerations may even then change the quality of the subjective experience. On the other hand, with profound regressions to functioning in archaic modes (in the hierarchical model, to Mode II), sexuality is divested of its later symbolic meanings; it becomes homologous in function with the addict's attempt to eliminate displeasure through pharmacological influence.[4] The same might be said, incidentally, about certain aggressive outbursts.

In such circumstances, the unconscious fantasy referable to the sexual act may be frankly autoerotic, i.e., it may completely ignore the existence of other beings. Perhaps more frequently, it may use someone (often only a portion of another person's body) as an animate tool; in other words, it will be perverse. In this light, we can better grasp Bak's (1974) contention that the basic perversion is fetishism, because the use of an animate tool amounts to the reduction of a human relationship to the employment of an infantile fetish (cf. Greenacre, 1969).

I believe that G. Klein was expressing a similar point of

---

[4]This fundamental equivalence is clearest in those instances where the ingestion of some substance constitutes the sexual perversion. Rado's theoretical construct of an alimentary orgasm (1926) has been fully vindicated by analytic experience: e.g., the discovery of perversions in which the fetishistic experience is the distention of the stomach by filling with a preferred substance (such as chocolate).

view when he wrote: "When a . . . sensual craving is pre-emptive and nagging—the clinician suspects . . . that the immediate sexual aim represents some more encompassing need in which self-conception and self-status are at issue" (1976, p. 97). Klein correctly espouses a system conception of sexuality as an "appetitive structure responsive to arousing and inhibiting activations." The latter emanates from the cognitive schemata into which the memories of previous sensual experiences have been organized (1976, pp. 114-115).

Klein's meaning can better be grasped by organizing the varieties of sexual behavior in accordance with the hierarchical schema. For each developmental stage, a phase-specific sexual activity is appropriate—successively, the erotic action patterns of the sensorimotor infant (Phase I), the action patterns used with transitional objects (Phase II), phallic-narcissistic sexual activity (Phase III), competitive sexual activity (Phase IV), and genitality (Phase V). In the adult, sexuality has multiple goals. Chiefly, it subserves the creation of personal relationships (Mode V); in Mode IV, it enhances the individual's personal worth; in Mode III, it serves to confirm gender identity; in Mode II, it confirms the integrity of the self; in Mode I, it restores organismic equilibrium. In case of developmental arrest or structural regression, the sexual aspects of pathological behavior can be seen as autoerotic actions (Mode I), fetishistic perversions (Mode II), genital bonds involving exploitation of the partner, often with perverse fantasies or activity, especially in the sadomasochistic mode or through homosexual object choice (Mode III), and those principally expressing competitive strivings (Mode IV).[5]

At any rate, there would be some advantages in eliminating from metapsychology that borderline between mind and body into which Freud inserted his drive concepts, i.e., to

[5]Note that the schema echoes Freud's division of the same line of development into autoerotic, narcissistic, and object-related phases. It lends itself less satisfactorily to the depiction of the leading body zones for sensual gratification in the prephallic child.

close the philosophically untenable Cartesian split between *res cogitans* and *res extensa,* mind and matter. Science in general has rejected this duality between body and mind. If we wish to remain within the scientific community, we are not entitled to claim that there is a concrete boundary area between them. Body and mind are not discrete entities; they are different ways of conceptualizing the same phenomena—methods on the part of the observer of apprehending the data of human functioning. The failure to keep these concepts properly differentiated amounts to a confusion of categories.

The decision to abandon the drives as metapsychological concepts, returning them into the realm of biology, necessitates rethinking a number of issues within psychoanalytic psychology which have hitherto been dealt with through constructs developed out of a drive-theoretical matrix. The concept of narcissism, for instance, is a direct component of the libido theory; a psychology of goals and values must find substitutes for this concept whenever it is used as an explanatory tool in psychoanalytic formulations. The concepts of the ego and the id, although they are less directly a part of drive theory, are impregnated with energic implications and must therefore also be reconsidered if they are to continue in use in the new theoretical framework. The same might be said of other traditional constructs used in the "reformulations" I have offered in previous chapters: in particular, repression, transference, and trauma.

A Revision of the Hierarchical Model of Psychic Functioning

In developing the hierarchical model (Gedo and Goldberg, 1973) we refrained from describing psychological development in terms of concepts at high levels of abstraction, such as the ego and the id, or libidinal and aggressive drives. We relied instead on the developmental lines of more specific psychic functions, which can be described in terms somewhat closer to the experiential: typical situations of danger, typical defensive operations, or reality testing, for example (see Figure 8).

The major exception to the policy of choosing develop-

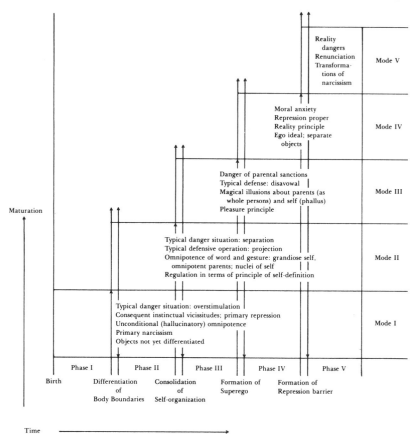

FIGURE 8
THE HIERARCHICAL MODEL: MODAL ORGANIZATION
(AFTER GEDO AND GOLDBERG, 1973)

mental lines of functions close to the observable and experiential level was our reliance on that of "narcissism." Because
of my decision to eliminate the concept of psychic energy
from my theoretical discourse, the behaviors traditionally included within the realm of narcissism must be accounted for
in some other way in the system I am proposing. If it were
feasible to detach the observational data hitherto called narcissistic from the libido theory, we would be in a position to
continue to use the term narcissism to refer to pathological
concerns about one's own person—the connotation the word
has in fact acquired in popular usage. All other aspects of the
self-organization could then be conceptualized outside of the
framework of a libidinal cathexis of one's own person. Such a
reform of our terminology would have the decisive advantage
of clearly differentiating expectable developments in the
structuralization of identity from pathological deviations in
this process—a distinction that cannot be drawn in terms of
past usage of psychoanalytic terms.

In any case, the development of a concept of self-
organization would raise serious obstacles to the continued
use of that of narcissism, even without considering the issues
that render this philosophically untenable. It is very difficult
to grasp what a presumed sexual cathexis of the self-
representation might in fact mean. Once we consider the
"self" to be a conceptual schema, we cannot continue to think
of the investment of feeling or interest in it as if that schema
were one of a number of actors upon a psychic stage. The
self-organization is not a direct reference to a person, but a
concept which stands for an individual's unique, personal
hierarchy of dispositions for action, i.e., his goals and values.
Such a schema cannot possibly be the target of the person's
instinctual drives.

As a result of the more or less permanent dispositions
built into such a primary identity, the child will have a series
of repetitive transactions with his environment which will be
preserved in the memory system as self-representations.
These will be continuously judged according to his ideals,

producing self-evaluations that can legitimately be termed self-love or self-hate. In using these compound words, however, we are no longer employing the term "self" in a technical psychoanalytic sense, but are reverting to common usage, referring to the individual's total person.

Parenthetically, relegation of drive theory to the realm of biology also means that we would be on safer ground than has been the case with past psychoanalytic parlance if we confined the terms object love (and hate) to the affective reactions and judgments people form in reaction to the activities of those around them. The permanence of object ties might be explained on a more reasonable basis if it were understood as the result of the adequacy of the other person's continuing fit with the subject's goals and values than it has been on the ground of some mysterious attachment of inner excitement, often literally described as a "stickiness of the libido," to the mental representation of the object.

The observable phenomena that have generally been classified as narcissistic consist, for the most part, of vanity, exhibitionism, and arrogant ingratitude; these are usually reflections of the fact that the person feels entitled to treat others without regard for mutuality in his human relationships. A detailed discussion of these problems belongs in the context of a work focused on psychopathology (but see Gedo, 1977b). In summary fashion, we may note that there is no difficulty in understanding these primitive action patterns as aspects of the person's childhood aims, especially disavowed or repressed ambitions which continue to exert a controlling influence on behavior. Whenever they have been relegated to an "id," early ambitions naturally maintain their archaic, infantile flavor, because they remain isolated from the mitigating influence of later experience.[6]

---

[6]Archaic ambitions have been declared to be grandiose (see Kohut, 1966, 1971) as a matter of developmental necessity, in line with Ferenczi's (1913) assertions about the universality of omnipotent thinking in the young child. My clinical experience (cf. Gedo, 1977b) has failed to substantiate the validity of these developmental hypotheses; in my experience,

These examples suggest that the observational data summarized and abstracted through the concept of narcissistic pathology lose none of their cogency if we divorce them from the libidinal concept of narcissism. On the contrary, by doing so we make it much easier to understand that inappropriate selfishness and attention-seeking in adult life more often betoken pathological vulnerability in the sphere of self-esteem than they signify excessive self-love. Comprehending this defect will encourage us to preserve analytic neutrality when confronted with so-called narcissistic behaviors.[7] To repeat, when we designate some aspect of an adult's behavior as narcissistic, we should be referring to a pathological fixation or regression to an infantile state of relatedness to the environment.

If narcissism is no longer to be viewed, therefore, as an expectable developmental line, we must substitute other constructs in its place within the hierarchical model in order to deal with certain phenomena of normal development. The epigenesis of the self-organization (see Chapters 12 and 13) in fact refers to all of the behaviors originally covered in the hierarchical model through the developmental lines of narcissism and of object relations. In other words, substitution of the epigenesis of the self-organization for these earlier concepts actually permits modification of the model in the direction of greater simplicity and elegance (see Figures 9 and 10). The developmental lines on which the model is based can

---

magical thinking is acquired only from the faulty instruction of the caretakers; it is not an innate maturational given. In this sense, I would agree with Kernberg (1975) that its presence is a pathological state; however, I see no intrinsic connection between omnipotent thoughts or other magical illusions, on the one hand, and "narcissism," on the other, so that I cannot accept Kernberg's concept of "pathological narcissism" either.

[7]Comprehending the fact that these behaviors are manifestations of psychological deficits should help the analyst to avoid countertransference errors, whether in the direction of taking a judgmental stance toward the person afflicted with these primitive and socially objectionable characteristics or in that of indulging his immaturity by condoning his behavior as expectable through unrealistic attitudes masked as "empathy."

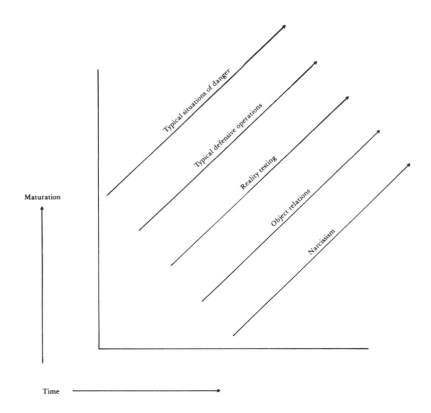

FIGURE 9
THE LINES OF DEVELOPMENT OF THE HIERARCHICAL MODEL

now be regrouped into just three classes, each of which illuminates one major psychological issue.

The transactions of the person with his environment are dealt with in terms of the development of his goals and values in relation to his objects, i.e., as a schema of his self-organization. Second, the traditional subject matter of psychoanalytic psychology as derived from the study of the transference neuroses, i.e., the issues involved in the psychology of intrapsychic conflicts, are represented in the model through the related lines of development of the typical situa-

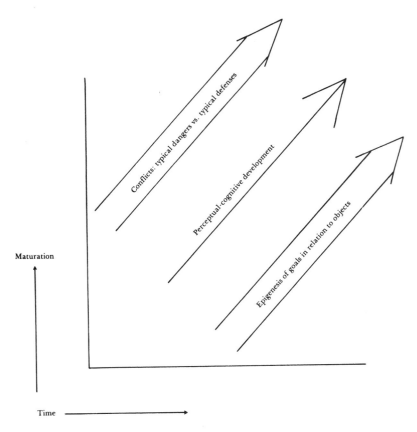

Maturation

Time

FIGURE 10
THE LINES OF DEVELOPMENT OF THE
REVISED HIERARCHICAL MODEL

tions of danger and the typical defensive operations employed to cope with these. And third, the line of cognitive development is included within the schema in the form of the maturation of reality testing.

Abandonment of drive theory as a component of the hierarchical model entails the redefinition of a second aspect of that schema, that of the series of regulatory principles of mental functioning that characterize the successive modes of the hierarchy (see Gedo and Goldberg, 1973, Chapter 12). As Schafer has pointed out (Panel, 1976), these regulatory principles have traditionally been conceived as instinctlike biological forces, a conception with psychoeconomic implications. In agreement with Schafer's argument, I must stress that the principles that seem to regulate psychic life are only guiding constructs to assist the scientific observer in his conceptualization and do not imply intentionality in the psychological organization of the subject.

The use of the concept of "repression" as one of the typical defensive operations also implies acceptance of Freud's psychoeconomic assumptions about cathexes and countercathexes (cf. G. Klein, 1976). However, the specific defensive operation called "repression proper," namely, the forgetting of mental content which was at some time in the past available to consciousness, is an observable phenomenon that can actually be freed of all metapsychological connotations. G. Klein agrees that the concept of repression can be established as a purely clinical theory, independent of any particular metapsychological presuppositions. I am in agreement with the desirability of retaining this term as a designation for defensive amnesias; it is, in fact, the *explanation* for repression, that of countercathexis, that is inadmissible in a theory devoid of physicalistic assumptions.

As Basch (1972) has already pointed out, it is not the occurrence of thinking without consciousness that requires special consideration; on the contrary, as Freud clearly showed in "The Interpretation of Dreams" (1900), unconscious mentation is the general rule, and it is the *achievement* of consciousness that constitutes the exception that calls for clarification. For the time being, I should like to leave this problem, with the provisional statement that repression involves the purposeful (i.e., regressive) suspension of those psychic activities which otherwise elevate thought content into consciousness, in circumstances that demand full awareness of the issues. Whenever such awareness is superfluous, it is the failure to keep mentation out of consciousness that is maladaptive.

The only other concepts with physicalistic connotations used in the construction of the hierarchical model were those of trauma and of the ego and the id. The transposition of the clinical phenomena behind these abstractions into a theoretical framework congruent with a psychology of goals and values is attempted in subsequent chapters: The concept of traumatization is translated into that of the incapacity to process stimuli (see Chapter 12), and the ego and the id are redefined (Chapter 14) in a manner that eliminates their connection to the hypothesis of psychic energy. This redefinition amounts to the replacement of the original tripartite model (Freud, 1923) by a new construct that retains some of its essential features but dispenses with many of the others. The same considerations apply to a redefinition of the topographic theory (Freud, 1900).

In spite of these suggested revisions, I believe it is acceptable to conceptualize Mode V in the hierarchy as characterized by potential self-awareness; Mode IV, on the other hand, is most usefully viewed in terms of the relative significance accorded to conflicting programs of action. These statements are already applicable to Freud's original descriptions of the clinical phenomena illuminated by the topographic and tripartite models, respectively.

Because the traditional theories of psychoanalysis did not possess explicit models of the mind based on object relations, we had to improvise such models for the hierarchical schema in order to clarify psychic functioning in Modes II and III (see Gedo and Goldberg, 1973, Chapter 6). These models were translations into graphic terms of a metaphor used by Freud to characterize the investment of libido in an object or its withdrawal from it: the metaphor is that of an amoeba extending or pulling back its pseudopodia. This imagery was used in *Models of the Mind* divorced of its original connection to the issue of object love. In other words, we were explicit about trying to find a model to portray conditions in the representational world, i.e., for the person's conception of himself and of the principal persons in his milieu. The major issues handled by such a model were therefore the question of unification of the self-schema (is there one hierarchy of goals and values, or are there several unintegrated "nuclei" or subsets of them?) and that of the degree of acknowledgment of the independent volition of others (are one's own goals and values separated from or merged with those of the caretakers?).

The necessity to change the conceptualization of Mode I from the traditional constructs we used in *Models of the Mind* to a more explicitly prepsychological model will be discussed in detail in Chapter 12 in terms of the biological regulation of behavior in the earliest stage of life. Mode II marks the transition from a prepsychological phase of organization to that of man capable of symbolic thought. This process is also to be taken up in Chapter 12. The correlation of these developments with Piaget's (1936) schemata of cognitive maturation is also attempted there.

On the basis of the foregoing modifications, we are now ready to reconsider the hierarchical model *in toto,* as Figure 11.

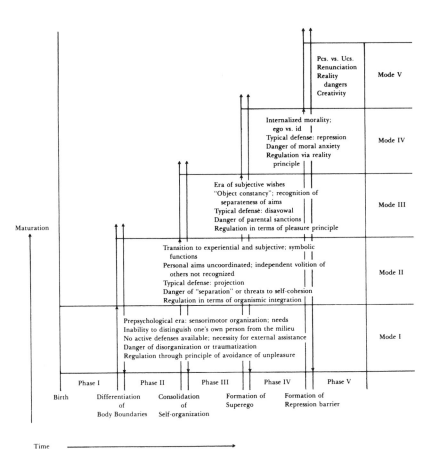

Maturation

| | | | | | |
| | | | | | Mode V |

Pcs. vs. Ucs.
Renunciation
Reality
dangers
Creativity

Internalized morality;
ego vs. id
Typical defense: repression
Danger of moral anxiety
Regulation via reality
principle

Mode IV

Era of subjective wishes
"Object constancy"; recognition of
separateness of aims
Typical defense: disavowal
Danger of parental sanctions
Regulation in terms of pleasure principle

Mode III

Transition to experiential and subjective; symbolic
functions
Personal aims uncoordinated; independent volition of
others not recognized
Typical defense: projection
Danger of "separation" or threats to self-cohesion
Regulation in terms of organismic integration

Mode II

Prepsychological era: sensorimotor organization; needs
Inability to distinguish one's own person from the milieu
No active defenses available; necessity for external assistance
Danger of disorganization or traumatization
Regulation through principle of avoidance of unpleasure

Mode I

| Phase I | Phase II | Phase III | Phase IV | Phase V |

Birth　　Differentiation　　Consolidation　　Formation of　　Formation of
　　　　　　of　　　　　　　　of　　　　　　　Superego　　Repression barrier
　　　　Body Boundaries　Self-organization

Time

↑ ↑ Area of "secondary autonomy" or
conflict-free function: "irreversibility"

↓ ↓ Function may undergo regression:
"reversibility"

FIGURE 11
THE HIERARCHICAL MODEL: FUNCTIONAL ORGANIZATION
IN THE VARIOUS MODES—REVISED

CHAPTER TWELVE

The Epigenesis of the Self-Organization: Formation of the Self

The developmental hypotheses of psychoanalytic psychology principally reflect clinical generalizations based on observations made within the psychoanalytic situation. Psychoanalytic authors usually state these generalizations without offering detailed records about how they arrived at them. In any case, consensual validation for psychoanalytic evidence is seldom possible, so that we generally rely on the clinical experience of our readers for the "confirmation" of the generalizations we utilize. Until relatively recently, this was indeed the only source of relevant observations about the subjective world of early childhood, specifically through reconstructive work based on interpretation of the transactions that form the analytic transference.

In the case of adult analysands, the nature of these observational tools has confronted psychoanalytic scholarship with a severe methodological dilemma. We are left with the necessity of making inferences about the probable nature of subjective psychological states at early stages of development from the "telescoped" transference material of persons who have passed through a number of later developmental phases. This telescoping of the derivatives of numerous successive psychological stages (reflected in the complex layering of the hierarchical model) means that the actualities of relatively earlier eras can never be observed in pure culture in adult life. They must be inferred, instead, in terms of the continuing effects they are presumably exerting on adaptation. In other words, they constitute vectors which codetermine the precise form of each later developmental solution. In view of the multiplicity of developmental phases, these influences may be extremely difficult to disentangle; the degree of this difficulty may be roughly proportional to the degree of primitiveness of the developmental phase in question. Reconstructions of the preverbal period of infancy are therefore highly conjectural at best.

This methodological problem has forced psychoanalysts into the field of the direct observation of children. Unfortunately, the fascinating data we have obtained through these studies have failed to solve the problems inherent in the proper conceptualization of developmental psychology. The data collected by means of "objective," external observation cannot be directly integrated with subjective, introspective accounts. Instead, a process of interpretation is necessary; unavoidably, this has had to be based on the existing hypotheses of psychoanalytic theory as applied to developmental processes. As a result, psychoanalytic child observations have failed to generate truly major new hypotheses (cf. Mahler et al., 1975); at best they have helped to fill in certain lacunae in our traditional views of development. As validation studies, they have been vitiated by the circularity of their reasoning: the hypotheses that were being tested by the research (e.g., the infant's investment of libido in its caretakers) were also adduced as explanations for some of the behaviors they should have predicted.

On the surface, one might suppose that these difficulties would be minimized by using the analysis of young children as an additional source of data. Actually, the methodological problems are even more severe in that endeavor. One reason for this seeming paradox is the fact that the clinical data of such analyses consist in large part of enactments rather than verbalizations. Hence, the validation of interpretations is a much more uncertain enterprise with these immature respondents than it is with adults with better developed rational faculties. Even more confusing is the simultaneity of the child's developmental progression, on the one hand, and the unrolling of the analytic transference, which repeats the patterns of earlier phases, on the other (see Diatkine and Simon, 1973).

All in all, we must still form our developmental hypotheses by piecing together inferences about various phases of infantile mental organization derived from the analytic treatment of individuals suffering from a variety of psychopathological conditions. The development and resolution of transference repetitions of the childhood transactions with the principal caretakers yield traces of the past that we arrange according to an epigenetic view of psychological development as a process. We thus regard "the formation of structure as the result of successive transactions between the organism and its environment; the outcome of each phase is understood to depend on the outcomes of all previous phases. Each new phase integrates the previous phases and has a new level of organization and regulation" (Gedo and Goldberg, 1973, p. 12).

The cases I have selected for presentation in this book were not only meant to illustrate the various therapeutic strategies dictated by psychic organization in terms of various modes reflecting different phases of infantile mental life; they also represent three rather typical clusters from the spectrum of problems I have found to be analyzable within the limits of my personal and theoretical development. In terms of their clinical course, these three analyses showed decided differences from each other. We might characterize the first case (Chapter 4) as an example of the problem of self-cohesion, in this instance caused by a limited period of stress after the establishment of the primary self-organization. The second case (Chapter 6) exemplifies a more archaic developmental disturbance, one that had necessitated the adoption of a symbiotic way of life, manifested in behavior in the form of severe masochism, including a sexual perversion. The third patient (Chapter 8) was a person in conflict between alternative subsets of goals and values, verging on the simultaneous existence of two parallel personalities.

With regard to the epigenesis of the self-organization, we therefore possess observational data in this volume covering three major spans of early development, each having a predominant bearing on a different kind of personality problem in adult life: threats to the integrity of the self-organization due to interference with its initial formation and to traumatic experiences following this developmental achievement, and "internal" conflicts among the major components of such an organization. These are, of course, highly abbreviated characterizations; they merely refer to the most central of each patient's psychological difficulties discovered within the psychoanalytic situation. Nonetheless, we may be in a position to attempt to use the reconstructive data provided by such case material to devise a tentative epigenetic schema for the formation and subsequent vicissitudes of the self-organization. Clearly, I am relying on the totality of my clinical experience as a psychoanalyst, as well as the writings of others, in addition to the specific cases cited earlier.

Formation of the Self-Organization: Phases I and II in Development

We possess no direct evidence about experience in the earliest stages of infancy because this era precedes the acquisition of consciousness as it exists in later life, after the achievement of communication through language and reflexive self-awareness. Perhaps some analogue of the "oceanic feelings" reported by mystics and other adults able to experience profound regressive states without personal disruption might describe the infant's position in the transactions with its environment at this stage. We must recall that the infant is unable cognitively to differentiate his own person from the "not-me" at this time.

Based on his own direct observations of infants, Freud

(1895, 1900) proposed a distinct model of behavior applicable to early infancy. We usually call this Freudian concept the "reflex arc" model (although it has sometimes been given other designations) because the metaphor it uses to throw light on the infant's functioning is that of the transmission of impulses through the nervous system, specifically as this occurs in simple reflex arcs. Holt (1976) has demonstrated that in the 1895 "Project" Freud was not using the concept of a reflex arc metaphorically; he was then proposing it as a testable neurological hypothesis. On that level, the idea has been shown to be in error. The switch to employment as a metaphor occurred in "The Interpretation of Dreams."

Because Piaget has characterized the behavior of infants in neurophysiological terms as a sensorimotor organization (i.e., one without regulation by the neocortex), it has become tempting to paper over the differences between Freud's original statements and these modern conclusions. We must acknowledge, however, that as a *psychological* concept, Freud's idea of the reflex arc is untenable in the light of recent evidence; he merely happened to use a metaphor from a branch of science familiar to him, and it is sheer coincidence that the appropriate conceptual approach to the problem has some similarities to the metaphor he selected. Hence, we are only entitled to go on using the reflex-arc model if we divest it of the original implication that the infant's behavior "discharges" a quantum of psychic energy.

The implications of this point of view have been explored in detail in a series of essential papers by Basch (1975a, 1975b, 1975c, 1976a, 1976b, 1976c). He started from the premise that Freud's assumption of hallucinatory wish-fulfillment in the neonate is untenable in the light of current knowledge about perceptual and cognitive development. Therefore, the infant's behavior cannot be explained on the basis of the accumulation or reduction of tensions caused by innate drives. Instead, Basch accepts prepsychological explanations based on the understanding of the function of the brain as a message-processing organ. In this context, the caretakers' failure to provide a comprehensible environment will ultimately lead to the state of disorganization which has been called "anaclitic depression" (Spitz, 1946). To put his explanations into general terms, Basch has proposed the replacement of Freud's physicalistic metapsychology by one founded on communication theory (as a number of others have done in recent years).

Recent psychoanalytic efforts to develop a metapsychology based on information theory are in the forefront of the latest developments in science as a whole. Toulmin (1978) has described the past century in the history of science as characterized by use of the central concept of energy, i.e., of the first law of thermodynamics. In this light, Freud's use of the concept of psychic energy as his first assumption was not only appropriate but, in the context of the 1890's, decidedly progressive. Toulmin sees the current disarray in physics as the harbinger of a new conceptual synthesis based on the idea of entropy, i.e., on the second law of thermodynamics.

Viewed thus, the biological "drives" amount to preprogrammed action patterns; these are characteristic of all mammalian species. These patterns are more selective than the simple stimulus-response patterns of organisms regulated by instincts. Hence we cannot escape from the conceptual dilemma posed by infantile behavior by a concretization of Freud's metaphor of the reflex arc. In mammalians, including the human infant, the actual choice of an activity is based on continuous monitoring of the environmental signals by the (old) brain. Contrary to other mammalians, man's repertory of action patterns at birth is relatively restricted, but he does possess the potential for a series of expressive signals, mostly facial, that come into operation soon after birth. These expressive patterns serve to alert the infant's caretakers to his basic needs. They are automatic signals, controlled by the old brain, and they must not be confused with subjectively experienced emotions. Subcortically controlled behavior patterns merely "provide the substrate for the later development of emotional experience which is cortically controlled and is an outgrowth of the symbolic function" (Basch, 1975b).

In Basch's terms, the economic point of view of psychoanalytic metapsychology is properly understood as measuring the degree to which an event "can arouse the original adaptive behavior patterns of infantile life." By extension, the regulation of behavior through the avoidance of unpleasure or trauma should be understood as the need to forestall disorganization.

The theory Basch has advanced to explain behavior regulation in the prepsychological phase is probably so different from Freud's hypotheses that it would be misleading to retain the name "reflex arc" model for it. However, we might note that, if we conceive of models as claiming no homology with the actualities they are intended to illuminate, the analogy of a reflex arc does not, in fact, misrepresent infantile behavior as it is understood by Piaget or Basch. Nonetheless, it may be preferable to label their views in terms of a "sensorimotor model," in order to avoid any false implication of cortical control, implicit in Freud's terminology.

In the phase of development that follows acquisition of the capacity to distinguish his own person from the external world, the infant still seems to experience the transactions between himself and his milieu (including the caretakers who form the most important aspects of that environment) as a series of global and uncoordinated perceptions. Behavior at this stage is still regulated in terms of inborn sensorimotor action patterns mediated through the old brain. Only somewhere in the second year of life does the neocortex gradually take over behavior regulation by means of "thinking." The characteristic rashness of toddlers noted by Mahler and her co-workers (1975) has usually been attributed to the use of magical thinking, i.e., to omnipotent attitudes, sometimes labeled a "grandiose self" (Kohut, 1971). These assumptions were derived from our uncritical acceptance of Ferenczi's hypotheses (1913) about the universality of infantile omnipotence. In view of what we now know about the development of cognitive capacities, the seeming rashness of toddlers is more likely to be the unintended consequence of thought-lessness and inexperience, i.e., of the continuing use of automatic patterns of action in circumstances for which they are not appropriate. It is behaviors of this kind that characterized the patient in my first case illustration at the start of his analysis.

I assume that it is the gradual confrontation of the child with the adaptive limitations of these inborn action patterns that leads to his explicit recognition of the need for parental assistance. The toddler's behavior changes at the point Mahler has characterized as "renewed" dependence on the mother for "refueling." In my view, this dependency, now to be understood as subjectively felt, is an entirely new development; it marks the beginning of truly psychological relatedness to other persons. In terms of the psychoanalytic treatment of an adult, a parallel development occurs when the patient begins to fear the consequences of interruptions of the analytic work, i.e., to see that his adaptive integration depends on the availability of the analyst as a monitor of his actions. Such transference patterns were established in two of the cases included in this book (Chapters 4 and 6). They involve fluctuation between a state of cohesive self-organization, present when the analysis is available and is effectively conducted, and a more regressive one, variously labeled as "fragmentation," loss of self-cohesion, disorganization, etc., which supervenes in the analyst's absence or through his failure to help the patient to maintain behavioral integration.

Neither the child, nor an adult organized in this archaic mode, is aware that he requires other people to adapt to his needs without fail and without qualification. As I have stated before, such a requirement is not a *wish* but an organismic need, i.e., it has no mental representation as such. In such conditions, the caretaking person is not perceived as an individual—only the results of his handling of the child (or the patient) impinge on the latter's subjective experience as pleasure or frustration. In adults, these states have been called psychic mergers between subject and object. From a misplaced rational perspective, the analytic observer may infer that these archaic requirements could only be fulfilled by a person endowed with omnipotence. Consequently, some have called the transference of such needs into the analytic relationship "idealizing." Because these issues at first have no subjective aspects, the true idealizing transference is of necessity a silent one, as exemplified by each of the case histories I have provided here. The obtrusive overidealization commonly seen in the analyses of patients with a wide variety of pathological conditions (it is by no means confined to the group Kohut has called the "narcissistic personality disturbances") is not to be confused with this archaic state of unthinking reliance on the milieu (see p. 107n, above).

Although both pleasurable and frustrating experiences are initially brought about through the agency of the caretakers, i.e., without being initiated by the infant, it seems to be a general attribute of human beings to attempt to bring about the repetition of passive experiences in an active manner. George Klein (1976) regards the "principle of self-initiated active reversal of passive experience" as one of the most essential psychoanalytic discoveries about the human mind. Passive experiences of particular qualities can thereby be encoded as cognitive schemata that will serve as guideposts for future behavior, i.e., as motives for seeking specific pleasures or frustrations, basic goals of individual behavior.

In *Models of the Mind* we named these building blocks of motivation "nuclei of the self" (Gedo and Goldberg, 1973), in the sense that each nucleus constitutes one of many parts which are eventually integrated into a whole.[1] None of the

[1]Kohut (1971) has also used the term "nucleus of the self," quoting an unpublished early draft of Gedo and Goldberg (1973) as his source. Unfortunately, although his view of the nature of such nuclei was different from the one we defined in *Models of the Mind*, Kohut did not make this dis-

patients I have described in this work functioned for any length of time in a manner characterized by a lack of integration of such specific action patterns; Atkin (1975), however, has recently provided an excellent clinical description of such a person.

Psychoanalytic references to the problems of this mode of organization have generally focused on what analysands demonstrate about their relationships to other people—on the "object relations" of the persons with these difficulties once they have reached adulthood. The school of Melanie Klein (see Segal, 1974) has been particularly preoccupied with the influence on adult behavior of "good" and "bad" objects. These terms may refer to fantasies about specific persons or about parts of their bodies, such as the breast or the phallus. Such fantasies are, of course, extremely common, but it is exceedingly difficult to determine at what point in development they may have been organized.

In view of the fact that the toddler's perceptual capacities are global and syncretistic (cf. Ehrenzweig, 1967), it is probably illegitimate to single out any one element from his experience in this way, i.e., in a manner that presupposes more developed perceptual-cognitive capacities than the infant possesses. It might be preferable to focus in our conceptualizations on "good" and "bad" early experiences as such. Even so, these judgments would remain entirely subjective, and experiences that appear "bad" to the observer may not only be acceptable to the person who continually seeks them out—they may actually constitute the only version of "goodness" for that individual. Each person may have a given optimum with regard to the input of stimuli, especially novel ones. Departures from these rates of stimulation, either in the direction

---

agreement explicit. His usage referred to early experiences involving single body parts or functions. More recently, Kohut (1975b) has repudiated this particular hypothesis; his abandonment of the concept of self nuclei may clear up the potential source of confusion in the use of this term.

of over- or understimulation, may well constitute what we later judge to have been a "bad" experience.

A similar point should be made about the omnipotent fantasies so often uncovered in the analyses of individuals with personality problems in part referable to these archaic developmental levels (see Gedo, 1977b). It is most probable that magical ideation can only be acquired at a later developmental phase, so that its appearance during analysis cannot legitimately be used as evidence for the nature of thought processes during the second year of life. In the mode of organization characterized by the coexistence of numerous "nuclei of the self," the child is barely able to differentiate his own person from others as a physical entity, i.e., with regard to body boundaries. When other issues are paramount, the independent volition of others cannot yet be appreciated. It is only learned insofar as their unavailability confronts the toddler with his inability to make appropriate choices among his varied goals, and the resultant confusion. Widely different, even mutually contradictory, aims are pursued without knowledge of the consequences, leading to a bewildering array of experiences. In line with the primitive cognitive capacities of the child, each of these will form the nucleus of a separate but global memory, only contributing to the eventual establishment of both self- and object representations.

If we look upon acquisition of the capacity to distinguish one's own person from others as the first nodal point in mental development, the second such nodal point might be the unification of the varied nuclei of the self into one cohesive hierarchical organization. This reorganization of psychic life is contingent on cognitive maturation into the stage of the capacity to use symbols. As a result of this advance, the child is enabled to grasp the sum total of his experiences in more general terms, as *his* own. Roughly speaking, this achievement might be correlated with acquisition of the use of the first-person pronoun. Lichtenstein (1971) offered a related but slightly different suggestion, that it is the emergence of the capacity to affirm or negate that may mark the child's recognition of his self as one entity. In any case, soon thereafter the child will find it impossible to maintain a multitude of uncoordinated aims and self-percepts as if each one were a valid whole. Thus, the formation of a coherent set of personal goals can also be thought of as the acquisition of a concept, one that Lichtenstein called the "primary identity" (1964).[2]

The concept of a nodal point in development is, of course, an arbitrary one, only intended to orient an observer about the mode of organization that typically prevails. In the specific instance under discussion, there is no abrupt change within the continuum of small increments in the maturation of the child's cognitive capacities. Developmental achievements thus take place quite gradually: the small child will be able to act in accordance with one coherent hierarchy of goals for short periods of time relatively early; we judge the self-organization to be consolidated only when the hierarchy of action patterns has become more or less enduring—let us say when it is no longer significantly impaired by the absence or empathic failure of a caretaker.

The capacity to say "no" (and its corollary, the development of negativism in behavior, as in the case of the analysand described in Chapter 4) may be an indicator of the acquisition of the "I" concept of a coherent set of goals because it implies the rejection of an aim suggested by someone else. In this sense, the acceptance of a "false self" (Winnicott, 1954) must signify some weakness in the capacity to reject alien goals. This results from a combination of intense external pressures for acceptance of someone else's aims and a lack of firm commitment to one's own past goals. Once the

---

[2]Steingart (1969) has previously described self formation as the acquisition of a concept. In contrast to my views, his conception of this achievement is referable to middle childhood.

child has formed his primary self-organization, he is not likely to be permeable to the pressures of others; the third case I have described (Chapter 8) is an outstanding illustration of this point.

Fluctuation between organization in accordance with a cohesive self and one characterized by uncoordinated subsets of goals is probably characteristic of most of the second year of life. Similarly, reversible regressions from the more advanced of these modes of organization to the more archaic one are the expectable vicissitudes that occupy center stage in the analysis of self-cohesion disturbances, such as the personality problem described in Chapter 4. Although these pathognomonic regressions can take a wide variety of external forms, probably one of the most frequent types we encounter in psychoanalytic practice is the occurrence of hypochondriacal symptomatology.[3] This phenomenon has hitherto been understood exclusively in the context of the libidinal conception of narcissism. In line with my obligation to reject explanations based on the libido theory (see Chapter 11), this may be the appropriate place to reconsider this issue.

From the point of view of the rational adult's consciousness, hypochondriacal symptoms are generally seen as some form of suffering, and their emergence is generally accompanied by considerable anxiety. In the context of primitive mental life, however, similar sensations may be age-appropriate phenomena. In other words, the symptoms are related to "memories of somatic pleasures," to use a happy phrase coined by Sonnenberg (1974). In the adult, a variety of secondary defenses may be erected against these archaic

---

[3]The other very common recurrent symptomatic manifestation encountered in the course of analyzing self-cohesion disturbances is the tendency to have subjective experiences of emptiness, hopelessness, lack of "energy," and depression. This set of contingencies does not involve a threat of dissolution of the self-organization; I shall therefore discuss it in connection with the next developmental phase, having to do with vicissitudes of the cohesive self.

intrusions into the preconscious because they are apt to be judged as bizarre experiences. Perhaps rationalization is the most commonly used defense; the sensations are then explained as some kind of somatic dysfunction (see the case history in Chapter 6). Sonnenberg has even brought certain sensory conversion phenomena into the context of the explanatory framework I have outlined through his ingenious hypothesis that such symptoms result from a defense against re-experiencing archaic mental states, i.e., that they stem from negative hallucinations.

Hypochrondriasis and related phenomena were originally explained psychoanalytically by Freud (1914) in terms which the foregoing account merely echoes and paraphrases. At the same time, Freud offered a metapsychological theory to account for these regressive manifestations. He postulated that the somatic sensations resulted from investment of narcissistic libido in the affected body part. This may have been the single instance in which Freud's use of the libido concept was most concretistic, i.e., the distribution of sexual interest was here regarded as a physical event. Moreover, Freud supposed that the quantum of libido which came to be invested in the body needed a new point of attachment because it had been detached from the person toward whom it had previously been directed. In spite of the unacceptably concretized version of narcissism used in this conceptualization, the lack of an alternative explanation to account for hypochondriasis has been the most powerful argument for the retention of that concept as an explanatory tool within psychoanalytic psychology.

Perhaps this is the main reason for Kohut's decision to cast his discussion of archaic mental states into the theoretical framework of the libido concept, i.e., in terms of the developmental line of narcissism (cf. Kohut, 1968, 1971). In contrast to Freud, Kohut explained "narcissistic personality disturbances" in terms of *insufficient* cathexis of narcissistic libido in one's own person, apparently understood as the mental representation of one's body. Kohut has introduced much confusion, however, because he paradoxically continues to accept Freud's formulation of hypochrondriasis as a regressive *hypercathexis* of libido in a body part (1971, p. 253). Moreover, he does not discuss in the framework of the libidinal conception of narcissism the overt arrogance and vanity so often found in the same individuals.[4]

Actually, theoretical alternatives for the understanding of hypochondriasis in terms completely divorced from the concept of narcissism are now available; these new hypotheses fit into the epigenetic view of the self-organization. In papers richly furnished with illustrative clinical data, P. Tolpin (1971, 1974) has postulated the occurrence of an expectable maturational sequence of experiences of pleasure. This line of development would form the counterpart to that of anxiety as outlined by Freud in 1926. In that conceptualization, Freud had been able to include all varieties of anxiety along one continuum, beginning with passively experienced unpleasure of traumatic proportions and culminating in the acquisition of the capacity to utilize signals of danger in the form of subliminal anxiety in the service of adaptation. According to Tolpin, the acquisition of similar control over the memories of former somatic pleasures may play an essential, if not exclusive, part in the regulation of anxiety. In this sense, the lines of development of anxiety and of pleasurable experiences become inextricably intertwined. This theory agrees with G. Klein's emphasis on the reversal of passive experience into activity (see also Rapaport, 1953).

Recent work on the development of cognition (well summarized by Basch, 1977) has demonstrated that the capacity for thinking in images is a relatively late acquisition; it is part

---

[4]Occasionally, Kohut has also used the libidinal conception of narcissism in a completely concrete way, as if it involved a somatic event, as when he seems to explain the blushing accompanying shame as a consequence of flooding with exhibitionistic libido (see Kohut, 1971, p. 64).

of the transformation of the young child from a sensorimotor organism to one capable of symbolic thought. This finding requires us to use Freud's term "hallucinatory wish fulfillment" with appropriate caution, i.e., always keeping in mind that there can be no question of organized visual or auditory hallucinations before this transformation is accomplished. In other words, the regulation of anxiety by means of Tolpin's mechanisms is not to be thought of as an exact waking counterpart to ordinary dreaming.

It is difficult to describe in words the preverbal experiences which are presumably being revived in these states: in the psychoanalytic situation, the Isakower phenomenon (Isakower, 1938) may be one derivative of such archaic somatic processes, although this adult experience has generally become infiltrated by visual elements from later stages of development. It will be recalled that the crux of the complex set of sensations Isakower described is tactile and concentrated around the buccal cavity. At any rate, Tolpin believes that the acquisition of the potential for the temporary damping down of unpleasure through resort to such memories of former gratifications may account for those qualities of personality that various authors have referred to as confidence, hope, or basic trust.

Through an extension of Tolpin's hypothesis we may now be in a position to explain hypochondriasis without resort to the concept of narcissism. Hypochondriasis might be regarded as a regressive phenomenon, one in which the signal function of the memories of former gratifications has been lost and the capacity to distinguish between memory and perception has been impaired in parallel fashion. In the context of such an explanation, it becomes easier to understand that hypochondriasis is generally the mark of a successful adaptive response to a threatened disintegration of the cohesive self through the reliving of a specific infantile experience. The person's attention is riveted to the discomfort of a particular body part (or, in analogous fashion, it may become focused on the possible "malfunction" of some aspect of the body or the mind). It is this experience of heightened self-awareness that preserves a modicum of behavioral integration.

In these instances, the Cartesian motto might well be paraphrased as, *"Dolet, ergo sum"*—it hurts, therefore I am. But the painful part continues to be experienced as only one aspect of a more complex whole. For that matter, Descartes' *"Cogito, ergo sum"* may also be seen as a successful affirmation of individual existence by means of obsessive rumination, which, in this context, may be understood as a hypochondriacal equivalent. In fact, the integrity of the self-schema is probably preserved even more frequently by such heightened awareness of thought processes than it is by focusing attention on some bodily dysfunction.

One can conceive of a series of obsessive concerns that serve these needs for organismic integration. This sequence might be listed in a logical order that reflects the depth of the regression utilized in terms of the degree to which the individual's concept of himself has become concretized or reified into a physical entity. Thus, obsessive ruminations which focus on a number of alternative plans of action on the stage of everyday life still conceive of the self as the selector of one among various subsets of goals and values. On a somewhat deeper level of regression, the ruminations may focus on the individual's capacity to solve problems through appropriate thought activity; at this stage, we can infer that the self as a potential agent has become regressively equated with a "mental apparatus" which might malfunction. The parallels to the traditional metapsychology of psychoanalysis need not be belabored here. The next regressive step involves resort to hypochondriacal anxieties about the capacity to regulate physiological activities over which some degree of volitional control should be possible (e.g., respiratory or gastrointestinal functions). At this stage, the concept of the self seems to hover on the "mysterious borderline" between psyche and soma. This is a conceptual error that also characterizes certain psychoanalytic hypotheses which concretize the notion of psychic energy, e.g., the idea of narcissistic libido investing certain body parts. The deepest level of regression which still permits the maintenance of self-cohesion is that of full-fledged hypochondriasis, i.e., preoccupation with actual sensations involving some organs or body parts. At this level, the self has become reified into the somatic apparatus. Psychological theories, such as certain schools of behaviorism, which correspond to such delusional thinking, conceive of man as a physiological preparation.

To recapitulate this discussion of hypochondriasis and related phenomena, all of these behaviors can be understood as defensive efforts to maintain the self-organization, albeit at some regressive level. The point most crucial for this explanation is that the specific regression involves the loss of symbolic capacities, i.e., a return to the sensorimotor mode of experience of infancy. The failure (or absence) of such adaptive efforts ushers in episodes of intense anxiety leading to confusional states or other forms of acute disorganization of behavior. In this sense, the loss of self-cohesion may be seen as an incapacity to process information in accord with preexisting schemata (Basch, 1975b). This concept corresponds to that of trauma or overstimulation within Freud's metapsychology (1895, 1900). From these observations of the regressive pathway in our clinical work, we may make certain inferences about the manner in which the change from behavior regulation in the sensorimotor mode to that characterizing psychological life proper must take place.

The Assimilation of Infantile Experience into Man's Symbolic Universe

Basch's accounts (1975b, 1975c) of the infant's transition from the prepsychological sensorimotor organization to one governed by thinking characterized by symbols follow Piaget's conceptual strategy in postulating sharply demarcated phases succeeding each other. In my view, the hierarchical model should not be read in that way; each mode it portrays is to be understood as the most typical one for any given period, but not as the exclusive one available to the person at the time.[5]

If we try to correlate the hierarchical model with Piaget's work, it might therefore be best to conceive of his succeeding perceptual-cognitive developmental stages as corresponding to Mode I and to Mode III, respectively. In other words, Mode II could be thought to represent the transition from Piaget's sensorimotor stage to his era of presentational symbolism. Although the present state of our knowledge by no means warrants making close correlations between the phases of early development and specific age levels, Mode II is generally achieved as the typical state of psychic organization near the end of the first year of life, and it probably characterizes much of the second, to be succeeded by Mode III sometime in the latter half of the second year.

Mode II, in the course of which the infant crystallizes his primary identity, may in some ways be regarded as the most decisive in its effect on adult character. To be sure, we may assume as a matter of principle that the experiences of the first year may have even greater impact; however, in spite of the putative claims of the followers of Melanie Klein (cf. Segal, 1974), reconstructions of subjective states from this earliest period of infancy on the basis of free associative verbalizations in psychoanalytic treatment are never feasible. As a matter of fact, even the psychic states of the second year will only emerge in psychoanalytic material under the guise of derivatives which reflect the profound modifications of these early experiences through the vicissitudes of later developmental phases into which they have been assimilated. Analysands often complain, with real justification, that the

[5]For the epistemological justification of the viewpoint I have taken on these issues, see Feldman and Toulmin (1975).

very act of putting their transference experiences into words subtly changes and denatures them (cf. Olinick, 1975). Consequently, the transference repetition of crucial infantile transactions almost always requires some degree of nonverbal re-enactment. It is imperative not to misinterpret such "acting out" within the psychoanalytic setting as a manifestation of resistance to verbalization and insight. The analyst's actual task in relation to these nonverbal communications is to find a vocabulary through which he can arrive at a consensus about their meaning with the analysand—a process that presumably parallels the caretakers' expectable efforts to teach the infant a shared language for the communication of subjective states.[6]

Whether the relevant content is communicated via enactments or verbalized in the form of altered derivatives, structural regressions involving the loss of capacity to function in a mode more differentiated than Mode II on the part of adults in analytic treatment are rare emergencies, accompanied by great anxiety.[7] In other words, even the derivatives of this mode are usually mixed with material referable to more mature psychic functioning; the most common manifestations take the form of dreams or of certain symptomatic behaviors which are experienced as subjectively alien. Although in their passage through later developmental phases

[6]In terms of the techniques of "unification" I have deemed to be optimal for resolution of the issues of Mode II (see Figure 5, p. 106), the teaching of such secondary processing of subjective experience may well be the principal vehicle for the (adult) analysand's consolidation of his hierarchy of goals and values. As such, it should become the accepted model technique for problems within this mode. To give the simplest of examples, we may have to instruct analysands in the meaning of certain body experiences such as "hunger" or "urinary urgency."

[7]For the distinction between functional and structural regression, see also Gedo and Goldberg (1973, pp. 101-110). The "mega-anxiety" accompanying structural regression to Mode II is generally misunderstood as fear of death. It is usually counteracted through the availability of a calm person who can accurately reflect the patient's actual situation—hence the clinging behavior of people in such emergencies.

these behaviors may become encrusted with certain symbolic meanings, in their essential core they lack such referents. At bottom they represent the infant's organization in the sensorimotor mode, i.e., his resort to his repertory of action patterns as a means of problem solving even after he has begun to acquire the rudiments of symbolic thought. To give only one illustration from adult life, the use of pharmacological agents to cope with psychological distress is best understood in terms of their direct effect on the addict's subjective state, in spite of the probability that the ingestion of various substances may have acquired certain magical symbolic meanings for such an individual: only that minority of addicts who get an equivalent response from a placebo may be said to be primarily motivated by the symbolic aspects of their actions.

It will be recalled (see Chapter 11, Figures 8 and 11) that Mode II is described in *Models of the Mind* as characterized by the coexistence of unintegrated nuclei of the self and illusions of omnipotence, which, however, are shattered if the ideal parent should become unavailable. Hence, the typical danger is that of separation, while the only defense available is that of projection. In terms of a psychoanalytic psychology centered on vicissitudes of the self-organization, it might be more illuminating to think of separation anxiety (a concept which assumes the perspective of an external observer) as a threat of lapsing into confusion in the absence of the caretakers' guidance. Should such a contingency arise, the small child (or the adult regressed to this mode of functioning) will fall back on reliance upon his preprogrammed action patterns: we could say that his behavior will be regulated by his instinctual drives, in a prepsychological sensorimotor manner. Hence, it may also be excessively adultomorphic to describe the mental activity guiding such behavior as indicative of omnipotent thinking; more accurately, it is devoid of the capacity to assess the consequences of actions. In this light, the magical fantasies often uncovered in the analyses of individuals who tend to regress to these archaic levels may well be retrospective pseudo-explanations of their maladaptive action patterns, rather than the actual motivations behind them.

In this regard, we must also keep in mind that when in psychoanalytic treatment we succeed in inducing a controlled, therapeutic regression to the very earliest psychological states which still preserve self-cohesion, we generally observe mental states devoid of verbal content. In other words, the most primitive conditions our analysands are able to re-experience in the psychoanalytic situation are not generally characterized by megalomania. These wordless experiences may have a wide variety of qualitative flavors. From the therapeutic point of view, the most important seem to be those states of subjective deadness, emptiness, blank depression, and pain that often underlie the pathological defensive operations that characterize archaic personality disturbances.

CHAPTER THIRTEEN

Later Stages in the Epigenesis of the Self-Organization

The formation of a cohesive schema does not mark the completion of the maturational sequence of the self-organization. On the contrary, this stage of the epigenesis merely forms the basis of an ongoing process of continuing rearrangements within the hierarchy of goals and values. Personal aims keep changing in the course of every lifetime, even if relatively slowly. We might think of this evolution as a series of changes in the configuration of the self-schema. In other words, the self-organization of the infantile phase may become superannuated and more or less replaced by a new integration of ambitions and ideals.

It should be understood that such new developments do not eliminate the previous configuration of the self-organization. This caution is especially important with regard to times of transition from one set of goals and values to another. The earlier hierarchy of aims is only relinquished gradually; it may then come to be disclaimed, to be regarded as an alien force, an "Id." From then on, only the new ambitions and ideals may be "ego-syntonic," i.e., subjectively experienced as authentically one's own. An example of such developments was provided in the case history described in Chapter 8. To put the matter in a slightly different way, it is only after the lengthy process of the formation of a cohesive self-organization that mental life can become divided into a "critical agency" and one criticized, as Freud originally put the issue in 1900. In other words, revisions and later repudiations of the primary hierarchy of goals and values correspond to the differentiation of the psyche into the modes of functioning Freud named the ego and the id.

Still another approach to the same process of differentiation is the statement that the ego comprises the aims that may actually be sought at a given phase of development and the id refers to the ones that must be avoided as dangerous.[1] This way of formulating the issue echoes the conclusion of Hartmann, Kris, and Loewenstein (1946): that it depends entirely on the specific context whether a particular mental content may be classified as ego or as id. The same opinion was later stressed by Gill (1963, pp. 145-147) and more recently by Schafer (1976, p. 218).

As stated elsewhere (Gedo and Goldberg, 1973, pp. 92-94), it is following the establishment of the superego that the observer is enabled to make relatively reliable judgments differentiating ego from id in the child. We may be in a better position to understand this empirical finding in terms of the correlation of ego-id differentiation with changes in the self-organization. Upon the consolidation of a set of learned moral principles for the regulation of behavior, the child must repudiate many of his initial goals or ambitions. Parts of his primary hierarchy of aims are then relegated to a hidden, archaic aspect of the self-organization. In the terminology preferred by Schafer (1973), these are then the springs of "disclaimed action."

---

[1]This way of looking at the matter disregards the fact that the pre-psychological aims that continue to exert influence on the individual's behavior share the qualities Freud called "the Id." Because they have no mental representation, they cannot, however, be experienced as dangerous or "avoided." These repetitive phenomena are passively experienced as alien forces.

Early Transformations of the Self-Organization:
Phases III to V in Development

The achievement of a cohesive hierarchy of personal aims coincides with the child's realization of his actual dependence on his caretakers (as discussed in Chapter 12). At first, however, while the child is already capable of perceiving the parents some of the time as whole objects with independent centers of volition, in other respects he still needs to use them as executors of his own goals for a long period. But at this stage, most of these aims will consist of subjective wishes, and the requirement of external assistance is actually understood by the child. In other words, the child continues to expect limitless assistance from his caretakers, but the unrealistic aspects of his wishes are now likely to be defensively discounted through disavowal.

This defense is necessitated by the child's inability to maintain self-esteem through his necessarily limited activites if he is deprived of the illusion of parental perfection (Schafer, 1967; Kohut, 1971). The consequences of traumatic disillusionment in the idealized other used as an auxiliary to confirm one's values may be observed in pure culture in those phases of psychoanalysis in which the idealizing transference has emerged in full force (Gedo, 1975a). In those circumstances, any sign of the analyst's imperfection (in practice, his actual or empathic unavailability usually constitutes imperfection enough!) produces a reaction of mixed sadness and rage, an emotional state generally characterized by a confusion of goals, feelings of underlying emptiness, and an impairment of self-esteem. Clinical illustrations of such contingencies have been provided in Chapter 6. Here it should be noted that this typical set of responses may not be easy to observe because of the vigorous adaptive efforts usually mobilized to cope with such an emergency. The disillusionment may quickly be disavowed, with the erection of compensatory pseudo-idealization, or there may be other compensatory developments, often in the direction of subject-centered grandiosity (see Kohut, 1971, p. 97).[2]

The idealization of the parent probably takes place when the child becomes capable of conceiving of another person as an individual, i.e., roughly at the time he forms a unified self-schema. Toward the middle of the second year of life, a characteristic turn for succor toward the mother has been noted by Mahler et al. (1975); this change probably betokens the toddler's realization of her existence as a source of assistance with functions not at his own command. Thus the child at first naïvely attributes perfection to the parent. On the surface, this omnipotent other is now recognized as a separate person—just as the nonpsychotic patient in analysis consciously acknowledges the analyst's separateness. On a deeper level, however, there is a fantasied psychological merger between the child and the parent (or, in these specific transference repetitions, between the analysand and the analyst). This means that the other person's goals are experienced as one's own, so that the child is buoyed up by his sense of the other's limitless capacities. The simultaneous recognition and disregard of separateness are kept apart by a "split in the self" (Gedo and Goldberg, 1973, p. 99), i.e., by a defense of disavowal. It is in this sense that the object continues to be utilized as part of the child, a state of relatedness Kohut has referred to, somewhat cryptically, as the use of a "self-object" (1971, pp. 3-6).

[2]Although Kohut's account of these vicissitudes is not entirely explicit on this score, it should probably be understood as a statement that the grandiose fantasies which result from such regressions are usually different from a younger child's healthy expansiveness. In this sense, what Kohut seems to mean is not significantly different from Kernberg's concept that in these analyses we uncover "pathological narcissism." Kohut has created further confusion, however, by claiming that every child goes through a phase of expectable grandiosity, which Kohut views as part of the universal developmental line of the narcissistic libido. In my clinical experience (see Gedo, 1977b), grandiose fantasies are not innate; they are invariably learned from the principal caretakers.

Reliance on the illusory perfection of the parent generally persists until a functional revolution is brought about through the achievement of a third major reorganization of the personality, the nodal point in development formed by the structuralization of the superego. This change occurs as a result of a sequence of events set in motion by the prior unification of the self-organization (Gedo and Goldberg, 1973). The rationale for this assertion is that, once the disintegration of goal-directed behavior no longer occurs in expectable circumstances, the child will find it increasingly difficult to avoid reacting with anxiety to his own archaic ambitions (which typically involve phallic aims at this stage). The reason for the occurrence of more and more conflict about wishes of this kind is the child's increasing acceptance of the moral standards of the parents, who are still endowed with perfect wisdom. At earlier phases of development, mutually contradictory emotional attitudes can still coexist without synthesis; but with increasing ascendancy of reality-oriented thinking, the child must begin to reconcile his conflicting interests. To conceal impulses from the parents thus becomes insufficient; henceforth, in order to avoid anxiety, these impulses have to be banished from consciousness altogether. In other words, with the acceptance of a system of morality based on that of the idealized parents, repression proper has to be instituted as the typical mode of defense.

It should be noted that this account of superego formation is somewhat at variance with standard psychoanalytic theories, which have usually attributed the "internalization" of this structure to the renunciation of incestuous wishes. Freud spoke of the superego as the "heir of the Oedipus complex" (1923). The view presented here completely reverses the sequence of events Freud postulated: the unacceptable erotic and aggressive aims of the oedipal child will be relinquished *because* he has accepted the morality of the admired parents. Freud concluded that this process is set in motion by the universal occurrence of castration anxiety in reaction to the child's oedipal wishes.

The supposed ubiquity of castration fear as a spur for superego formation may have been an artifact of the specific child-rearing practices around the turn of the century that determined the personality development of Freud's patients.[3] Empathic parents should in fact be able to provide optimal maturational experiences for their children which may yield what Schafer (1960) has aptly called "the loving and beloved superego." From this point of view, we can also eliminate one of the least tenable aspects of Freud's (1925b, 1933) psychology of women: his conviction, based on the lack of relevance of castration anxiety in their expectable development, that females do not usually form a superego comparable to that of men.

The view of superego formation I am advocating dispenses with the confusing and unnecessary distinction often made between superego and "ego ideal." At the same time, it allows us to change our conception of the acquisition of ideals into that of a learning process, in essential respects no different from other learning. This would obviate the vexing, not to say insuperable, theoretical problem of explaining the so-called "transformations of narcissism" (i.e., the change in the quality of personal ambitions from infantile ruthlessness and absolutism to wisdom, humor, and empathy) on the basis of putative structure-building out of the energy of the drive (cf. Kohut, 1966). This metaphorical idea seems to use an analogy to the synthesis of uranium produced through nuclear reactions. To be sure, the more reasonable developmental hypotheses I am now proposing will have to be widely documented through clinical evidence, such as the case material in Chapter 8. An additional case report that exemplifies

[3]See the case history of Little Hans (Freud, 1909a) for an example of the unempathic brutality of these practices in the most enlightened of households, that of one of Freud's early followers. From a current perspective, castration anxiety could be understood as a particular form of hypochondriacal concern, limited to the most valued of body parts. In other words, it is a childish concretization of the confused aims of the oedipal conflict.

my point has recently been provided by Terman (1976).

It should by now be clear that I am in agreement with Schafer's (1967) view that the moral ideals embodied in the superego constitute but one aspect of the system of values codified in the self-organization. The addition of this set of moral standards to the ideals and values that make up one principal component of the child's primary hierarchy of aims may be seen as the first of the series of transformations of the self-organization that characterize the optimal maturation of the personality.

The clinical evidence for these developmental conclusions comes from the analytic treatment of patients whose overall personality organization suffers from an arrest of development at a very archaic phase. Among the case histories illustrating this book, the patient described in Chapter 6 most obviously fits this category. As in that instance, so, in much of my clinical experience, I have found that successful analysis of individuals arrested at these primitive phases of development is most feasible if they turn out to have the capacity to establish an idealizing relationship within the analytic transference. In some instances this may be the first occasion in the patient's experience of being able to idealize another person; in other cases, this transference pattern constitutes the reliving of a position given up in childhood as a result of some enforced regression. These possibilities are illustrated by the childhood histories of the first and second patients I have described, respectively in Chapters 4 and 6. Mahler et al. (1975, Chapter 14) have reported interesting behavioral parallels to these intrapsychic states from the direct observation of toddlers in the midst of the "separation-individuation" process.

The complexities of the idealizing transference patterns encountered in clinical psychoanalysis cannot be reviewed in detail here (see, however, Gedo, 1975a); suffice it to say that, with appropriate interpretive work on the part of the analyst, a genuine idealizing transference will gradually lead to the acceptance of a new set of ideals; these will, in turn, influence the hierarchy of personal ambitions. In this way, psychoanalytic treatment can produce a transformation of the self-organization without any departure from its classical technique, i.e., without reliance on "corrective emotional experience." Be it noted that I consider an idealizing transference to be "genuine" only if the patient has projected these fantasies onto a "blank screen." I would look upon the presentation of the personal values of the analyst for emulation as an ideal model, or other invitations to accept his "superior" approach to life, however subtly and unobtrusively these were offered, as departures from appropriate analytic neutrality.

Education of the patient in adapting more effectively might be quite useful as psychotherapy for certain aimless individuals, but it does not qualify as psychoanalytic treatment. I would define psychoanalysis as the process of acquiring self-knowledge through reliving crucial childhood transactions within the treatment setting. In other words, idealization of the analyst can be regarded as a manifestation of *transference* only if it occurs as a spontaneous development, against the grain of the analyst's actual behavior, so to speak. Witness the instantaneous idealizing transference formed by the patient described in Chapter 8 simply on the basis of the analyst's recognition of the quest for perfection implicit in his plan of suicide. In those cases where the idealizing relationship is without childhood precedent, the transference proper consists of reliving the recurrent disappointments of childhood whenever the idealization is interfered with.

Once the idealization of the analyst is established, the patient will experience him as perfect in every sphere: in knowledge and wisdom, power, beauty, and morality. The actualities of the analyst's behavior, insofar as they fail to substantiate these impossible fantasies, either are disavowed or will be experienced as severely disillusioning. Beyond the analyst's human limitations, however, the patient will discern the goals and values inherent within psychoanalysis as a scientific and therapeutic enterprise. In contrast to the private value system and personal ambitions of the analyst, these qualities of the discipline (to name only the most obvious, our commitment to the truth, to human dignity and autonomy, to helpfulness and responsible conduct, etc.) cannot and need not be concealed from the analysand.[4]

As in the instance of expectable developmental progress in childhood, so in these successful analyses the archaic self-organization is not eliminated by the acquisition of a more mature successor. The more primitive goals and values emerge again in the course of regressive episodes in everyday life, in dream material, in creative products, or as a result of regressions set in motion by further psychoanalytic treatment. Perhaps, in fact, the adequacy of general adaptation might best be measured in terms of the individual's success in integrating as much as possible of the archaic self-organization into his currently acceptable hierarchy of aims, so that as few as possible of his earlier goals and values will have to be relegated to the status of disclaimed motives, i.e., transformed into id.

The foregoing account of structural change within the personality may help to explain the fact that Freud's concepts of the ego and the id have turned out to have only marginal relevance in illuminating primitive mental life (Gedo and Goldberg, 1973, pp. 18, 55). Before the formation of the primary hierarchy of aims, the principal issues of psychic life concern the reconciliation of uncoordinated subsets of goals and values (Basch, 1975b); until the acquisition of a structured morality, the child's hierarchy of aims does not create intrapsychic conflict.

In the developmental phase that follows the formation of the superego (in the hierarchical model, this is Phase IV), the

---

[4]For a detailed discussion of the goals and values of science in general and of psychoanalysis in particular, see Gedo (1972).

child will, in expectable circumstances, be able to maintain his autonomy with regard to his goals and values; therefore, he will also be relatively self-regulating with regard to self-esteem. The child can now relinquish the parents as idealized extensions of himself. When he no longer uses them in that way, his assessment of others gradually assumes a more realistic course. It is during this period, however, that the child's conscious view of his parents is often characterized by unrealistic overestimation. In order to differentiate these phenomena from the archaic idealizations that coincide with the consolidation of the self-organization, I have advocated calling the later attitudes "pseudo-idealizations" (see Gedo, 1975a).[5]

The first transformation of the child's primary hierarchy of aims through the formation of the superego, i.e., by the acceptance of the moral values of the idealized parents, will change the typical situation of danger from that of threatened separation (or loss of love, or punishment in retaliation for the child's aggressions) to that of moral anxiety. To be more precise, superego formation initiates the era of loss of self-esteem resulting from failure to live up to one's ideals (cf. Gedo and Goldberg, 1973, pp. 77-79).

Maturation in the cognitive sphere will gradually foreclose the possibility of holding on to mutually exclusive aims by refusing to consider their lack of congruence, i.e., through disavowal alone. With this advance in rationality, threatened dangers can be warded off only by removing the offending ideas from consciousness, i.e., through the institution of repression proper as the typical mechanism of defense. This de-

---

[5] I have tried to show that the later overestimation of the parents is brought about by the expectable ambivalence stirred up in the child by two concurrent emotional processes: his angry disappointment and potential depression as he learns to see his parents in a more realistic way, and the hostile aspects of oedipal competitiveness. A "pseudo-idealization" can be erected as a reaction formation against either or both of these hostile attitudes. In summary, it may be distinguished from true idealizations by the fact that, however unrealistic the qualities attributed to the object may be, that person is clearly experienced as a whole and separate entity.

velopmental achievement can be viewed as the definitive de-
marcation of the ego from the id. It is by promoting this differentiation that the Oedipus complex serves as a normative
maturational crisis (see also Gedo and Goldberg, 1973, pp.
89-100).

The repression or compromise resolution of the archaic,
unrealistic fantasies of the oedipal child does not constitute a
radical revision of the hierarchy of goals and values established through the formation of the superego. In this regard,
the period between the acquisition of a structured morality
and the transformations of adolescence is truly a phase of
latency. Prior to the experience of adolescence, it is probably
quite rare for anyone to be able to view his archaic self with
tolerance, detachment, or humor, instead of reacting to it
with anxious disavowal and a mortified loss of self-esteem.

If the transformation of the self-organization following
consolidation of the superego is the first of a series of expectable metamorphoses in the course of a lifetime, adolescence (as a phase of psychological development, to be differentiated from the merely biological maturation of puberty)
should certainly be understood as the second member of
such a sequence. In defining the process of adolescence as
just this kind of developmental transformation of the self-
organization (see Wolf, Gedo, and Terman, 1972), we did not
take up the question of what becomes of the hierarchy of
childhood goals and values abandoned by the adolescent in
favor of his new, more mature self-organization. Our thesis
was focused, instead, on the radical effects on future behavior of the establishment of new governing ideals, and the
consequent alteration of the adolescent's central ambitions.

By conceiving of adolescence as a transformation of the
self-organization, one of a series of metamorphoses that
characterizes human development through the life-span, we
proposed a logical explanation, for the first time, of the fact
that the psychological changes accompanying puberty are by
no means universal. As we know, it is not at all infrequent

for character structure to become inflexibly set during latency. This finding remained a paradox as long as adolescence was regarded as a reaction to the universal experience of sexual awakening at puberty. The actual role of these biological changes in promoting the adolescent process can be grasped only if they are seen as one of the many sources of motivation for a revision of the young person's ideals and ambitions, i.e., in terms of the symbolic *meaning* assumed by these biological developments.

Although psychoanalysis does not as yet possess a detailed developmental psychology for the postadolescent years, we do know that transformations of the hierarchy of goals and values can occur in adult life, either spontaneously or as a result of therapeutic interventions—witness the results of all three analyses described in this book. Eissler (1972) has pointed out that creative personalities may differ from other people in their unusual propensity for repeated metamorphoses of this kind. The revolutionary impact of religious conversion on personality structure could also be seen in a similar explanatory framework. Jaques (1965) has postulated that certain changes are expectable at the "mid-life crisis," roughly between the ages of 35 and 40, as well as at the beginning of old age, perhaps. These changes might best be conceptualized in the manner I have proposed here. In his own terminology, Jaques has made statements that imply that the capacity to shed the confining limitations of an existing self-organization and to acquire a more appropriate, fresh set of goals and values may determine the success of an individual's subsequent adaptation.

Perhaps, after all, these ideas merely form a return to one of Freud's *premières pensées* about the topography of the mind. In a letter of December, 1896 to Wilhelm Fliess, he surmised that the succession of registrations he was then assigning to the stratified layers of his neural model that were later to be turned into his "psychic systems" "represent the psychical achievement of successive epochs of life" (1892-1899, p. 235).

CHAPTER FOURTEEN

The Status of Structural Theory

Some Conceptual Problems in Ego Psychology

Overextension of the Ego Concept

Some years ago, G. Klein (1968) called for a retrenchment of the broadened ego concept introduced by Hartmann on the ground that this extension of Freud's original conceptualization had led to confusion. Specifically, the ego had come to be used in two contradictory ways: as a term denoting a supraordinate regulatory system, on the one hand, and as one of the three subordinate agencies involved in psychological conflict, on the other. As a matter of fact, Kris (1951) had already pointed out this internal inconsistency in Freud's definition of the ego. Recently, Holt (1975) has explicitly tried to distinguish between "two ego psychologies"—the narrower one initiated by Freud in 1923 and the broader, which came into use after 1939, and he has rightly pointed out that failure to distinguish these separate theories has led to a great deal of confused thinking within the psychoanalytic literature.

Among psychoanalytic authors of the past half century, only Rapaport was cautious enough to have reservations about classifying the "quasi-stationary functions" of the personality, such as memory or cognition, as ego functions pure and simple (see Gedo, 1973). In the vulgarization of Hartmann's ideas that has recently been in use under the rubric of "ego psychology," it has been generally overlooked that it makes no sense to list functions known to be organized according to drive determinants as part of the ego—if by "ego" we mean the agency defined by Freud in 1923 as antithetical to the drives.

The confusion of ego as a label for the program opposed to dangerous satisfactions with ego as a supraordinate regulatory system that determines the choice of principles governing the totality of behavior should be avoided. Starting from the assumption that mental conflict implies the existence of an "integrating organization" capable of self-observation, self-criticism, and choice with regard to emotional needs, G. Klein (1976) demonstrates that this structure cannot be the ego (as defined by Freud, i.e., as one of the conflicting agencies involved in these choices): "If an 'ego aim' is in conflict with a 'drive,' how can the ego itself *create* the conflict, and what would be the criterion of adequate resolution? Some provision is necessary for an integrating center *beyond* the ego, in terms of which 'ego functions' and aims are recorded as compatible or incompatible with each other. . . . [C]onflicts involve the adjudication of aims—ego aims, superego aims, or 'pleasure' aims. We now require a concept that provides for the *integration* of aims and for sensibility to contradictions among them. The notion of *self,* to provide what is lacking in the concept of ego, now seems indispensable" (pp. 171-172).

In a recent review of W. T. Powers' model of behavior regulation, Basch (1975a) correctly identified the supraordinate system as the self; in Powers' hierarchical schema, this occupies the highest or ninth level, while specific programs (such as the mechanisms of defense to be subsumed under the "ego") are assigned a level two notches lower. The intervening (eighth) level consists of the system of principles that determines the choice of programs. In terms of the theory I am proposing, this would correspond to the system ego, i.e., to one subset of specific goals and values. The sum total of all such subsets constitutes the self. The possibility for differentiating these two concepts was already laid down in *Models of the Mind,* where the use of the word "ego" was confined to the narrowest definition possible for the term, that of a hierarchy of defensive operations.

Schafer (1972), one of the foremost critics of traditional metapsychology, advocates the abandonment of the structural point of view altogether. In his "action language" for the description of behavior, the relevant psychic contents are simply classified as intended to satisfy an instinctual situation or to avoid a situation of danger. Insofar as these motivations tend to remain stable over long spans of time, however, what Schafer advocates still represents a structural viewpoint. We are therefore justified in inventing names for the "structures" involved, i.e., for these configurations of potentials for action, in spite of the fact that concepts of "mental structure" are particularly prone to be abused through reification.

With the proviso, then, that these terms—like the concept of the self-organization throughout this statement of theory—must never be misunderstood as designations for concrete things or entities, it might be useful to retain the familiar terms of "ego" and "id" as names for the persisting dispositions to act in the service of avoiding danger and in that of seeking satisfaction, respectively. To put this another way, if we translate our concepts into an action language, as Schafer would have us do, we shall have to make provision for those actions which must be expressed in the future tense; it is to these potentialities that we are actually referring whenever we make use of the substantives "ego" and "id." It may be recalled, however, that I have committed myself to the view (Gedo and Goldberg, 1973), which I still uphold, that such a distinction only makes sense in situations that arouse internal conflict. In other words, whenever counter-motives for an action are lacking, it cannot be characterized either in terms of ego or in those of id (cf. Kohut and Seitz, 1963).

Legacy of the Topographic Theory

Beyond the confusion engendered as a result of the over-extension of the ego concept in recent years, a second disadvantage of the structural theory results from its derivation from Freud's topographic model of the mind. In that earlier theory, Freud had already conceptualized psychological functioning in terms of the interaction of two discrete systems or agencies. This basic idea was preserved when he substituted the systems Ego and Id for those of the topographic theory, the *Pcs.* and the *Ucs.* The principal change resulting from this substitution was the abandonment of the criterion of accessibility to consciousness as the distinguishing characteristic of the systems. Indeed, Freud felt compelled to relinquish the topographic theory as a universal explanatory framework because he thought he had discovered that the phenomena of resistance in the course of psychoanalytic treatment were not conscious ones, as they should have been in accordance with that theory. (He meant that not only was repressed content unconscious—so was the defensive operation of repression itself.)

This discovery did not constitute the only discrepancy between Freud's expanding clinical findings and his 1900 theory of the mind; to cite only one other, the discovery of negative therapeutic reactions had also demonstrated the inadequacy of the topographic model as a universal framework for the observational data of psychoanalysis. By giving proper recognition for the first time to the role of internal morality, the structural theory of 1923 therefore went beyond a simple transformation of the *Pcs.* and the *Ucs.* into the ego and the id. Here, however, I wish to focus on the common features of the two theories, instead of stressing their significant differences.

The concepts of the ego and of the id refer to organized sets of mental dispositions by virtue of their derivation from their predecessors in Freud's first theory of the mind, the systems *Pcs.* and *Ucs.* As Loewald (1971b) has recently stated, by *definition* the ego and the id have been differentiated from each other on the basis of the assumption that they possess differing cathexes of psychic energy. Perhaps a similar way to state this would be that the ego, like the *Pcs.*, is supposedly characterized by secondary-process mentation regulated by the reality principle, while the id, like the *Ucs.*, is assumed to consist of primary processes governed by the pleasure principle. In this connection, it might well be recalled that Freud introduced the term "ego" in the "Project" (1895) to designate a neural organization that interferes with the discharge of excitations through some process of inhibition. He explicitly stated at that time that the establishment of an ego amounts to the formation of "psychical secondary processes" (p. 327), and was clearly thinking of secondary-process capacities as relatively late acquisitions that develop out of the earlier, primary modes of mentation. This assumption later gave rise to the seemingly absurd explanation of "regression in the service of the ego" (Kris, 1952) to account for the finding, paradoxical only in terms of the structural theory, that man's greatest creative achievements require primary-process thinking.

Within the psychoanalytic community, it was Rapaport who first raised objections to this hypothesis about the development of thinking in the child. Rapaport (1960a) stated: ". . . the secondary process does not simply arise from the primary process under the pressure of environmental necessity, but, like the primary process, arises from an undifferentiated matrix in which its intrinsic maturational restraining and integrating factors are already present" (pp. 842-843). This conclusion was based primarily on Rapaport's understanding of Piaget's empirical data about cognitive development. More recently, Noy (1969, 1973) has joined in this serious challenge to the Freudian view of these two types of thinking. He has proposed an alternative hypothesis which fits all of the available observational data more exactly. As did Rapaport and, somewhat later, Holt (1967b), Noy believes that both primary and secondary processes develop in parallel, i.e., that neither changes into the other by means of developmental progress or regression. Noy also believes that the two types of thought have entirely different functions from their inception. According to this view, secondary processes deal with information about the world of actuality, including, of course, that of the person's body, and must therefore be capable of objectivity and realism; primary processes, by contrast, deal with one's own person in a subjective mode. If we accept Noy's persuasive arguments, it would follow that Freud's original distinction of the systems *Pcs.* and *Ucs.* was faulty: neither can be characterized exclusively by one of these modes of thinking alone. (See also G. Klein, 1976, p. 250.)

Basch (1976c), tracing the history of this mistake, has shown that in the metapsychological chapter of "The Interpretation of Dreams" Freud unwittingly reverted to a theory of thinking he had discarded as unworkable when he abandoned his 1895 "Project." Basch goes on to show that the *Pcs.* and *Ucs.* as structural agencies are therefore illegitimately transposed from that speculative excursion into neurobiology into a hypothesis about psychic life. The idea started out as a geological metaphor of stratified layers, but by degrees, almost imperceptibly, Freud changed his usage into the reification of an "apparatus" consisting of parts or systems.

As a matter of fact, Freud himself recognized many of these flaws in his formulations of 1900, and in his "Papers on Metapsychology" (1915-1917) he noted certain objections, apparently without realizing the need radically to redefine the psychic systems he had postulated. The flaws of the topographic theory are related to the manner in which unconscious and preconscious processes had been converted into systems. These flaws were later more or less casually passed on to its successor, the structural theory of the mind. Hence, a redefinition of the ego and the id should avoid assigning either primary- or secondary-process thinking exclusively to either one of these "systems."

More recent clinical experience has also seriously compromised one of the supposed advantages of the structural theory over the topographic one—its ability to account for the clinical generalization that defensive operations, i.e., the manifestations of resistance in the course of psychoanalysis, are largely unconscious. To be sure, at the time Freud substituted the structural theory for his formulations of 1900, this was a perfectly sound observation at the phenomenological level. Today, however, we are no longer constrained to assign any behavior that is not immediately capable of becoming conscious to some unconscious system—specifically, to the unconscious portion of the "ego." In this regard, as it happens, we have reaped one of the fruits of Freud's abandonment of exclusive reliance on a topographic theory. His espousal of the functional viewpoint (in the structural theory) led to the elaboration of a psychoanalytic theory of adaptation, commonly but erroneously known as "ego psychology." As part of this development, Hartmann (1939) began to assign certain unconscious processes to the conflict-free sphere of the personality by explaining them as automatisms, i.e., as thoughts that ordinarily take place beneath the threshold of consciousness as a matter of adaptive efficiency. Mental events of this kind can be made conscious through the requisite deployment of attention; the analyst's interpretations about the specific operations of resistance in the course of treatment constitute precisely this sort of re-education in self-observing activity. By means of accurate confrontations with the actualities of his behavior, the nature of the anlysand's defensive operations—if not the content he has been striving to ward off—can be made available to his consciousness without undue difficulty.

As a matter of fact, it is probably most difficult to accomplish this with regard to the mechanism of repression proper, although even this subtle operation can be spontaneously detected by analysands well trained in the introspective method. It should be recalled in this connection that in the psychoanalytic era of the topographic theory, Freud had allowed the distinction between the concepts of "defense" and "repression" to become blurred, in spite of the fact that in the mid-1890's he had actually described a number of defense mechanisms other than repression. The focus of analytic attention on dreams, slips, and discrete neurotic symptoms during this period made it expedient to regard repression as the prototypical defensive operation. One of the proximate results of the development of the tripartite model was to remove the "repression barrier" from the conceptual role of serving as a boundary between the psychic systems. It can hardly be a coincidence that Freud's major clinical contributions thereafter concerned problems, such as that of fetishism (Freud, 1927), in which the mechanism of disavowal was the typical defense (see also Freud, 1925a, 1940b). In comparison to repression, the operation of disavowal is rather noticeable—it is often overt and verbal, at other times easily identified by such expressive behaviors as laughter, a shrug of the shoulders, or the like. (See Gedo and Goldberg, 1973, pp. 97-100.) The same is true of many of the other defense mechanisms catalogued by Anna Freud in 1936. It is now a matter of everyday clinical experience to be able to raise the hitherto unconscious aspects of defensive operations into consciousness.

Lest it be claimed that analysands are not really able to detect these mechanisms through introspection and are merely repeating explanations offered to them in the past by the analyst, it is pertinent to note the results of one of Robert Gardner's technical experiments (personal communication, 1975). Gardner has attempted to maximize the use of "assisted introspection," i.e., to confine the analyst's role as much as possible to rendering assistance to the analysand in the latter's introspective task. Because he tries to avoid teaching his patients about their thinking, including their defensive thought processes, Gardner's analysands learn about their defenses mostly through their efforts at self-observation. Gardner's report that his patients often succeed in these introspective attempts strongly suggests that the detection of the operation of resistances and of their specific mechanisms is not merely the result of training by the analyst even in treatments conducted according to more traditional analytic technical precepts.

Hence I believe we are entitled to conclude that Freud's assumption that the ego is in principle largely an unconscious agency was truly a misconception. The entire issue of the individual's lack of awareness of his defensive operations fits most cogently into Basch's explanation (1975b) for raising mental activities into awareness. In a brilliant effort to replace physicalistic models in psychoanalytic theory construction with others based on communications theory, Basch has pointed out that conscious awareness of self will occur *only* on occasions when unsuccessful behavior will have aroused the need for negative feedback.

In order to grasp the theoretical implications of this conclusion, it should be recalled that Freud felt compelled to revise the structural concepts embodied in his topographic theory precisely because they could not accommodate the finding that analysands were not aware of their resistances and of the motives for these. If the defenses *can* be made conscious, however, merely through a concentration of attention, it is not necessary to alter the topographic model in order to fit the phenomena of resistance into it; they are properly seen as aspects of preconscious thinking. It is particularly easy to fit such an understanding of the defenses into Freud's 1915 version of the topographic model, in which he postulated a "second censorship" between consciousness and the system Preconscious. I have stressed this argument only to show that the presumed advantages of the structural theory over the topographic one have been erected on unsound foundations: both formulations stand or fall together with regard to their adequacy as structural concepts.[1]

A Structural Theory for a Psychology of Goals and Values

The foregoing considerations lead to the conclusion that a redefinition of the ego and id concepts is not merely a necessity forced upon us if we are to elevate the epigenesis of the self-organization into the central organizing principle of psychoanalytic psychology; in addition, this step should be taken in order to effect certain modifications within these hypotheses that are desirable on totally different grounds. Modell (1975) has also reached the conclusion that clinical evidence about primitive object relations now requires a revision of Freud's structural theories—yet Modell's preferred solution is offered in the context of an overall psychoanalytic psychology based on the theory of instincts.

I shall therefore attempt a redefinition of the structural theory (Freud, 1923) as it befits a psychoanalytic psychology

---

[1]The concept of the id has of late been subjected to criticisms even more scathing than the arguments I have reviewed at length with regard to the ego. In a searching paper, Hayman (1969) has shown that a proper definition of "id" has never been attempted; it has always been characterized in terms of one or another feature that contrasts it to the ego: "The word is at present used as if defined to have a number of different abstract meanings, having something to do with ideas about unconscious mental activity—structural instance, energic hypothesis, primitive mode of discharge, etc.; and also refers generally to the 'dark inaccessible part of our personality.' " (p. 378). Hayman concludes that "the word 'id' as at present used has no specific definable meaning as an abstract term" (p. 379). The concept may have been rescued from relegation to the status of a fiction by the theoretical work of Gill (1963, 1967), with which the views to be proposed here are in some ways parallel. Gill stated, ". . . the id would be more usefully characterized by seeing in it the beginnings of the functions which exist on a continuum with their more highly developed forms in the psychic hierarchy" (1967, p. 297). Although I do not agree with the implication of greater maturity in one portion than in another, Gill's conception of a continuum serves as a useful starting point for the reconsideration of Freud's structural agencies.

focused on the self-organization. I propose conceiving of both "ego" and "id" as hierarchies of potentials for action. Both sets of these potentials keep changing throughout life under the impact of changes in the overall self-organization, especially in terms of changing value systems, which always entail necessary shifts in ambitions.

Such a redefinition of structural concepts eliminates the energic implications of the original Freudian concepts of ego and id. Moreover, it does not imply any correlation of primary- and secondary-process thinking with either currently acceptable aims or with disclaimed ones. Most important of all, it does not assign thinking motivated by defensive needs to an unconscious system. I believe these features of the theory I have proposed to be major advantages.

An additional advantage of this revision is that it avoids the difficulties inherent in the extreme abstractness of Freud's structural concepts of 1923 (see Meissner, in Panel, 1976). It brings structural concepts closer to the realm of subjective experience than did their traditional definitions. In this way, the theoretical terms referable to the subsystems of the personality are brought into congruence, with regard to their level of abstractness, with the central organizing concept of the theoretical framework I have employed, that of the self-organization as a hierarchy of human aims.

I should add that this proposed reform of the structural theory is equally applicable to the topographic theory (Freud, 1900). When both theories are reformulated in accordance with a psychology of goals and values, only one major distinguishing feature between these phase-specific structured dispositions of man remains. This is the fact that in Mode V, for which the topographic model is the most appropriate explanatory tool, the disclaimed goals and repudiated values of the former self-organization have become inaccessible to consciousness. In contrast, in Mode IV, which is best illuminated through use of the tripartite model, neither the currently acceptable hierarchy of aims nor the disclaimed one is inaccessible to consciousness. The foregoing statement paraphrases a conclusion we reached in *Models of the Mind:* namely, that the topographic model is optimally applicable to conditions in which repression proper is the typical mechanism of defense. In developmental terms, this transition has commonly been called the "laying down" of the repression barrier.

Before this step has been taken and in instances of its regressive loss or abandonment, the typical mechanism of defense is that of disavowal. Instead of altogether removing threatening ideation from consciousness, in using disavowal the person merely shrugs off its actual significance. The capacity to disavow intentions that might provoke anxiety is based on reliance on thinking incapable of drawing logical inferences from the totality of experience. On the other hand, this very irrationality may also be shrugged off through disavowal, so that the person may be able to claim that he is adhering to realistic standards of thought. Because of the persistence of such internal contradictions, these conditions have been referred to as "splits in the self" (Gedo and Goldberg, 1973, p. 99).

The ego and the id, as well as the corresponding structures of the topographic model, as I propose redefining them, cannot be regarded as "systems" as these structures were defined by Freud. In other words, the hierarchy of currently acceptable aims cannot be conceived to be organized in some fundamentally different *manner* from that of the currently disclaimed goals and values of the past, i.e., those that now create dangers because of their power to arouse conflict. Whether we would choose to call a model of the mind that merely distinguished the preconscious aspects of the self-organization from the ones that are unconscious-repressed a "topographic" one may well be a matter of taste. In the same way, it depends on our attitude toward terminological questions whether we would regard the acknowledged and the disavowed aspects of the self-organization, whenever the latter are warded off through defenses other than repression, as acceptable modern redefinitions of the ego and the id. Do we prefer to pour new wine into old bottles in order to emphasize the historical continuity of our conceptual evolution, or should we strive to prevent potential confusion by inventing new names for them whenever our ideas have undergone significant conceptual evolution? It should be apparent that my personal preference in this instance is for the maintenance of our tradition in terminology.

CHAPTER FIFTEEN

Metapsychological Considerations

The foregoing chapters have presented a new synthesis of psychoanalytic psychology focused on the concept of a self-organization as a hierarchy of goals and values. I have attempted to develop this clinical theory inductively, i.e., to account for the entire spectrum of observational data currently available from the psychoanalytic treatment setting. This effort was in part dictated by the conviction that some of these clinical observations are completely ignored by the traditional theories of psychoanalysis—the case presented in Chapter 8 is a clear example of such lack of relevance between existing theories and the data (see also the discussion of that material in Chapter 9). In other instances, traditional theories did address themselves to the clinical material, but new ways of looking at the data seemed to have certain advantages (see especially Chapter 11).

I have tried to articulate my hypotheses in a manner that would be congruent with recent critiques of Freud's metapsychology (e.g., Basch, 1975c; Toulmin, 1978), which reject the materialist and positivist bias of the natural science of the nineteenth century. It is well known that many serious students of psychoanalysis have become so discouraged in the face of the epistemological dilemmas confronting us that they propose dispensing with metapsychology altogether (e.g., Gill, 1976; G. Klein, 1976). Gill has attempted to justify this position on the ground that metapsychology is an effort to bridge the gap between psychological observations and our understanding of the functioning of the nervous system. He is doubtless correct in asserting that such a bridging effort cannot be made on the basis of psychoanalytic data.

Although the radical abandonment of metapsychological speculation may seem like an attractive solution, we are, unfortunately, not entitled to such an evasion of our difficulties. Psychoanalysts have no expertise in neurophysiology as a result of their clinical activities, to be sure; they are nonetheless obliged, as I have tried to show through the illustrative data in this book, to deal with behaviors derived from a realm beyond subjectivity and introspection. This nonexperiential sector of behavior regulation must therefore be dealt with on the basis of theories borrowed from other disciplines, such as neurophysiology, cognitive psychology, or communication science.

It has often been pointed out, most recently by Polanyi (1974), that all science constitutes a commitment to *some* specific set of beliefs about the Nature of Things. Consequently, a refusal to specify our assumptions about the human organism would not amount to *having* none. In other words, just as they are destined to speak in prose, so psychoanalysts are also condemned to using some manner of metapsychology. Therefore, we cannot avoid the responsibility of making the metapsychology we choose as explicit, as coherent, and as universal as possible. Rubinstein (1976) has discussed the philosophical issues involved in these arguments in convincing detail.

In agreement with Waelder (1962), I prefer to define metapsychology as a set of psychoanalytic propositions further removed from observational data than are our clinical theories. I would add that such theories invariably make use of presuppositions about human nature derived from nonpsychological sources. Clinical theories must be judged in accordance with the criterion of psychological validity. In contrast, metapsychological propositions must be evaluated in terms of their congruence with the conclusions of other disciplines, as well as their relevance, coherence, economy, and beauty. As Loewald has said (Panel, 1976), the most general theories of psychoanalysis are like works of art in the medium of pure thought.

Many theoreticians have stated the desirability of discarding some of the mainstays of Freud's theoretical scaffolding because of the lack of scientific standing of its conceptual armamentarium, which had been borrowed wholesale from Newtonian physics (see especially Rubinstein, 1974). In *Models of the Mind* we heeded these epistemological warnings and omitted from consideration the most objectionable components of traditional metapsychology—the concepts of psychic energy and of cathexis. As Rubinstein has shown, retention of these energic concepts would require psychoanalysis to continue to accept the premise of mind-body duality, although Descartes' division of the cosmos into *res cogitans* and *res extensa* has been totally rejected by every branch of science (see also Rubinstein, 1967 and Swanson, 1977).

Traditionalists within psychoanalysis have largely abandoned the defense of the concept of psychic energy against these philosophical objections; they have generally fallen back on the argument that this notion should be understood not concretely but only as a metaphor (cf. Wurmser, 1977). That position is, of course, unarguable, but it is also extrascientific. Those who pursue that option are under an obligation to eliminate from psychoanalytic psychology every concept that depends on the idea of psychic energy as an *explanation* for actual changes in behavior—concepts such as conversion, sublimation, etc. As Basch once informally put it, it is legitimate to speak of being driven by the winds of adversity, but it is absurd to attempt to sail one's boat before them! In summary, I believe that the task of adjusting psychoanalytic theory to an understanding of the psychic-energy construct as a metaphor is even more difficult than to develop a new psychology, one without borrowings from nineteenth-century physics.

A decision to discard the use of the psychic-energy

hypothesis poses a tremendous problem for psychoanalytic psychology because of the implications this has for the theory of instinctual drives. In *Models of the Mind* we chose to strad-dle this difficult issue: the hierarchical model was designed to remain viable whichever way we ultimately answer the ques-tion of the use of drive theory. It is true that drive theory might conceivably be divested of its original association with the concept of psychic energy. Loewald, for instance, has ad-vocated retention of the drive theory, without committing himself about the question of psychic energy. He sees in-stincts as psychic motivational forces that cannot be taken as givens at birth. Loewald thinks that they are themselves or-ganized through *"interactions within a psychic field consisting of a mother-child unit"* (1971b, p. 118).

This whole issue derives its fundamental importance from the fact that Freud used drive theory (in its early form, "libido theory") explicitly as the central organizing construct for his entire psychological system. It cannot be emphasized too strongly that the extreme reluctance of psychoanalytic theoreticians to abandon the use of the drives as meta-psychological concepts (i.e., to understand them as biological ones), in spite of mounting and ever more cogent criticisms on both empirical and philosophical grounds, has found its justification in the logical necessity for postulating *some* such organizing construct to anchor the sprawling system of psychoanalytic psychology.

The first challenge to the libido theory as a universal ex-planatory framework came from Jung on the basis of his clin-ical experience with psychotic patients. In response to these criticisms, Freud modified his theory, postulating that libido must occur in two varieties, that invested in objects, "object libido," and that invested in one's own person, "narcissistic libido" (Freud, 1914). Further clinical work with non-neurotic patients, especially those suffering from certain severe char-acterological disturbances (which Freud initially described in 1916) and with the traumatic illnesses observed in wartime, then confronted Freud with the impossibility of attributing all pathogenic conflicts to the *sexual* drive. Freud eventually attributed the self-damaging phenomena observed in more regressive syndromes to the "repetition compulsion."

In postulating this nonsexual force in psychic life in *Beyond the Pleasure Principle* (1920), Freud switched from a libido-centered to a dual-drive theory. It has generally been overlooked that the conceptualization of a drive that might fuel the archaic manifestations he attributed to the repetition compulsion was necessitated by Freud's preference for preserving drive psychology as the cardinal feature of psychoanalytic theory. This option for theoretical *coherence* is clearly a metapsychological consideration.

The drive Freud postulated for the phenomena of the repetition compulsion was the death instinct. As is well known, this concept has not been widely espoused, in large measure because it operates at a level of abstraction so far removed from the data of clinical observation that it has not proved to be heuristically useful. One of the major theoreticians who has continued to use the concept is Loewald (see 1971a); his retention of the death-instinct hypothesis has led him to a series of consistent theoretical choices quite different from the ones I have proposed. Objections to Loewald's position must address themselves to the biological foundations of the concept of a death instinct. Such a critique has been supplied by Jules Weiss (1961). Arguing from a broad biological perspective, Weiss has shown that repetition phenomena are necessarily reflections of the maintenance of pre-existing structure; they do not signify its dissolution, as Freud had wrongly assumed. I believe this argument to be a decisive one against retention of a theoretical system founded on Freud's concept.

The specific rebuttal of Freud's biological conception of the death instinct has no bearing on my *historical* argument: right or wrong, that hypothesis had become necessary to hold together Freud's metapsychological edifice. To be sure, Freud's dual-drive theory of 1920, the dichotomy of Eros and Thanatos, has been superseded, with Hartmann's (1948) by far the preferred alternative. This was also a dual-drive theory, one that postulated a primary aggressive drive. Its clinical usefulness has seldom been questioned.

The replacement of primary masochism by a more relevant hypothesis has been widely accepted because of its advantages in terms of clinical theory. It has been generally overlooked, however, that in one particular the implications of primary aggression are diametrically opposed to those of Freud's original concept. If one accepts the view that masochism is a turning of aggression against one's own person, as Hartmann's hypothesis proposes, one must also accept the theoretical consequences of that change of position, namely, the fact that such an explanation for masochism abandons the effort to include the phenomena attributable to the repetition compulsion within the field to be illuminated by drive theory. In other words, the phenomenon of the repetition compulsion is no better explained on the basis of presumed aggressive cathexes than it had been by means of sexual ones.

Schur (1966) may have been the first to note that it hardly makes sense to conceive of organismic "flight reactions" as manifestations of aggression; yet many of the phenomena of the repetition compulsion are best understood as automatic responses designed to avoid traumatic unpleasure. The same point might be granted with regard to the numerous repetitive phenomena that produce the valued activities we label "creative." Many behaviors that may seem severely disadvantageous from the viewpoint of adaptation in adult life turn out, upon analytic scrutiny, to be efforts to preserve the self-organization, and by no stretch of the imagination, conceivable as attacks upon oneself. Other instances of repetitive maladaptive behaviors, such as the regressive episodes in the course of the analysis of the patient described in Chapter 4, do not seem to have any subjective motivations at all, so that they cannot be explained as results of self-destructive wishes.[1]

---

[1]In this context, we do not have to take into account another category of repetitive maladaptive behaviors (e.g., so-called "negative therapeutic

To sum up the historical argument I have advanced thus far: Freud postulated the concept of a death instinct in order to maintain drive psychology in its position as the universal framework for psychoanalytic psychology. In discarding this concept on the ground of its clinical shortcomings, psychoanalysts have failed to offer an alternative that could fill its previous role within the metapsychological realm. No concept now performs the function of providing a dynamic basis for the phenomena attributable to the repetition compulsion. Drive theory is thus no longer adequate to the task of being the universal explanatory framework for psychoanalysis, and we cannot escape the necessity of finding an alternative construct to fulfill that role if we wish to elaborate a psychoanalytic psychology that will form a unitary theory based on consistent premises.

My preference for creating a single framework for psychoanalytic psychology may seem incongruous in view of my insistence on the need to consider multiple modes of mental functioning at all times. But I believe that this simultaneous demand for simplicity and complexity is a false paradox. We must never lose sight of the complexity of clinical phenomena, in conformity with the principles of epigenesis; by contrast, the only proper principle on which to base any scientific effort with regard to theoretical abstractions is Occam's razor: the principle of economy in conceptualization.

To recapitulate: to the numerous cogent critiques of traditional metapsychology on epistemological grounds, I have added an objection based on the *coherence* of the theory as a system. Although Freud's metapsychology possessed unity and consistency by virtue of his adherence to the conception

---

reactions") which are motivated by unconscious needs to expiate guilt—these responses do not, in fact, belong in the realm "beyond the pleasure principle." But certain unfavorable developments in treatment, akin to negative therapeutic reactions, do occur in the absence of guilt conflicts (Loewald, 1972). Such contingencies cannot be accounted for on the basis of either "fight" or "flight" reactions.

of life and death instincts, general abandonment of this aspect of his theory has thrown psychoanalytic psychology into disarray. As I have already mentioned, Rapaport (1960b) expressed discomfort with the lack of internal consistency between Freud's drive psychology and more recent theories of object relations: ". . . it is probable that besides reality relationships established by frustration and motivations deriving from instinctual drives in consequence of frustration, we must postulate autonomous and inborn apparatuses of contact with reality and perhaps even corresponding, and therefore reality-attuned, autonomous motivations" (p. 887).

In spite of its success in demonstrating that all of the major clinical theories of psychoanalysis are still relevant and usefully organizing given segments of its observational data (even if sometimes in an approximate manner), *Models of the Mind* did not, in fact, meet these objections to the incoherence of traditional metapsychology. The hierarchical schema had to employ subsidiary models based on object-relations theories (cf. Gedo and Goldberg, 1973, Chapter 5) in order to provide explanations for early stages of development without using the concept of the death instinct. It is easy to overlook that these new theories are not based on drive psychology, especially if we make the unwarranted a priori assumption that any object relationship must imply the cathexis of the representation of that object with libidinal or aggressive energy. However, it is equally legitimate to assume that drives do not form an invariable feature of object relationships; as I have already stated, Loewald (1971b) is trying to salvage drive theory by postulating that the drives are organized as a *result* of the child's transactions with his mother (see also, Gedo, 1979a).[2]

---

[2]Should Loewald's concept about the organization of the drives prove to be tenable, we would be in a position to preserve the concepts of sexual and aggressive drives as valid clinical hypotheses by eliminating their energic implications (cf. G. Klein, 1969).

Just as it is not possible to reduce the object-relations theories of recent psychoanalysis into drive-psychological terms, so the models useful in clarifying functioning at the more mature end of the developmental continuum completely ignore the issue of object relations. Nor did we succeed in weaving these disparate models together through the consideration of any number of developmental lines in *Models of the Mind*. The only issue relevant in this matter is that of object relations. The end point of their development, the attainment of "object constancy," is generally considered to antedate the formation of the superego. In other words, object-relations theories have little explanatory power for conditions in which psychic functioning is sufficiently differentiated to be understood through use of the tripartite model. The flexible employment of the various models extant in psychoanalysis is therefore satisfactory for clinical purposes, but from the theoretical viewpoint it is the equivalent of a patchwork quilt.

The implications of my current proposals for psychoanalytic theory include the replacement of both drive and object-relations theories by that of the self-organization. Thus, in addition to creating conceptual coherence by avoiding the simultaneous use of two disparate fragments in psychoanalytic psychology, to center our theoretical focus on man's hierarchy of personal aims will obviate the shortcomings of previous views of object relations. The most significant of these was the common feature of all conceptualizations focused on interpersonal transactions. These theories always try to illuminate the most important issues of psychology by considering only one part of the individual's experience, that of his relations to the people who matter to him. These concepts are invariably developed from the viewpoint of an observer and therefore leave out of account the subject-centered core of these experiences of human interaction. Moreover, such theories often use the third-party viewpoint with an adultomorphic and rationalistic bias, so that they misrepresent even the limited sector of human experience they are intended to describe.

From the person's subjective viewpoint, both his relations with significant others and his sexual and aggressive motivations (the latter understood in biological terms as well as psychologically as derivative wishes) can be understood as subsets within the hierarchy of goals and values. The epigenesis of this hierarchy (cf. Chapters 12 and 13) yields relevant information about every phase of development; in other words, it has universal clinical applicability. A summary of this epigenesis was included in *Models of the Mind.* We suggested there that the natural history of the self-organization could be divided into three major periods: that of the self-in-formation, completed with the establishment of a single hierarchy of potentials for action; later, that of the self-in-conflict among its repudiated wishes, its morality, and its sense of reality; and finally, that of the self-in-internal-harmony, beyond conflict (Gedo and Goldberg, 1973, pp. 61-66).

Our view has recently been endorsed by G. Klein (1976), who proposed the concept of a supraordinate regulator of behavior he called the self-schema. The only significant difference between his solution and my current hypothesis stems from Klein's seeming acceptance of an Aristotelean epistemology, i.e., one in which motivation is understood exclusively as a product of *cognitive* schemata (see also Basch, 1976a). As I have stated before, I prefer a view of psychic functioning that makes no distinctions between thought, affectivity, and volition. Hence I stress the self-organization as a hierarchy of *aims,* i.e., of potentials for action that implicitly include cognitive and affective aspects.

CHAPTER SIXTEEN

Reprise: On the Mode of Action of
Psychoanalytic Therapy

The traditional view of the division of labor between the participants in each psychoanalytic encounter has assigned the task of free association to the analysand; by the same token, the work of interpretation has been placed in the hands of the analyst. Whereas it is undoubtedly true that for best results the patient cannot interrupt his associative efforts—although he is of course expected to do so in order to pay attention to the analyst's responses!—the capacity of most patients to reach valid conclusions about the introspective data they produce in analysis has been generally underestimated. The fantasy that analysts have a monopoly on significant insights is a legacy of the authoritarian medical tradition from which psychoanalysis has issued. This same attitude tends to lead to the erroneous assumption that segments of analytic material can usually be understood on the basis of their (more or less exact) congruence with pre-existing psychoanalytic "knowledge." Both presumptions derive from inappropriately applying "objective," natural-science criteria in the realm of human intentionality. In fact, the statement of some wish, whether it be explicit or merely covertly embedded in the associative material, does not call for a conclusion related to factuality; it demands an understanding of the *meaning* of the occurrence, a process for which the analysand may often be better equipped than is the analyst. It is quite probable that empathy hardly applies to the recognition of subjective configurations; when analysts arrive at interpretations of such material, it is either on the basis of some pre-existing schema (i.e., the accepted clinical generalizations of psychoanalytic psychology) or through complex cognitive inferences. Errors of empathy should refer to instances in which the analyst fails to recognize a psychological need. They should not refer to the analyst's "failure" to recognize the subjective meaning to the patient of some given material, usually because he assumes that this material has the same subjective meaning for the patient that it would have for himself. In the last analysis, such an assumption is *always* unwarranted, except for universal psychobiological needs.

To underscore this crucial point, let us consider, for example, a common situation which betrays a sexual wish: that of an attractive young woman who with considerable embarrassment and anxiety brings up repeated associations about the possibility of sexually stimulating her male analyst. Probably all competent clinicians would agree that these facts in isolation do not permit any reasonable interpretation to be made, beyond noting the patient's conflict and discomfort. Even in a series of analysands, each of whom may have experienced similar fantasies and discomforts in relation to her father in middle childhood—and such a historical background is by no means an invariable antecedent of the therapeutic situation we are trying to understand—the specific meaning of their repetition in the present would depend on a wide variety of contextual factors. To name only a few obvious possibilities, almost at random: the patient may be correct in her assessment of the threat of an unmanageable reaction on the part of the analyst; she may be enacting a sadistic game of teasing men by means of her sexuality; she may be lapsing into delusional erotomania; she may be on the verge of a transference neurosis in which her childhood longings for her father will come into focus; and so forth. I have deliberately oversimplified the example, for I am merely attempting to demonstrate that the interpretive task consists of discerning a meaningful pattern of which the "facts" in question form one part. Although it is more or less true that such pattern recognition depends on accurate perceptions of as many details as possible, no accumulation of data, however detailed and reliable, will add up to a valid "truth"; instead, in order to make it meaningful, the entire observational field must be apprehended as a significant gestalt.

In the analytic literature, these issues have been most cogently discussed with regard to genetic interpretations—in my opinion, because of excessive optimism concerning the possibility of valid inferences about current dynamics. At any rate, the focus of attention with regard to the significant childhood data has gradually shifted from specific historical events to the individual's inner world (cf. Schimek, 1975). As psychoanalysts have had to reconcile themselves to the subjectivity of their observational data, it has also become clearer to them that the childhood experiences that mold the human personality are not objective happenings but the child's subjective perceptions of them. In line with my preceding discussion of the earliest stages of development, it should never be forgotten that certain processes that may be detected by an external observer do influence man's psychobiological destiny. The legacy of these transactions may not have any mental representation, however; hence it does not form a part of what we experience as personal motivation. The world of human intentionality is born from the child's subjective experience of his life within his milieu; the actual events, as they might be perceived by an objective observer, cannot even be registered in memory.[1] In principle, therefore, the

---

[1]Basch (1978) has perceptively classified the psychoanalyst's therapeutic interventions in terms of their capacity to teach the analysand to think in a manner characteristic of a higher stage along the line of cognitive development. In this sense, psychoanalytic therapy serves to correct for the cognitive deficits at the time the individual went through certain experi-

essential data about the past we look for in psychoanalysis concern the child's perceptions of the patterns of his significant experience.

Insofar, then, as psychoanalytic interpretations deal with conflicting sets of wishes, or, to put it into the construct language proposed in this work, with clashes of goals and values, their impact does not depend primarily on their truth value. They are effective, instead, to the degree of their power to alter for the patient the meanings of his experiences. Psychoanalysis has probably been overly confident about the extent of the correlation between the validity of an interpretation and its effectiveness. With the progressive evolution of our clinical understanding, we have had to face the disconcerting fact that the successful analytic results of the past were obtained on the basis of interpretations which could not be regarded as valid by contemporary standards. The mutually exclusive systems of interpretation of rival schools of thought within psychoanalysis, all of which seem to gain similar therapeutic results, also suggest that successful treatment does not stem in any direct manner from valid "insights."

These conclusions do not imply that psychoanalysis can afford to abandon the criterion of validity for its interpretations; they merely point to the fact that this criterion is of *limited* relevance with regard to the question of therapeutic results. To approach the issue from the opposite direction, an interpretation will succeed in altering the patient's view of the meaning of his experience to the extent of its approximation to the "truth" probably because its validity will enhance the power of such a statement to create a new nexus of meaning for the analysand. But this factor is only one among many which have a bearing on the outcome; in other words, the

---

ences crucial for his future development. The change tends to replace a predominantly subjective understanding of transactions by more "objective," i.e., consensually validated, versions.

foregoing statement is correct only insofar as other things in the situation are equal.

Strangely enough, it has been known for a very long time that, in a therapeutic setting, "other things" are hardly ever equal. Freud became keenly aware of the enormous influence of the therapist's personality upon the outcome of treatment as a result of his exposure to Charcot (Miller et al., 1969), to mention only one other variable. Never did he claim for psychoanalysis any advantage in therapeutic results over treatment methods that exploit the transference to gain leverage for behavior modification. We should never forget that the choice of using self-knowledge for therapeutic purposes, in preference to methods that do not strive for the truth, is not a pragmatic one, but is a decision dictated by our ethical commitments to freedom and dignity (see Gedo, 1977a).

Many therapeutic systems doubtless produce good results on the basis of indoctrinating patients instead of facing the facts usually uncovered by psychoanalysis; to name only one of these, the school of Jung, dedicated to a search for man's cosmic significance, has for over 60 years offered a clear alternative to our commitment to facing the hidden depths of man (cf. Gedo, 1978). The power of religious conversion to effect profound changes in personality has also been generally acknowledged. In other words, the psychoanalytic theory of therapy has never underestimated the power of inexact interpretations (see Glover, 1931). At the same time, analysts have continued to insist that their own therapeutic results (if not necessarily those of their colleagues!) are obtained because of the validity of their interpretive insights. In my view, it would make better sense to acknowledge that our interpretations are not effective because of their validity, which they may possess or they may not; they work insofar as they happen to supply the analysand with a new pattern for organizing the information available to him (see also Neu, 1976). This understanding of the mode of action of psychoanalytic treatment would relieve the puzzlement of those who cannot grasp why their discovery of certain facts does not seem to alter the psychological world of their patients; it may even mitigate the ill-concealed outrage of others, who feel abused by the patients' ungrateful refusal to get well when confronted by "the truth."

Lichtenstein (1974) has pointed out that our truths may seem especially irrelevant to those separated from us by a "generation gap," whose world of subjective meanings is often entirely alien to our own. Loewald (unpublished material quoted by Schafer, 1976) has also espoused a point of view similar to the one I have attempted to describe, in his elegant statement: "In a sense, every patient, and each of us, creates a personal myth about our life and past, a myth which sustains us and may destroy us. The myth may change, and in analysis, where it becomes conscious, it often does change. The created life history is neither an illusion nor an invention, but gives form and meaning to our lives..." (p. 50n.).

To repeat: like other treatment experiences, psychoanalytic therapy creates new potentialities for adaptation by reformulating the meanings of the analysand's personal history. Psychoanalysts have shied away from the inescapable implication that their search for the truth, however essential it may be for the formulation of scientific hypotheses, is only a means toward the educational goals of treatment. In spite of Freud's characterization (1916, p. 312) of psychoanalysis as *nach-Erziehung*, i.e., an after-education or a second bringing-up, as a community, we have been uneasy about acknowledging the inevitable subjectivity of our contribution to treatment, embarrassed by comparisons to gurus and Zen masters.

I believe such embarrassment to be out of place on several grounds. First of all, the meanings we teach are neither idiosyncratic nor arbitrary. One of Freud's stunning empirical discoveries, that infantile sexuality plays a determining role in personality development, formed the backbone of the manner in which early psychoanalysis reformulated the meaning of personal histories. It is quite naïve to claim that psychoanalysis has taken a neutral stance toward these "facts."[2] In the aftermath of Victorian prudery, Freud taught the victims of the discontents produced by a civilization simultaneously moralistic and prurient that one must live one's life within the body. He thereby altered the meaning of universally experienced sensual impulses for his analysands—and ultimately for large populations caught up in the wave of modernization in the twentieth century. Through this revision of moral values, Freud effected a major change in the very fabric of our culture, one that decisively altered our conception of reality. To put his achievement into the theoretical framework I am proposing now, Freud raised the goal of appetite satisfaction to a position of relative primacy within the hierarchy of acceptable aims in life.

Although psychoanalytic therapy no longer consists solely in advocating this restricted version of what it means to be human, this is not the place to enter into an exhaustive discussion of the full range of legitimate and sound principles for living which are conveyed, either explicitly or covertly, by our treatment endeavors (but see Gedo, 1972). I merely wished to illustrate, by means of this example about the general thrust of psychoanalytic interventions at the beginning of Freud's career, that the rational educational aims we carry out have always formed the core of psychoanalysis as a therapy. Consequently, there is no reason to be hesitant about acknowledging these aims.

The second major justification for accepting the tutorial role of psychoanalysis that I wish to discuss here is an epistemological one. As Toulmin (1978) has shown, psychoanalysis, a scientific discipline created as an offshoot of

---

[2]It may suffice to recall, in this connection, Freud's attitude toward the horror with which his patient Dora (1905) reacted to the advances of Herr K., a father-surrogate. From Freud's perspective, such an event should have been experienced as pleasurable. This does not mean, of course, that Freud would have favored any particular course of action in the situation.

late nineteenth-century neurophysiology, shared the contemporary philosophical assumptions of the natural sciences as a matter of course. The intervening century has seen the reorganization of Western cosmology on two separate occasions as a result of advances in physics. First, our epistemology turned from materialism to the central concept of energy; this change was reflected in the conceptualization of Freudian metapsychology. We are currently witnessing the abandonment of energy as the central idea of our cosmology in favor of the concept of information. In acknowledging that our therapeutic endeavors consist in conveying new meanings to our patients, rather than in altering the economics of mental energies, far from succumbing to a shameful and unscientific dogmatism, we are actually restoring our discipline to the forefront of contemporary thinking, in the tradition of the Freud of 1900.

Thus in our explanations of the mode of action of psychoanalysis, we must face the uncomfortable knowledge that all interpretations, even those which are essentially invalid, may have profound effects, provided they are not mere repetitions of existing ways of organizing information. The fate of the adaptational changes brought about by any intervention which has introduced some alteration in the analysand's understanding of the meanings of his life experience is probably subject to the hazards of chance. Freud (1937) was quite aware of the fact that the practical outcome of analytic treatment depended on the opportunities and difficulties the analysand subsequently encountered in actuality. The adaptational value of a new pattern of meaning is therefore quite unpredictable.

Seen from this perspective, various psychoanalytic theories codify the significant meanings of life in terms of the subjective preferences of their advocates. I have already described the view of man embodied in the libido theory as an attribution of primary significance to the satisfaction of the appetites. At this point, I would mention only the most prominent examples of alternative theories which similarly stress a single dimension of human existence. I believe it is no exaggeration to characterize the psychoanalytic system of Melanie Klein as a doctrine teaching the need to make reparation for man's constitutional wickedness. Kohut (1975a, 1977) has laid comparable emphasis on the unique healing power of empathy; his point of view ultimately amounts to acknowledging man's entitlement to an affectively gratifying milieu.[3]

I have chosen these specific theoretical proposals as my illustrations not only because large numbers of psychoanalysts have found them to be effective guides to successful therapeutic activity; I have singled them out for mention because I believe them to possess, as I believe the original Freudian theories to have possessed, a measure of validity in their general outlines. On the other hand, I see all such clinical theories as statements which cannot serve as the exclusive basis of our theory of mind because each of them focuses too narrowly on one specific meaning of human existence.

Recapitulation

I began this exposition with a brief history of the evolution of the psychoanalytic theory of treatment, focused in particular on explanations of the therapeutic action of psychoanalysis. I have offered a hypothesis which views the effectiveness of treatment as a result of the correction of the unfavorable outcome of various developmental crises. A corollary of this theory is the inference that different modalities of intervention are indicated to deal with the consequences of pathogenic experiences at varying developmental levels. At the more archaic end of this continuum, analysis

---

[3]This point of view implies that empathy is not merely a tool used by the analyst to arrive at his conclusions but a therapeutic agent conveyed to the analysand through various channels of communication. I am in sharp disagreement with this belief.

must supply for the patient a "holding environment," the provision of which is made possible only by the analyst's accurate perception of the analysand's objective needs through empathy. By contrast, at the more mature end of the scale, the principal issues center on the conflicts around the analysand's subjective wishes. Because such intentions are not simply matters of fact, but need to be understood in terms of their significance in the context of the analysand's life situation, their meaning must be interpreted. The task of discerning the patterns of meaning in free-associative material is dependent not on empathy but on the analyst's capacities for recognizing *Gestalten,* some of which may actually be unfamiliar to him.

Psychoanalysts have been guided in this difficult enterprise by a series of competing clinical theories in which the primary meanings implicit in human existence have been encoded. Many of these theories have emphasized one of these meanings to the exclusion of the others. The logic of my argument leads toward the conclusion, however, that psychoanalytic therapy should be able to produce a maximal variety of meaningful reformulations of the analysand's experience. These must include both the meanings of his need for a holding environment in the analytic setting—i.e., his objective psychobiological goals—and the significance of his subjective wishes. Preferably, analysands should arrive at as many of these insights as possible through their own introspective efforts, for in the world of subjective meanings no outside observer, however empathic he may be, is really competent to judge the relative importance of various determinants.

To encompass the infinite variety of meaningful human goals and values encountered in clinical practice, no theory of the mind consisting of combinations and permutations of aggression, libido, narcissism, and the defenses against their derivatives can suffice. In the place of such overly restrictive categories, I am attempting to develop a theory organized around the central concept of a relatively permanent hierarchy of aims, both organismic and subjective. I believe that this hierarchy of goals and values should be conceptualized as the self-organization, a concept that can anchor psychoanalytic psychology simultaneously in the world of biological needs and in that of subjective wishes. At the same time, such a theoretical system avoids the pitfall of postulating fictive, reified entities to straddle the gap between natural science and the existential concerns of our psychology.

References

Applegarth, A. (1971), Comments on aspects of the theory of psychic energy. *J. Amer. Psychoanal. Assn.*, 19:379-416.

Atkin, S. (1975), Ego synthesis and cognition in a borderline case. *Psychoanal. Quart.*, 44:29-61.

Bak, R. (1974), Distortions of the concept of fetishism. *The Psychoanalytic Study of the Child*, 29:191-214. New Haven: Yale University Press.

Basch, M. F. (1972), Psychoanalytic interpretation and cognitive development. Presented to the Chicago Psychoanalytic Society.

——— (1975a), Perception, consciousness, and Freud's "Project." *The Annual of Psychoanalysis*, 3:3-19. New York: International Universities Press.

——— (1975b), Psychic determinism and freedom of will. Presented to the Chicago Institute for Psychoanalysis.

——— (1975c), Toward a theory that encompasses depression: A revision of existing causal hypotheses in psychoanalysis. In: *Depression and Human Existence*, ed. E. Anthony & T. Benedek. Boston: Little Brown, pp. 483-534.

——— (1976a), The concept of affect: A re-examination. *J. Amer. Psychoanal. Assn.*, 24: 759-777.

——— (1976b), Psychoanalysis and communication science. *The Annual of Psychoanalysis*, 4: 385-422. New York: International Universities Press.

——— (1976c), Theory formation in Chapter VII: A critique. *J. Amer. Psychoanal. Assn.*, 24: 61-100.

——— (1977), Developmental psychology and explanatory theory in psychoanalysis. *The Annual of Psychoanalysis*, 5: 229-263. New York: International Universities Press.

——— (1978), Psychoanalysis and cognitive psychology. Unpublished manuscript.

Beres, D. (1965), Structure and function in psychoanalysis. *Internat. J. Psycho-Anal.*, 46:53-63.

Diatkine, R. & Simon, J. (1973), *La psychanalyse précoce*. Paris: Presses Universitaires de France.

Ehrenzweig, A. (1967), *The Hidden Order of Art*. Los Angeles and Berkeley: Univ. of California Press.

Eissler, K. R. (1953), The effect of the structure of the ego on psychoanalytic technique. *J. Amer. Psychoanal. Assn.*, 1:104-143.

———— (1972), *Talent and Genius*. New York: Quadrangle Press.

Erikson, E. (1959), *Identity and the Life Cycle. Psychological Issues*, Monograph 1. New York: International Universities Press.

Feldman, C. & Toulmin, S. (1975), Logic and the theory of mind. In: *Proceedings of the Nebraska Symposium on Motivation*. Lincoln: University of Nebraska Press, pp. 409-475.

Ferenczi, S. (1913), Stages in the development of the sense of reality. In: *Contributions to Psychoanalysis*. New York: Basic Books, 1950, pp. 213-239.

———— & Rank, O. (1924), *The Development of Psychoanalysis*. New York and Washington: Nervous and Mental Disease Publishing Co.

Frank, A. (1969), The unrememberable and the unforgettable: Passive primal repression. *The Psychoanalytic Study of the Child*, 24:59-66. New York: International Universities Press.

Freud, A. (1936), *The Ego and the Mechanisms of Defense. Writings*, 2. New York: International Universities Press, 1966.

Freud, S. (1886-1940), *The Standard Edition of the Complete Psychological Works of Sigmund Freud*, ed. J. Strachey. London: Hogarth Press, 1953-1974.

———— (1888-1892), Papers on hypnotism and suggestion. *Standard Edition*, 1:63-172.

———— (1892-1899), Extracts from the Fliess papers. *Standard Edition*, 1:175-280.

———— (1893), On the psychical mechanism of hysterical phenomena. *Standard Edition*, 3:27-39.

———— (1895), Project for a scientific psychology. *Standard Edition*, 1:295-391.

———— (1898), Sexuality in the aetiology of the neuroses. *Standard Edition*, 3:261-285.

———— (1900), The interpretation of dreams. *Standard Edition*, 4,5.

———— (1905a) Fragment of an analysis of a case of hysteria. *Standard Edition*, 7:3-122.

———— (1905b), Three essays on the theory of sexuality. *Standard Edition*, 7:123-243.

———— (1909a), Analysis of a phobia in a five-year-old boy. *Standard Edition*, 10:3-147.

———— (1909b), Notes upon a case of obsessional neurosis. *Standard Edition*, 10:153-249.

———— (1914), On narcissism: An introduction. *Standard Edition*, 14:69-102.

———— (1915), The unconscious. *Standard Edition*, 14:219-235.

———— (1915-1917), Papers on metapsychology. *Standard Edition*, 14:105-260.

———— (1916), Some character-types met with in psycho-analytic work. *Standard Edition*, 14:311-333.

———— (1917a), A metapsychological supplement to the theory of dreams. *Standard Edition*, 14:219-235.

———— (1917b), Mourning and melancholia. *Standard Edition*, 14:239-258.

———— (1920), Beyond the pleasure principle. *Standard Edition*, 18:3-64.

———— (1923), The ego and the id. *Standard Edition*, 19:3-66.

———— (1925a), Negation. *Standard Edition*, 19:235-242.

———— (1925b), Some psychical consequences of the anatomical distinction between the sexes. *Standard Edition*, 19: 243-258.

———— (1926), Inhibitions, symptoms and anxiety. *Standard Edition*, 20:77-174.

———— (1927), Fetishism. *Standard Edition*, 21:149-157.

———— (1933), New introductory lectures on psycho-analysis. *Standard Edition*, 22: 3-182.

———— (1937), Analysis terminable and interminable. *Standard Edition*, 23:211-253.

———— (1940a), An outline of psycho-analysis. *Standard Edition*, 23:141-207.

———— (1940b), Splitting of the ego in the process of defence. *Standard Edition*, 23:271-278.

———— (1940-1941), Sketches for the preliminary communication of 1893. *Standard Edition*, 1:146-154.

Gardner, R. (in prep.), A psychoanalytic characterology.

Gedo, J. (1964), Concepts for a classification of the psychotherapies. *Internat. J. Psycho-Anal.*, 45:530-539.

———— (1966), The psychotherapy of developmental arrest. *Brit. J. Med. Psychol.*, 39:25-33.

———— (1967), On critical periods for corrective experience in the therapy of arrested development. *Brit. J. Med. Psychol.*, 40:79-83.

———— (1968), The wise baby reconsidered. In: Gedo & Pollock, 1976, pp. 357-378.

———— (1972), The dream of reason produces monsters. *J. Amer. Psychoanal. Assn.*, 20:199-223.

———— (1973), Kant's way: The psychoanalytic contribution of David Rapaport. *Psychoanal. Quart.*, 42:409-434.

———— (1975a), Forms of idealization in the analytic transference. *J. Amer. Psychoanal. Assn.*, 23:485-505.

———— (1975b), To Heinz Kohut: On his 60th birthday. *The Annual of Psychoanalysis*, 3:313-322. New York: International Universities Press.

—— (1976), The psychology of genius revisited. (Unpublished.)

—— (1977a), Sigmund Freud and the Socratic tradition. *Dialogue*, 1: 2-15.

—— (1977b), Notes on the psychoanalytic management of archaic transferences. *J. Amer. Psychoanal. Assn.*, 25: 787-804.

—— (1979a), Magna est vis veritatis tuae, et praevalebit! *The Annual of Psychoanalysis*, 7. New York: International Universities Press, in press.

—— (1979b), Theories of object relations: A metapsychological assessment. *J. Amer. Psychoanal. Assn.*, 27. In press.

—— (in press), Dreams and primitive modes of psychic organization. In: *The Dream in Clinical Practice*, ed. J. Natterson. New York: Jason Aronson.

—— & Goldberg, A. (1973), *Models of the Mind: A Psychoanalytic Theory*. Chicago: University of Chicago Press.

—— & Pollock, G. H., eds. (1976), *Freud: The Fusion of Science and Humanism*. Psychological Issues, Monograph 34/35. New York: International Universities Press.

—— & Wolf, E. (1973), Freud's *Novelas Ejemplares*. In: Gedo & Pollock, (1976), pp. 87-113.

Gill, M. (1963), *Topography and Systems in Psychoanalytic Theory*. Psychological Issues, Monograph 10. New York: International Universities Press.

—— (1967), The primary process. In: Holt, 1967c, pp. 259-298.

—— (1976), Metapsychology is not psychology. In: Gill & Holzman, 1976, pp. 71-105.

—— & Holzman, P., eds. (1976), *Psychology Versus Metapsychology: Psychoanalytic Essays in Memory of George S. Klein*. Psychological Issues, Monograph 36. New York: International Universities Press.

Gitelson, M. (1962), The curative factor in psychoanalysis. In: *Psychoanalysis, Science and Profession*. New York: International Universities Press, 1973, pp. 311-341.

Glover, E. (1931), The therapeutic effect of inexact interpretation: A contribution to the theory of suggestion. *Internat. J. Psycho-anal.* 12:397-411.

Greenacre, P. (1969), The fetish and the transitional object. In: *Emotional Growth*. New York: International Universities Press, 1971, pp. 315-334.

Greenson, R. R. (1965), The working alliance and the transference. In: *Explorations in Psychoanalysis*. New York: International Universities Press, 1978, pp. 199-224.

Grossman, W. & Simon, B. (1969), Anthropomorphism: Motive, meaning, and causality in psychoanalytic theory. *The Psychoanalytic Study of the Child*, 24:78-114. New York: International Universities Press.

Hartmann, H. (1939), *Ego Psychology and the Problem of Adaptation*. New

York: International Universities Press, 1958.

———— (1948), Comments on the psychoanalytic theory of instinctual drives. In: Hartmann, 1964, pp. 69-89.

———— (1952), The mutual influences in the development of ego and id. In: Hartmann, 1964, pp. 155-181.

———— (1964), *Essays on Ego Psychology*. New York: International Universities Press.

————, Kris, E. & Loewenstein, R. (1946), Comments on the formation of psychic structure. In: *Papers on Psychoanalytic Psychology*. *Psychological Issues*, Monograph 14. New York: International Universities Press, pp. 27-55.

Hayman, A. (1969), What do we mean by "Id"? *J. Amer. Psychoanal. Assn.*, 17:353-380.

Holt, R. (1965), A review of some of Freud's biological assumptions and their influence on his theories. In: *Psychoanalysis and Current Biological Thought*, ed. N. S. Greenfield & W. C. Lewis. Madison: Univ. of Wisconsin Press, 1967, pp. 93-124.

———— (1967a), Beyond vitalism and mechanism: Freud's concept of psychic energy. In: *Science and Psychoanalysis*, vol. 11, ed. J. H. Masserman. New York: Grune & Stratton, pp. 1-41.

———— (1967b) The development of the primary process: A structural view. In: Holt, 1967c, pp. 344-383.

———— ed. (1967c), *Motives and Thought: Psychoanalytic Essays in Honor of David Rapaport*. *Psychological Issues*, Monograph 18/19. New York: International Universities Press.

———— (1975), The past and future of ego psychology. *Psychoanal. Quart.*, 44:550-576.

———— (1976), Drive or wish? A reconsideration of the psychoanalytic theory of motivation. In: Gill & Holzman, 1976, pp. 158-196.

Isakower, O. (1938), A contribution to the patho-psychology of phenomena associated with falling asleep. *Internat. J. Psycho-Anal.*, 19:331-345.

Jacobson, E. (1964), *The Self and the Object World*. New York: International Universities Press.

Jaques, E. (1965), Death and the mid-life crisis. *Internat. J. Psycho-Anal.*, 46:502-514.

Jones, E. (1953), *The Life and Work of Sigmund Freud*. vol. I. New York: Basic Books.

Kernberg, O. F. (1975), *Borderline Conditions and Pathological Narcissism*. New York: Jason Aronson.

Klein, G. (1968), The ego in psychoanalysis: A concept in search of identity. In Klein, 1976, pp. 121-160.

———— (1969), Freud's two theories of sexuality. In: Klein, 1976, pp. 72-120.

———— (1973), Is psychoanalysis relevant? In: Klein, 1976, pp. 17-40.

—— (1976), *Psychoanalytic Theory: An Exploration of Essentials.* New York: International Universities Press.

Kohut, H. (1966), Forms and transformations of narcissism. In: Kohut, 1978, pp. 427-460.

—— (1968), The psychoanalytic treatment of narcissistic personality disorders: Outline of a systematic approach. In: Kohut, 1978, pp. 477-509.

—— (1970), Discussion of D. Levin's "The self: A contribution to its place in theory and technique." In: Kohut, 1978, pp. 577-588.

—— (1971), *The Analysis of the Self.* New York: International Universities Press.

—— (1972), Thoughts on narcissism and narcissistic rage. In: Kohut, 1978, pp. 615-658.

—— (1975a), The psychoanalyst in the community of scholars. In: Kohut, 1978, pp. 685-724.

—— (1975b), Remarks about the formation of the self. In: Kohut, 1978, pp. 737-770.

—— (1977), *The Restoration of the Self.* New York: International Universities Press.

—— & Seitz, P. (1963), Concepts and theories of psychoanalysis. In: Kohut, 1978, pp. 337-374.

—— (1978), *The Search for the Self,* ed. P. H. Ornstein. New York: International Universities Press.

Kris, E. (1951), The development of ego psychology. In: *The Selected Papers of Ernst Kris.* New Haven: Yale University Press, 1975, pp. 375-389.

—— (1952), The psychology of caricature. In: *Psychoanalytic Explorations in Art.* New York: International Universities Press, pp. 173-188.

Lichtenstein, H. (1963), The dilemma of human identity: Notes on self-transformation, self-objectivation, and metamorphosis. *J. Amer. Psychoanal. Assn.* 11:173-223.

—— (1964), The role of narcissism in the emergence and maintenance of primary identity. *Internat. J. Psycho-Anal.,* 45:49-56.

—— (1965), Towards a metapsychological definition of the concept of self. *Internat. J. Psycho-Anal.,* 46:117-128.

—— (1971), The malignant no: A hypothesis concerning the interdependence of the sense of self and the instinctual drives. In: *The Unconscious Today,* ed. M. Kanzer. New York: International Universities Press, pp. 147-176.

—— (1974), The effect of reality perception on psychic structure: A psychoanalytic contribution to the problem of the "generation gap." *The Annual of Psychoanalysis,* 2:349-367. New York: International Universities Press.

Loewald, H. (1960), On the therapeutic action of psycho-analysis. *Internat. J. Psycho-Anal.,* 41:16-33.

—— (1971a), Discussion of M. Schur's "The id and the regulatory prin-

ciples of mental functioning." In: *The Unconscious Today*, ed. M. Kanzer. New York: International Universities Press, pp. 86-96.
——— (1971b), On motivation and instinct theory. *The Psychoanalytic Study of the Child*, 26:91-128. New York: Quadrangle.
——— (1971c), Some considerations on repetition and repetition compulsion. *Internat. J. Psycho-Anal.*, 52:59-66.
——— (1972), Freud's conception of the negative therapeutic reaction, with comments on instinct theory. *J. Amer. Psychoanal. Assn.*, 20:235-245.
——— (1973), Review of *Analysis of Self. Psychoanal. Quart.*, 42:441-451.
Mahler, M., Pine, F. & Bergman, A. (1975), *The Psychological Birth of the Human Infant: Symbiosis and Individuation*. New York: Basic Books.
McGuire, W., ed. (1974), *The Freud/Jung Letters*. Princeton: Princeton University Press.
Miller, J., Sabshin, M., Gedo, J., Pollock, G., Sadow, L., & Schlessinger, N. (1969), Some aspects of Charcot's influence on Freud. In: Gedo & Pollock, 1976, pp. 115-132.
Modell, A. (1975), The ego and the id—fifty years later. *Internat. J. Psycho-Anal.*, 56:57-68.
——— (1976), "The holding environment" and the therapeutic action of psychoanalysis. *J. Amer. Psychoanal. Assn.*, 24:285-308.
Neu, J. (1976), Thought, theory, and therapy. *Psychoanalysis and Contemporary Science*, 3:103-144. New York: International Universities Press.
Noy, P. (1969), A revision of the psychoanalytic theory of the primary process. *Internat. J. Psycho-Anal.*, 50:155-178.
——— (1973), Symbolism and mental representation. *The Annual of Psychoanalysis*, 1:125-158. New York: Quadrangle.
Nunberg, H. (1932), *Principles of Psychoanalysis*. New York: International Universities Press, 1955.
——— & Federn, E., eds. (1967), *Minutes of the Vienna Psychoanalytic Society*, vol. 2. New York: International Universities Press.
Olinick, S. (1975), On empathic perception and the problems of reporting psychoanalytic processes. *Internat. J. Psycho-Anal.*, 56:147-154.
Oremland, J., Blacker, K., & Norman, H. (1975), Incompleteness in "successful" psychoanalyses: A follow-up study. *J. Amer. Psychoanal. Assn.*, 23:819-844.
Panel (1970), Negative therapeutic reaction, S. Olinick, reporter. *J. Amer. Psychoanal. Assn.*, 18:655-672.
——— (1973), Technique and prognosis in the treatment of narcissistic personality disorders, L. Schwartz, reporter. *J. Amer. Psychoanal. Assn.*, 21:617-632.
——— (1976), New horizons in metapsychology, W. W. Meissner, reporter. *J. Amer. Psychoanal. Assn.*, 24: 161-180.
Piaget, J. (1936), *The Origins of Intelligence in Children*. New York: International Universities Press, 1952.

Polanyi, M. (1974), *Scientific Thought and Social Reality. Psychological Issues,* Monograph 32. New York: International Universities Press.

Rado, S. (1926), The psychic effects of intoxicants: An attempt to evolve a psycho-analytical theory of morbid cravings. *Internat. J. Psycho-Anal.,* 7:396-413.

Rapaport, D. (1953), Some metapsychological considerations concerning activity and passivity. In: Rapaport, 1967, pp. 530-568.

———— (1959), *The Structure of Psychoanalytic Theory: A Systematizing Attempt. Psychological Issues,* Monograph 6. New York: International Universities Press, 1960.

———— (1960a), Psychoanalysis as a developmental psychology. In: Rapaport, 1967, pp. 820-852.

———— (1960b), On the psychoanalytic theory of motivation. In: Rapaport, 1967, pp. 853-915.

———— (1967), *The Collected Papers of David Rapaport,* ed. M. M. Gill. New York: Basic Books.

———— & Gill, M.M. (1959), The points of view and assumptions of metapsychology. In: Rapaport, 1967, pp. 795-811.

Rosenblatt, A. & Thickstun, J. (1970), A study of the concept of psychic energy. *Internat. J. Psycho-Anal.,* 51:265-78.

Rubinstein, B. (1965), Psychoanalytic theory and the mind-body problem. In *Psychoanalysis and Current Biological Thought,* ed. N. S. Greenfeld, & W. C. Lewis. Madison: University of Wisconsin Press, pp. 35-56.

———— (1967), Explanation and mere description: A metascientific examination of certain aspects of the psychoanalytic theory of motivation. In: Holt, 1967c, pp. 20-77.

———— (1974), On the role of classificatory processes in mental functioning: Aspects of a psychoanalytic theoretical model. *Psychoanalysis and Contemporary Science,* 3:101-185. New York: International Universities Press.

———— (1976), On the possibility of a strictly clinical psychoanalytic theory: An essay in the philosophy of psychoanalysis. In: Gill & Holzman, 1976, pp. 229-264.

Sadow, L., Gedo, J., Miller, J., Pollock, G., Sabshin, M. & Schlessinger, N. (1967), The process of hypothesis change in three early psychoanalytic concepts. In: Gedo & Pollock, 1976, pp. 257-285.

Sandler, J. & Rosenblatt, B. (1962), The concept of the representational world. *The Psychoanalytic Study of the Child,* 17:128-148. New York: International Universities Press.

Sapirstein, J. & Gaines, J. (1973), Metapsychological considerations on the self. *Internat. J. Psycho-Anal.,* 54:415-424.

Schafer, R. (1960), The loving and beloved superego in Freud's structural theory. *The Psychoanalytic Study of the Child,* 15:163-188. New York: International Universities Press.

——— (1967), Ideals, the ego ideal, and the ideal self. In: Holt, 1967c, pp. 129-174.

——— (1970a), An overview of Heinz Hartmann's contributions to psychoanalysis. In: Schafer, 1976, pp. 57-101.

——— (1970b), The psychoanalytic vision of reality. In: Schafer, 1976, pp. 22-56.

——— (1972), Internalization: process or fantasy? In: Schafer, 1976, pp. 155-178.

——— (1973), Action: Its place in psychoanalytic interpretation and theory. In: Schafer, 1976, pp. 102-122; 127-154.

——— (1976), *A New Language for Psychoanalysis.* New Haven: Yale University Press.

Schimek, J. (1975), The interpretations of the past: Childhood trauma, psychical reality, and historical truth. *J. Amer. Psychoanal. Assn.,* 23:845-866.

Schlessinger, N. & Robbins, F. (1975), The psychoanalytic process: Recurrent patterns of conflict and changes in ego functions. *J. Amer. Psychoanal. Assn.,* 23:761-782.

Schur, M. (1966), *The Id and the Regulatory Principles of Mental Functioning.* New York: International Universities Press.

Segal, H. (1974), *Introduction to the Work of Melanie Klein.* Second edition. New York: Basic Books.

Sonnenberg, S. (1974). An hypothesis concerning the nature of sensory conversion. Presented to the Baltimore-Washington Psychoanalytic Society.

Spitz, R. (1946), Anaclitic depression. *The Psychoanalytic Study of the Child,* 2:313-342. New York: International Universities Press.

——— (1959), *A Genetic Field Theory of Ego Formation.* New York: International Universities Press.

Steingart, I. (1969), On self, character, and the development of a psychic apparatus. *The Psychoanalytic Study of the Child,* 24:271-303. New York: International Universities Press.

Swanson, D. (1977), A critique of psychic energy as an explanatory concept. *J. Amer. Psychoanal. Assn.,* 25:603-633.

Terman, D. (1976), Distortions of the Oedipus complex in severe pathology: Some vicissitudes of self development and their relationship to the Oedipus complex. Presented to the American Psychoanalytic Association.

Tolpin, P. (1971), Some psychic determinants of orgastic dysfunction. In: *Adolescent Psychiatry,* ed. S. Feinstein, P. Giovacchini, & A. Miller. New York: Basic Books.

——— (1974), On the regulation of anxiety: Its relation to "the timelessness of the unconscious and its capacity for hallucination." *The An-*

nual of Psychoanalysis, 2:150-180. New York: International Universities Press.

Toulmin, S. (1975), Self-knowledge and knowledge of the "self." Presented to the Center for Psychosocial Studies, Chicago.

———— (1978), Psychoanalysis, physics, and the mind-body problem. *The Annual of Psychoanalysis,* 6. In press.

Waelder, R. (1930), The principle of multiple function. In: *Psychoanalysis: Observation, Theory, Application.* New York: International Universities Press, 1976, pp. 68-83.

———— (1962), Psychoanalysis, scientific method, and philosophy. In: *Psychoanalysis: Observation, Theory, Application.* New York: International Universities Press, 1976, pp. 248-274.

Wallerstein, R. & Smelser, N. (1969), Psychoanalysis and sociology: Articulations and applications. *Internat. J. Psycho-Anal.,* 50:693-710.

Weiss, J. (1961), Repetition and structure. Unpublished manuscript.

Winnicott, D. (1951), Transitional objects and transitional phenomena. In: *Collected Papers.* New York: Basic Books, 1958, pp. 229-242.

———— (1954), Metapsychological and clinical aspects of regression within the psychoanalytical set-up. In: *Collected Papers,* New York: Basic Books, 1958, pp. 278-294.

———— (1960), The theory of the parent-infant relationship. *Internat. J. Psycho-Anal.,* 41:585-595.

Wolf, E., Gedo, J. & Terman, D. (1972), On the adolescent process as a transformation of the self. *J. Youth Adolesc.,* 1:257-272.

Wurmser, L. (1977), A defense of the use of metaphor in analytic theory formation. *Psychoanal. Quart.,* 46:466-98.

Zaleznik, A. (1975), Review of Gedo & Goldberg's *Models of the Mind. J. Phila. Assn. Psychoanal.,* 2:41-44.

Zetzel, E. (1956), The concept of transference. In: *The Capacity for Emotional Growth.* New York: International Universities Press, 1970, pp. 168-181.

Index

274